THE COMPLETE
INDIAN
COOKBOOK

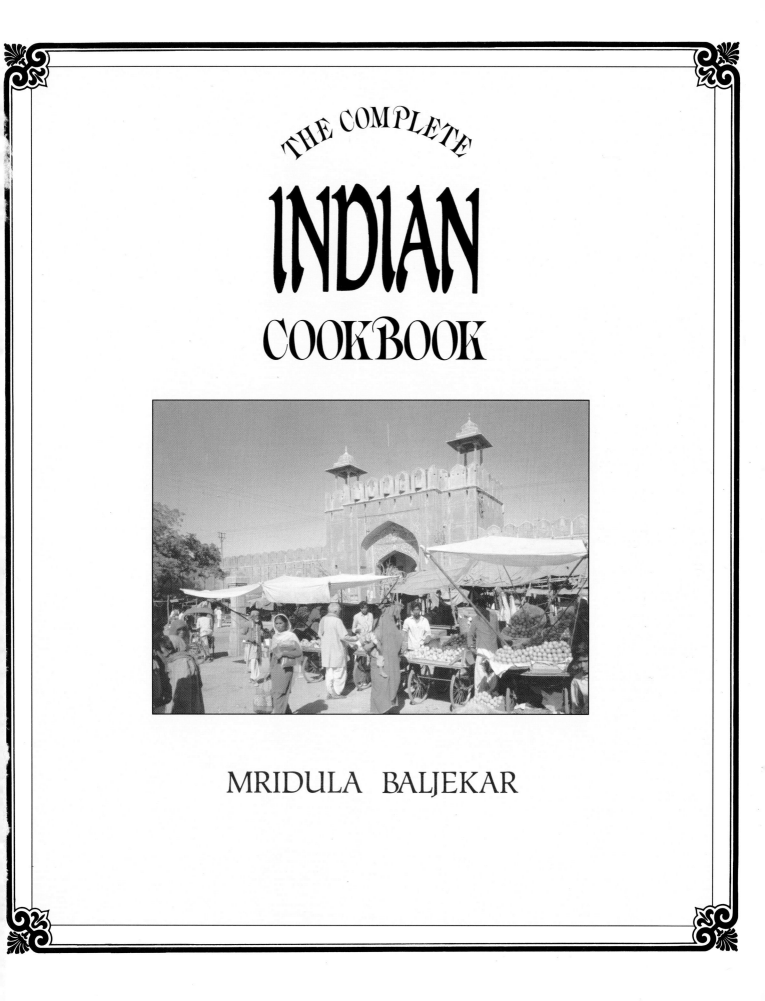

MRIDULA BALJEKAR

Photographed by Peter Barry

Recipes prepared and styled by
Bridgeen Deery and
Wendy Devenish

Edited by Jillian Stewart,
Jane Adams and
Judith Ferguson

Designed by Philip Clucas and
Claire Leighton

AUTHOR'S ACKNOWLEDGMENT

I wish to thank all my pupils for the inspiration
they gave me by showing tremendous interest
in and appreciation for my recipes.

I offer my sincere thanks to my close
friends Gek Starkey and Louise Read for
looking after my children while I was busy
compiling the recipes for this book.

A multitude of loving thanks goes to my
husband for his support and understanding
during the entire period of writing this book.

Lastly, I must mention the book *Herbs,
Spices and Flavorings,* which proved to be an
invaluable guide in compiling the glossary. The
author; Tim Stobart, deserves thanks for an
excellent piece of work.

This edition published in 1994 by
SMITHMARK Publishers, Inc.,
16 East 32nd Street, New York, NY 10016.

SMITHMARK books are available for bulk purchase
for sales promotion and premium use. For details,
write or call the manager of special sales,
SMITHMARK Publishers, Inc. 16 East 32nd Street,
New York, NY 10016; (212) 532-6600

CLB 2462
Produced by CLB Publishing
Godalming Business Centre
Woolsack Way, Godalming, Surrey, England
ISBN 0-8317-1487-5
Printed in Singapore
10 9 8 7 6 5 4 3 2 1

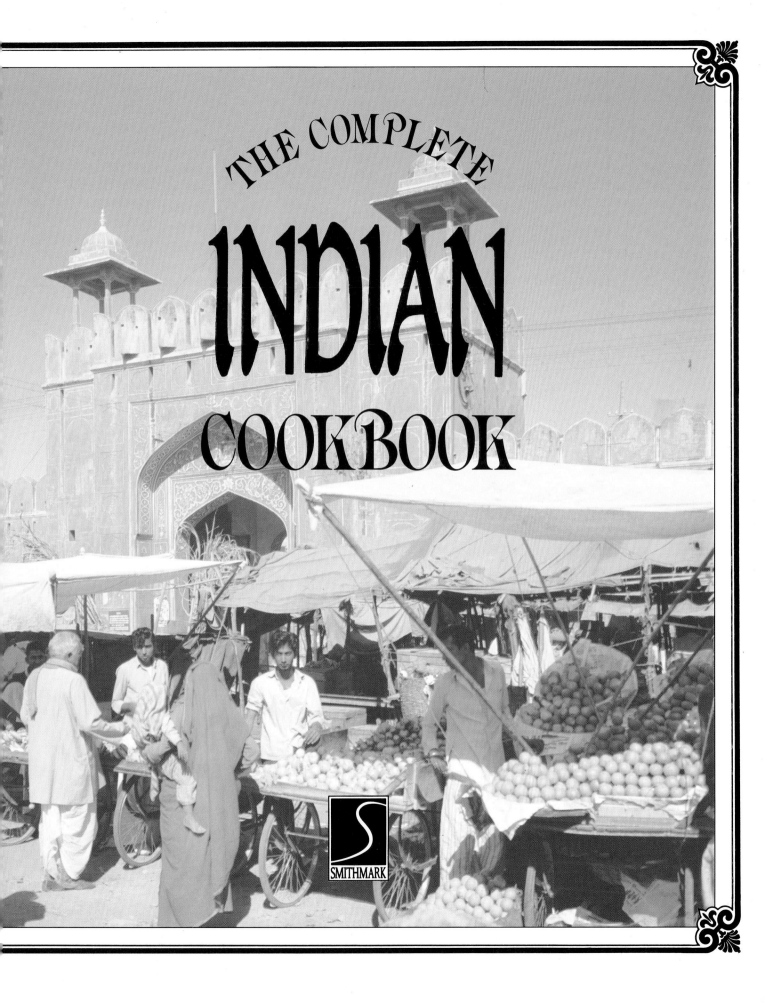

THE COMPLETE
INDIAN
COOKBOOK

SMITHMARK

contents

Introduction 5

Snacks and Appetizers 16

Main Meals

Fish and Seafood 48

Vegetarian 68

Classic Chicken Dishes 72

Classic Meat Dishes 118

Microwave 166

Bread and Rice 226

Side Dishes 262

Drinks and Desserts 348

Glossary 395

Index 400

introduction

India is a country full of striking contrasts; this is evident not only in its cuisine, but also in its climate, geography, culture and customs. The vastness of the country, together with its great regional diversity, is the main factor that places Indian cuisine in its unique and interesting position in the culinary history of the world. Indian food reflects the colorful and varied life led by its people as well as the external and internal influences that have shaped its particular style of cooking.

The Mughals, a regal race of Muslims, invaded India from their traditional homeland in Afghanistan and the Middle East, bringing with them exotic spices and dried fruits and nuts, which they combined with milk and cream to concoct rich "Mughlai" dishes. These are among the finest in Indian regional cuisine.

During their journey to India via Persia (modern-day Iran), the Mughals adapted the much-admired Persian cooking to their own style and later introduced this into India. They then settled in northern India and made "Mughlai" cuisine famous throughout the country. Dishes cooked in this particular style, with their delicately flavored, rich, smooth sauces, include kormas, pasandas and wonderfully fragrant birianis and pilaus, all of which have become extremely popular both in India and the West.

The Kashmiris from the north used saffron and other rare condiments, giving Indian recipes, especially candies and desserts, a festive touch. It is also in Kashmir that the origins of the Saraswat community are found. They originally lived in the valley of the Saraswati river in Kashmir and journeyed southward, finally settling in the districts of North and South Kanara. Their contribution to the cuisine of the country has been considerable. Kashmiris are mainly vegetarians, though many will also eat the beautiful fresh fish found along the vast coastline. Most Saraswat recipes, as is evident from those contained in this book, are quick, easy, delicious and, above all, very healthy.

About thirteen centuries ago a group of Persians came to India and made their home in the southern half of the country. They adapted to the rich and varied culture they found there, but made their own particular contribution to the Indian culinary world. Persian food has a very distinctive flavor which the Parsees, as they are known in India, cleverly integrated into the exotic and colorful cooking of the Indian subcontinent. A fine example of their contribution is the "Dhansak" style – chicken or lamb cooked with lentils and spices and served with brown rice.

The influence of religion on the country's cooking has been, and continues to be, quite profound. There are many religions practiced in India, of which the major ones are Hinduism with its three main divisions – Buddhism, Jainism and Sikhism – and Islam, which was first brought to India by foreign traders.

There are a number of taboos, or restrictions, that apply to the food eaten by followers of the different religions. Devout Hindus, for example, will not eat beef because Indian mythology depicts the cow as a sacred animal, while Muslims will not eat pork, and their religion requires that animals are killed by the halal method.

In the early days, when travel and communication between different areas were virtually nonexistent, each region used the herbs and spices that were to be found growing naturally. As a result, housewives were compelled to experiment by using the same ingredients, but frying, grinding and mixing them in different sequences and proportions. The same ingredients, when cooked differently, gave dishes their diverse tastes, colors and textures, and resulted in the same recipes having quite a few variations. Today, though certain recipes have specific geographic strongholds, a large number of the dishes and cooking methods have spread the length and breadth of the country.

People are often confused by the different ways in which the names of ingredients and dishes are spelled in English. Should it be Tandoor or Tandur? Aloo Ghosh or Alu Ghosht? Because all the fourteen main Indian languages and their 144 dialects are phonetic, the translation of Indian phonetics into non-phonetic English spelling causes this confusion.

Since ancient times Indians have known about the medicinal properties of herbs, spices and other ingredients used in cooking. Garlic, for example, is known to control the level of cholesterol in the blood and, therefore, reduces the risk of high blood pressure and heart attacks. Cloves and cinnamon act against coughs and colds and help to keep the body warm in extreme weather. Ginger reduces acidity in the stomach and thus minimizes the risk of ulcers. Green chili peppers, which normally thrive in dry, arid areas where not much else grows, are a good source of vitamins; cumin helps settle an upset stomach; turmeric purifies the blood; mustard, which grows in cooler climates, has a warming effect and prevents hypothermia – the list is endless!

These different properties created a varied, healthy cuisine that is now known by the all-embracing term "Indian food" or "curry." It is a common misconception, however, that everything that is spicy is a curry. The word curry means sauce, and dry-spiced Indian dishes cannot therefore strictly be called curries. Dishes all have their own identifying terms. For example, a vegetable dish that has no sauce is known as a bhaji, while food cooked by the dum method, which creates little or no sauce, is simply referred to as, say, Dum Aloo (potatoes) or Dum Murghi (chicken).

Indian recipes are generally handed down from one generation to the next. A fair attempt has now been made to formalize and record all recipes. Weights and measures were never used and the quantities of all the ingredients were simply estimated. It therefore took a long period of apprenticeship for anyone to become a good cook. This practice is followed even to this day in India.

For the Western world, however, the recipes have to be written down, which involves the laborious measuring of estimated quantities; skill and experience have had to give way to the urgency and mass-production needs of today's busy lifestyle.

INDIAN SPICES AND CONDIMENTS

The range of Indian spices and condiments is vast and varied. The selection of spices that go into any given recipe has evolved through the generations and great care has to be taken to ensure that the chosen spices complement, rather than counteract, each other. Correct use of spices is the key to successful Indian cooking.

Spices usually add taste and texture to the dish. They integrate totally into the sauce and cannot be identified at the end of the cooking process; examples are asafoetida, ginger, garam masala and most ground ingredients.

Condiments generally add flavor and bouquet to the dish. They do not blend into the sauce and are put to one side after cooking, not eaten. Examples are whole chili peppers, cinnamon sticks, whole cloves and cardamom.

Interestingly, whether an item is a spice or condiment is sometimes determined by its usage rather than by the ingredient itself: coriander seed is a condiment, but ground coriander is a spice.

Spices are usually freshly ground just before cooking to ensure that the best possible results are obtained. In many cases meat is marinated overnight in the spice mixture so that the spices have a chance to reach the innermost "grain" of the meat. Careful and correct use of previously ground and stored spices, if a few tips and hints are followed, will produce perfectly good results. These tips have been included in most of the recipes.

Once the spices to be used are selected, the cook is faced with several options:

1 The quantity of each spice to use
2 Which of these spices to roast and grind
3 In what sequence to add these spices to the dish

Thus, even if only three spices are chosen, it is still possible to concoct many different flavors! Obviously only a few of these have found favor through the generations, but this point serves to illustrate the vast number of combinations that are possible. The process can be likened to musicians playing a piece of music; even with the same notes and the same players the end result can be totally different depending on the skill of the conductor in blending, mixing and emphasizing the different contributions made by individual players.

Some five thousand years ago, the sages of India discovered the medicinal properties of various roots, barks, leaves, seeds and flowers. They were the first to formalize and systemize the effects and usage of these ingredients. Natural human reluctance to accept these dictats forced the sages to incorporate these instructions into the Holy Indian Scriptures, the *Vedas*. Once these instructions were given a religious bias they were more readily accepted into the Indian way of life.

THE TECHNIQUES OF PREPARING AND COOKING INDIAN FOOD

Maintaining the delicate balance of spice mixing is an art that can be acquired with a little care and imagination. The taste given by the spices to any dish depends on their combination and on the method of cooking used. The same basic spices used in different combinations and with different methods of cooking will produce a dramatically different taste. The combinations are many and varied, but the best results can be achieved by following the simple guidelines below.

Preparing Spices

In India, spices are usually freshly ground before cooking each meal, as this ensures the best results. However, it is not always possible for today's busy cook to follow this method. Careful and correct use of ready-ground or home-ground, stored spices will produce perfectly delicious results.

Using whole spices Clean the spices, remove any debris, stalks and pieces of grit. Heat a cast-iron or other heavy-based skillet without adding any fat, and dry-roast the spices gently until you can smell the aroma. Allow the spices to cool completely, then grind in a spice or coffee mill and store in airtight jars. These spices will remain fresh for three to four months.

Using ready-ground spices Ground spices have a limited shelf life as they tend to lose their essential flavor and aroma during storage. Better results can be achieved by revitalizing dull spices. To do this, heat them through gently in a dry, heavy-based pan. Heat the spices just until you can smell the aroma being released, then cool thoroughly and store in airtight jars. Spices prepared in this way will produce a much more delicious dish than if used straight from the packet.

Frying Spices

It is essential to follow the timings given for frying spices at different stages of cooking. Frying and braising the spices at different temperatures for the same recipe is an art that ultimately helps to blend the flavors of the various spices that are used.

Frying dry spices Care should be taken in frying dry, ground or whole spices. The fat should not be allowed to overheat as this will burn the spices very quickly, imparting a bitter flavor to the dish.

Frying "wet" spices This category consists mainly of puréed onions, ginger and garlic, to which other dry, ground spices are added during frying. It is crucial not to rush the process of frying. The raw smell, which will ultimately lead to a rancid curry, must be eliminated before adding the meat.

Frying onions When frying chopped or sliced onions to make a curry sauce, the onions should not be allowed to brown. They should be fried gently over medium-low heat and stirred frequently to ensure that they are an even, pale golden color. Sometimes onions have to be browned if they are to be used to garnish pilaus and birianis. For this purpose, the onions should be fried over medium heat, stirring frequently to ensure even browning.

The fat used for frying onions should be carefully measured because, in the beginning, when the moisture content of the onions cloud the fat, it is tempting to add a little more. Once the moisture begins to evaporate, the fat will separate and become more visible, indicating that the onions are now ready to take on other spices. When dry spices are added at this stage the heat should be adjusted to low and, after two to three minutes, a little water (about one tablespoon) should be sprinkled over to ensure that the mixture does not stick to the bottom of the pan and that it fries evenly.

Using Water
The temperature of the water used in preparing a curry is an important consideration. Cold water should not be added to the carefully blended ingredients as this will impair the flavor. Warm water helps to maintain the degree of flavor that has been achieved by blending the spices at a given temperature.

Using Salt
Most westerners seem to find the quantity of salt used in Indian recipes rather alarming. There are perfectly valid reasons for maintaining these levels of salt in the food, the most important being that salt subdues the flavor of the spices and chili peppers. Without the correct amount of salt, the spices taste rather overpowering. Unlike in Western cooking, salt in Indian cooking is used at the beginning of, or during, the cooking process to ensure the proper blending of flavors created by the different spices used. Another reason is that when salt is added to some dishes, particularly vegetables, these release their own juices and the food is cooked entirely in these. This in turn dilutes the effect of the spices, creating a proper balance of flavors.

If the amount of salt is drastically reduced in a recipe, it is advisable to adjust the quantity of spices too. This, though, will mean losing some of the authentic taste of the dish.

Using a Pressure Cooker
The pressure cooker is an almost indispensable item in an Indian kitchen. A large proportion of the Indian population is vegetarian, and protein in their daily diet is therefore obtained from foods such as lentils, chickpeas, and all kinds of dried beans. In a pressure cooker, pulses as well as meat will cook in less than half the time required by the conventional method. Peas and beans should be prepared according to the instructions in the recipe, but, instead of prolonged simmering, they can be cooked in a pressure cooker. Remember, however, to follow the manufacturer's instructions regarding cooking times.

Preparing Rice Before Cooking
Long-grain rice is generally used in Indian cooking. There are different types of long-grain rice and choosing a good quality rice is just as important as cooking it successfully.

Basmati is the superior long-grain rice and is used in all pilaus and birianis. Basmati rice differs from other long-grain rice in that it is matured for as long as four to five years after harvesting. The older the rice, the better it is, as it will cook easily without sticking. Basmati rice varies a great deal in quality and this largely depends on how mature the rice is. The best variety, grown in the foothills of the mighty Himalayas, is known as "Tilda." There are other varieties of good quality basmati rice, such as Dehra Dun Basmati, Patna Basmati and, of course, Pakistani Basmati.

Young long-grain rice has a high proportion of starch and is more prone to sticking. However, as basmati rice tends to be expensive, other long-grain rice, such as Patna rice, can be used successfully if it is washed and drained at least two to three times in cold water. After draining it, soak the rice in cold water for an hour or so, then stir it and drain thoroughly. This will reduce the starch content and prepare the grains to absorb the moisture during cooking without getting sticky. Basmati rice should also be washed at least twice, soaked for thirty minutes, and then drained.

One important point to remember for successful rice cooking is that it should never be stirred as soon as it is cooked. Freshly cooked rice tends to be fragile and it must be allowed to stand before being handled. The rice should be forked through gently before serving.

In India rice is also of significance in religious and social ceremonies. At weddings, for instance, small handfuls of rice are thrown, rather like confetti, at the bridegroom when he arrives at the bride's home for the wedding ceremony. Similarly, when the bride arrives at her new home, after the ceremony, a large bowl of rice is offered to her and she scatters some of it on the ground before entering the house. This signifies that the bride brings good fortune with her.

Preparing Dough for Indian Bread

The type of dough used for Indian bread tends to be easy to prepare, and can be prepared in advance. The point to watch out for is that the right amount of water is used to ensure that the dough has the correct elasticity without any stickiness. The level of absorbency varies a great deal between different types of flour. It is therefore advisable to add the water a little at a time until the correct consistency is achieved. Prepared dough should be wrapped in waxed paper and placed in a plastic bag if it is to be stored in the refrigerator. The dough will always benefit from a little standing time. If left at room temperature, wrap the dough first in waxed paper and then in a cloth to prevent it from drying out. It should not be left at room temperature for more than a few hours. Dough stored in the refrigerator should be brought to room temperature before rolling out.

Preparing Chicken

Chicken is never cooked with the skin left on and it is almost always cut into small portions. This is because the skin does not allow the spices to permeate the meat, and the smaller the pieces are cut, the better the chances of the spices reaching the innermost grain of the meat. As well as removing the skin, all excess fat should be trimmed off. The chicken should then be washed and dried thoroughly with paper towels or a cloth. If not dried properly, the excess water content will not allow the chicken to fry with the spices and it will start braising instead. Frying the chicken with the other ingredients before adding the required amount of water is extremely important.

Chicken is also normally cooked on the bone, except when making kababs, because the flavor of the meat is always best nearest the bone. The bones also add flavor to the sauce. In India, a special bone stock, called *Yakhni*, is prepared for cooking certain types of curries and pilaus which use boned meat.

Preparing Meat

Meat is generally cooked on the bone for the reasons stated above. The same procedure for skinning, trimming off the fat, and washing and drying as for chicken, should be followed when preparing meat. Again, drying the meat is very important.

Cooking with Oil and Ghee

Traditionally, most Indian cooking was done in ghee (clarified butter), but recently people have been made aware of the dangers of too much saturated fat in their diet and hence oil is now more commonly used. No particular recommendation is necessary as to which cooking oil to use. This is purely a matter of personal choice, though a light variety such as sunflower oil is easier on the digestive system. Ghee, however, is necessary for certain dishes, such as pilaus, birianis and some Mughlai curries.

TECHNIQUES

Although full instructions accompany each recipe, a description of the techniques themselves is necessary to help the cook understand them better. Once these techniques are fully understood, you will be completely at ease cooking Indian food and will be able to use your own creative skills to adapt the recipes.

Braising (Korma)

This is one of the most important techniques. Korma is essentially braised meat or vegetables, cooked using only a minute quantity of liquid. Traditionally, a korma is made by very slow cooking and hot charcoal is placed on the lid to ensure the even distribution of heat. To simplify this, a heavy-based pan with a tight-fitting lid should be used, because slow cooking is the key to success with this method. There are several different types of korma dishes, all of which use only prime cuts of meat. For most kormas, the meat or chicken is first marinated in a yogurt-based mixture and cooked in the marinade itself, with little or no water. The more elaborate kormas need an aromatic stock, or *Yakhni*, which is prepared by prolonged simmering of bones with whole spices. This is then strained and used to cook the meat.

The delicious creamy taste and the smooth velvety texture come from ingredients such as thick set plain yogurt, cream, ground almonds and coconut milk. These, of course, are not all used in the same dish.

Pot Roasting (The Dum Method)

Though this method is like Western pot roasting, there is a very special technique involved. The dish is cooked over charcoal and hot charcoal is also placed on the lid of the pot. The pot is sealed using a sticky dough made of flour to prevent any loss of steam. Accurate judgement of cooking times is necessary because the lid is removed only once the food is fully cooked. The food is not stirred during cooking, but the pot is gently shaken from side to side to ensure that the food does not stick to the pan.

To adapt this method for use in a modern kitchen, use a heavy-based saucepan which has a non-stick surface and a tight-fitting lid. The non-stick surface is essential because the food is generally cooked without any water. Sometimes a little water is added to cook certain dishes such as Kashmiri Dum Aloo, and this method is known as "Dum Bhoona." The meat and vegetables cooked by this method are normally cut into large pieces, and since little or no water is used in the dum method, a generous amount of ghee or oil is used to cook the food. Present-day, health-conscious food habits make it difficult to follow this traditional method and the recipes contained in this book therefore tend towards the use of cooking liquid to replace some of the fat. To seal the saucepan, use a piece of aluminum foil or waxed paper, then put the lid on.

Frying (Bhoona)

This important technique produces beautifully aromatic, dry dishes. The most important stage in cooking a successful bhoona dish is frying the spices until they are a rich brown color. Sometimes puréed onions, garlic and ginger root are fried first at varying temperatures to achieve the required color, and the other spices are added halfway through. Chopped or sliced onions with crushed garlic and ginger, fried in the same way, produce a different flavor in a bhoona dish. The meat is cut into small pieces and very little water or stock is used to cook it. At the end of the cooking time the meat is occasionally fried again over a high heat to give it that final "bhoona" flavor. Meat or fish is sometimes browned over a fairly high heat to form a crust, then the spices are fried separately and combined with the meat or fish to cook with a small amout of liquid, which forms a dryish dish such as Fish Bhoona. Meat or chicken can be cooked in a spicy liquid first until almost tender. The pieces are then lifted out of the liquid and fried in hot fat, and a little cooking liquid is added from time to time until the liquid has reduced to a paste-like consistency; Murghi Jhal Frezi is a perfect example.

Seasoning (Tarka)

Tarka simply means seasoning. This method involves frying spices in hot oil and incorporating these into the dish after it has been cooked. Sometimes, only whole spices such as mustard and cumin seeds, dried red chili peppers and curry leaves are fried, and sometimes finely chopped or sliced onions and garlic are added to the whole spices, as in Tarka Dhal.

Tandoori Cooking

The word *tandoor* means clay oven, and all food cooked in a tandoor is referred to as Tandoori. A tandoor is cylindrical in shape and charcoal is used to cook the food. The heat generated in the tandoor is rather fierce and the clay is able to retain this heat well and   to distribute it evenly. This is the reason why Tandoori Chicken and kabab dishes such as Chicken Tikka and Boti Kabab have a crust on the surface while the inside is beautifully moist and succulent. Small whole chickens and whole fish can also be cooked to perfection in a tandoor.

The preparation of Tandoori dishes involves marinating first to tenderize the meat, a process which also enables the flavor of the spices to penetrate deep inside. The pieces of meat, chicken or whole fish are threaded onto specially designed skewers and lowered into the oven. Food generally takes only a few minutes to cook because the tandoor is able to cook both the outside and the inside of the food simultaneously.

Besides cooking meat, fish and chicken, the tandoor is also used to bake breads such as Naan and Tandoori Roti. The dough is not rolled, but stretched to the desired shape and slapped onto the inner walls of the tandoor. The color used in Tandoori food has no flavor, and is used simply to distinguish Tandoori dishes from others. The traditional colouring is a natural dye, though artificial Tandoori color is widely used now. The color can be omitted from the recipe, if desired. On the other hand, if you like the color, but are unable to buy it, tomato paste mixed with a few drops of red food coloring makes a good substitute. The food coloring on its own will turn the food pink rather than red. One tablespoon of tomato paste is generally enough for the recipes contained in this book.

A traditional tandoor is meant for commercial use where mass production is necessary. Perfectly delicious Tandoori food can be prepared in a very hot gas or electric oven, although the characteristic charcoal flavor will be missing. Food cooked in this way should be turned over and basted during cooking and the excess liquid should be drained off before the food is transferred to a serving dish.

REFRIGERATING, FREEZING AND REHEATING

Indian food is ideal for entertaining because the preparation can be done in advance and the food refrigerated or frozen.

When refrigerating Indian food it is advisable to cover the dish with a piece of plastic wrap or aluminum foil before placing the lid on it. This not only ensures freshness, but also prevents the leakage of strong smells inside the refrigerator.

Although freezing, defrosting and reheating need no special techniques, a few important points should be remembered for the most successful results.

Freezing and Defrosting Dishes with Sauce

The dish should be cooled thoroughly and chilled for several hours before freezing. Defrosting should be done slowly, preferably overnight in the refrigerator, and the dish should be thoroughly defrosted before reheating. The dish should also be reheated fairly slowly. This is most important in reheating Mughlai, or creamy, dishes.

When a dish is defrosted it can look rather alarming to the novice because the liquid separates and collects at the bottom of the container. At this stage there is no need to stir and mix the food. Simply transfer the food to a saucepan and cover with a lid. Place the saucepan over a low heat and bring the contents to a gentle simmer. Then stir the food gently, replace the lid and allow the dish to simmer until it is heated through. This way, the meat will reabsorb all the liquid and the texture of the dish will return to its original state.

Freezing and Defrosting Dry Dishes

Foods such as kababs, Tandoori dishes, all types of pakoras, bhajiyas and samosas should be cooled and wrapped in a double thickness of aluminum foil to prevent them from drying out. Place the packed food in a freezer bag, then label and freeze it. The food should be defrosted slowly and thoroughly before reheating.

Reheat kababs and Tandoori dishes in the oven, in their foil package. The oven temperature should be moderately hot with the food placed in the center. Most of these dishes will reheat adequately in ten to fifteen minutes, with the exception of Tandoori Chicken which will need approximately twenty to twenty-five minutes. These can also be successfully reheated in the microwave; the food must be covered to prevent dehydration during reheating. The pieces of meat and chicken should be turned over halfway through the reheating cycle.

Reheat pakoras and bhajiyas in the center of a moderately hot oven in an open dish. The foil should be removed and the food arranged in a single layer. They can also be reheated under a preheated medium broiler and turned over halfway through. Both methods will restore the crispness. The microwave is not suitable for this purpose. To reheat samosas, unwrap and arrange them on a baking sheet in a single layer. The sheet should be placed in the centre of a moderate oven for fifteen to twenty minutes, turning the samosas over once. They can also be reheated under a preheated low broiler for ten to fifteen minutes, turning frequently.

It is not strictly necessary to defrost bread before reheating. The foil package can be placed in the center of a hot oven for about twenty minutes, and the package turned over halfway through. Allow ten to twelve minutes if the bread has been defrosted.

Breads such as Naan and Tandoori Roti can be reheated successfully in the microwave. Thinner varieties, such as Chapattis, become rather hard and dry if reheated in the microwave. Puris and Loochis are not recommended for freezing.

To reheat Cauliflower Cutlets and Masala Machchi, unwrap and reheat under a preheated low broiler for eight to ten minutes, turning them over carefully halfway through.

All other dry dishes that are suitable for freezing can be reheated on top of the stove over a low heat. The food should be stirred gently from time to time.

All rice dishes, whether refrigerated or frozen and defrosted, can be reheated as follows. Put the rice into an ovenproof dish and cover it with a piece of greased foil before putting the lid on. This will prevent the top layer of the rice from drying out during reheating. Preheat the oven to 350°F. Reheat the rice in the center of the oven; the time required will depend on the quantity. Usually, 3½ cups rice will heat through in thirty to thirty-five minutes.

The easiest way to reheat rice is in the microwave. It should be placed in a covered dish and the rice forked through once or twice during reheating to ensure that it heats evenly.

COOKING UTENSILS AND EQUIPMENT

No extra-special cooking utensils are required to produce the authentic flavor of Indian food. Traditionally, cast iron and earthenware pots and pans are used in India. A round-bottomed cast-iron pan (*Kadhai*), similar to a wok but smaller in size, is used for deep-frying. Its shape means that it does not require as much cooking fat or oil as a deep-fat fryer and the cast iron enables the food to cook at an even and steady temperature. A cast-iron griddle (*Tava*) is used to make most Indian breads. Heavy pots and pans with tight-fitting lids and a frying pan with a non-stick surface are ideal for Indian cooking because they enable the food to cook evenly without sticking.

For preparing the ingredients, a blender or food processor and a coffee or spice grinder are absolutely necessary. In a modern kitchen these replace the traditional grinding stone.

A blender or food processor is essential for pulverising onions, root ginger and fresh garlic, while a coffee or spice grinder is required for grinding special spice mixtures. It is advisable, however, not to use the same grinder for coffee unless you like coffee with a spicy flavor!

A pestle and mortar or a wooden pestle are useful for crushing garlic and root ginger.

A food processor is an excellent investment. Indian recipes call for finely chopped or sliced onions and these are the key to a successful, smooth sauce. To achieve the necessary degree of fineness manually can be rather difficult and time consuming. A food processor will do this in a few seconds, as well as chopping vegetables and making a beautiful purée of onions, root ginger and fresh garlic. This purée can be frozen in the required quantities. In fact, just about any ingredients that need blending can be prepared in the food processor in a few seconds.

The greatest advantage of a food processor is that it will mix and knead the dough for all Indian breads to perfection, saving you all the hard work.

PLANNING AND SERVING AN INDIAN MEAL

Unlike in the West, Indian dishes are not strictly categorized into appetizers and main courses. An Indian meal consists of several dishes, and the traditional style of serving these would be to bring all the dishes to the dining table and for everyone to help themselves, rather like a sit-down buffet. Generally, people have second helpings of most of the dishes. In the classic style, however, the food is actually served in a large plate known as a *thali*. The staple, such as rice or bread, along with the dry dishes, is served on the thali and small bowls are used to serve dishes with sauces. Traditional methods are being adapted to suit the changing pattern of life and there is no reason why an appetizer cannot be served before the main meal, indeed this practice is now becoming increasingly popular.

A carefully chosen appetizer is the way to fill guests with curiosity as well as enthusiasm for the meal to follow. With this in mind, enticing and delicious recipes have been chosen for the section called "Snacks and Appetizers."

Alcoholic drinks are not traditional accompaniments to an Indian meal; this is because the majority of the population in India prefer water which, they feel, better enables them to enjoy and appreciate the flavor of the spices. If you wish to serve alchohol, beer is by far the best drink to accompany an Indian meal. Well-chilled, dry white wine is a suitable alternative. A chilled, light red wine can be served if desired, though red wine does not usually complement an Indian meal very well.

Nonalcoholic drinks, such as Nimbu Pani, Jeera Pani and Mango Sherbet, can all be enjoyed with Indian food.

MICROWAVE INDIAN COOKING

Cooking Indian food in the microwave might sound like an impossible idea. However, a careful analysis of the way in which spices are used in the conventional method will show that adapting this to the microwave is actually fairly simple and straightforward.

In the conventional method of cooking, spices are fried first, both to eliminate their raw taste and to enhance their flavor before the meat, fish or vegetables are added. This is the very essence of successful Indian cookery. Two easy steps will ensure that these requirements are met when cooking in the microwave. Firstly, pre-roast the spices using conventional methods (full instructions for this are given in "The Techniques of Preparing and Cooking Indian Food"). Then freshen up the spices just before using them. Instructions on how to do this are given with each recipe. This normally involves roasting or heating the spices at specified power levels for specified times and then allowing a certain amount of standing time.

When preparing Indian dishes in the microwave, you should bear in mind several factors:

1 Spices tend to taste much stronger than in conventionally cooked dishes. For this reason, they must be used only in the quantities specified. Fewer spices in smaller quantities is the key to success here. Pay particular attention to turmeric and saffron; if not used carefully in the specified quantities, these two spices will give a bitter taste to the dish.

2 Cooking the dishes in advance and reheating them will enhance their flavor by a significant amount. This is particularly evident in microwave-prepared dishes.

3 Remember that it is important to stir the food as you would do in the conventional method.

4 It is very important to use the correct size of cooking dish – these are specified in most recipes.

5 Cut all meat, vegetables and fish into even-sized pieces so that the is able to penetrate the food uniformly, thereby cooking all the pieces evenly and to the required degree.

6 Allowing standing time after cooking is another important point to remember, as the microwave energy will continue cooking the food even when the oven is switched off.

Follow the above steps carefully and you will find that the food is just as delicious as that cooked in the conventional way. Microwave cooking is also the perfect way to prepare Indian meals without strong cooking smells.

The most important benefit, of course, is that the microwave cuts cooking time by at least a third and, in some cases, by as much as half. Last, but not least, food cooked in the microwave is healthier as it retains all its goodness as well as the fresh colors of the vegetables, making the dish look more attractive and appetizing.

Microwave Indian cooking is sure to be an exciting new experience which will not only bring you a great deal of pleasure but also many compliments from family and friends!

All microwave recipes featured in this book were prepared using a 700 watt oven. For ovens of a lower rating, timings should be increased accordingly:
500 watt: add 40 seconds to every minute stated in the recipe
600 watt: add 20 seconds to every minute stated in the recipe
650 watt: only a slight increase in the overall time is necessary

Dry spices have been known to ignite when heated in a microwave and should be watched throughout their cooking time. Always follow microwave manufacturer's guidelines.

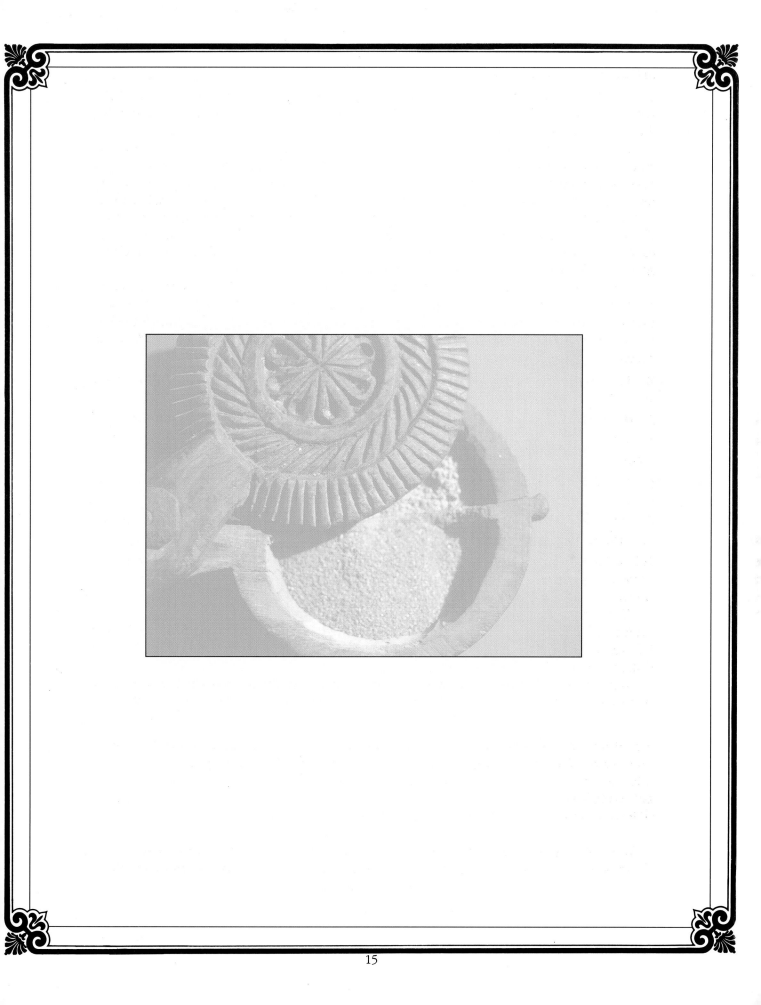

snacks and
appetizers

MEAT AND POTATO PATTIES

MAKES 14 Patties

6 medium-sized potatoes

½-1 tsp chili powder

1½ tsps salt or to taste

3 tbsps cooking oil

½ tsp fennel seeds

1 large onion, finely chopped

½-inch cube of root ginger, peeled and finely grated

2-4 cloves garlic, peeled and chopped or crushed

12oz fine lean ground lamb or beef

Make a paste of the following 5 ingredients by adding 3 tbsps water

1 tsp ground cumin

1½ tsps ground coriander

1 tsp ground fennel

½ tsp ground turmeric

½ tsp garam masala

1 small can of tomatoes

⅓ cup water

1 fresh green chili pepper, finely chopped

2 tbsps chopped coriander leaves

1 egg, beaten

2 tbsps milk

2 tbsps flour

1 cup breadcrumbs

Oil for deep frying

1. Boil the potatoes in their skins, peel and mash them. Add half the chili powder and ½ tsp salt from the specified amount. Divide the mixture into 14 golf-ball sized portions, cover and set aside.

2. Heat the oil over medium heat and fry the fennel seeds until they are brown.

3. Add the onions, ginger and garlic, and stir and fry until the onions are lightly browned (6-8 minutes).

4. Add the ground meat and fry until all moisture evaporates, stirring frequently (6-8 minutes).

5. Add the spice paste, stir and fry for 5-6 minutes reducing heat towards the last 2-3 minutes.

6. Add the tomatoes, stir and mix, breaking them up with the back of the spoon. Adjust heat to medium and cook for 3-4 minutes stirring frequently.

7. Add the water, the remaining chili powder and salt, cover and simmer for 15 minutes. Adjust heat to medium, uncover and cook for 4-5 minutes or until the mixture is completely dry but moist. Stir frequently.

8. Stir in the chopped green chili pepper and the coriander leaves. Cook for 1-2 minutes stirring constantly, remove from heat and allow to cool completely.

9. Mix the beaten egg with the milk and set aside.

10. Take a portion of the potato and roll it between the palms to make a neat smooth ball. Make a depression in the center and form into a cup shape. Fill this cavity with the meat mixture leaving approx. ¼-inch round the border. Cover the filling by gently pressing the entire circular border together. Roll between the palms and flatten to form a round cake, about ½-inch thick.

11. Dust the cake in the flour then dip in egg and milk mixture and roll in the breadcrumbs. Make the rest of the patties the same way.

12. Deep fry the patties until they are golden brown. Drain on paper towels.

TIME Preparation takes 45-50 minutes, cooking takes 35-40 minutes.

CHICKEN TIKKA

Chicken Tikka is one of the most popular chicken dishes cooked in the Tandoor, the Indian clay oven. This recipe is adapted to cook the chicken in the conventional oven at a high temperature.

SERVES 4

1lb boneless, skinned chicken breasts
1 tsp salt
Juice of ½ a lemon
½ tsp tandoori color or a few drops of
    red food coloring mixed with
    1 tbsp tomato paste
2 cloves garlic, peeled and coarsely
    chopped
½-inch cube of root ginger, peeled and
    coarsely chopped
2 tsps ground coriander
½ tsp ground allspice or garam masala
¼ of a whole nutmeg, finely grated
½ tsp ground turmeric
⅔ cup thick set plain yogurt
4 tbsps corn or vegetable oil
½ tsp chili powder

1. Cut the chicken into 1-inch cubes. Sprinkle with ½ tsp salt from the specified amount, and the lemon juice – mix thoroughly, cover and set aside for 30 minutes.

2. Put the rest of the ingredients into a food processor or blender and blend until smooth.

3. Put this marinade into a strainer and hold the strainer over the chicken pieces. Press the marinade through with the back of a metal spoon until only a very coarse mixture is left.

4. Coat the chicken thoroughly with the strained marinade, cover the container and leave to marinate for 6-8 hours or overnight in the refrigerator.

5. Preheat the oven to 450°F.

6. Line a roasting pan with aluminum foil (this will help to maintain the high level of temperature required to cook the chicken quickly without drying it out).

7. Thread the chicken onto skewers, leaving ¼-inch gap between each piece (this is necessary for the heat to reach all sides of the chicken).

8. Place the skewers in the prepared roasting pan and brush with some of the remaining marinade.

9. Cook in the center of the oven for 6-8 minutes.

10. Take the pan out of the oven, turn the skewers over and brush the pieces of chicken with the remaining marinade.

11. Return the pan to the oven and cook for a further 6-8 minutes.

12. Shake off any excess liquid from the chicken. (Strain the excess liquid and set aside to make Chicken Tikka Masala)

13. Place the skewers on a serving dish. You may take the tikka off the skewers if you wish, but allow the meat to cool slightly before removing from the skewers.

TIME Preparation takes 30-35 minutes plus time needed to marinate, cooking takes 15-18 minutes.

Barrah Kabab (Marinated Lamb Chops)

*A wonderful dish which can be served as an appetizer or a main course.
The chops are marinated in a spice-laced yogurt mixture.
The yogurt tenderises the chops and also prepares the meat to absorb
the spices better.*

SERVES 6-8

2lbs lamb shoulder chops
½ tsp ground nutmeg
½ tsp ground black pepper
½ tsp ground cinnamon
½ tsp cayenne or chili powder
½ tsp ground turmeric
2 cloves garlic, peeled
2 tbsps coarsely chopped onions
½-inch cube of root ginger, peeled and
     chopped
⅔ cup thick set plain yogurt
½ tsp salt or to taste
1 tbsp cooking oil
1 tsp ground cumin
1 tbsp sesame seeds

1. Trim off excess fat from the chops and flatten each chop with a meat mallet or a rolling pin. Wipe clean with a damp cloth.

2. Put all ingredients except chops, oil, cumin and sesame seeds, into a blender or food processor and blend to a purée.

3. Put the chops into a large bowl and pour the blended ingredients over them.

4. Using your fingers, rub the marinade well into each chop.

5. Cover the container with plastic wrap and leave to marinate for at least 8 hours in a cool place or overnight in the refrigerator.

6. Preheat oven to 425°F.

7. Line a roasting pan with aluminum foil (this will help reflect heat and keep your roasting pan clean).

8. Arrange the chops on the roasting pan in a single layer (reserve any remaining marinade) and cook in the center of the oven for 10 minutes – turning the chops over once. Reduce heat to 400°F.

9. Mix the remaining marinade with the oil and cumin. Brush the chops with this and sprinkle half the sesame seeds on top. Return the pan to the upper part of the oven for 10 minutes. Turn the chops over and brush this side with the remaining marinade mixture and sprinkle the rest of the sesame seeds as before. Cook for a further 10-15 minutes.

TIME Preparation takes 20-25 minutes plus 8 hours to marinate, cooking takes 30-35 minutes.

SERVING IDEAS Serve one chop per person as an appetizer with plenty of raw onion rings, sprinkled with lemon juice, wedges of cucumber and crisp lettuce leaves; or as a main course with Plain Boiled Rice and Mixed Vegetable Curry.

ONION BHAJIYAS

(ONION FRITTERS)

These crisp and delicious onion fritters are popular for snacks all over India.
They are made by coating finely shredded onions with a spicy batter.

SERVES 6-8

1½ cups besan (lentil or chick-pea flour)
1 tsp salt or to taste
Pinch of baking soda
1 tbsp ground rice
2 tsps ground cumin
2 tsps ground coriander
½-1 tsp chili powder
1-2 fresh green chili peppers, finely
    chopped and seeded for a milder flavor
2 large onions, sliced into half rings and
    separated
Scant cup water
Oil for deep frying

1. Sieve the besan and add the salt, bicarbonate of soda, ground rice, cumin, coriander, chili powder and green chili peppers; mix well.

2. Now add the onions and mix thoroughly.

3. Gradually add the water and keep mixing until a soft but thick batter is formed and the onions are thoroughly coated with this batter.

4. Heat the oil over medium heat (*it is important to heat the oil to the correct temperature – 300-350° F*). To test this, take a tiny amount of the batter, about the size of a pea and drop it in the oil. If it floats up to the surface immediately but without turning brown, the oil is at the correct temperature.

5. Put in as many small amounts (about half a tablespoon) of the onion/batter mix as the pan will hold in a single layer. Don't fry too many fritters at once as this will result in the outsides overcooking while the insides remain uncooked.

6. Reduce the heat to low as the fritters need to be fried over a gentle heat to ensure that the batter at the center stays soft, while the outside turns golden brown and crisp. This should take about 10-12 minutes for each batch.

7. Drain the fritters on paper towels.

TIME Preparation takes 15-20 minutes, cooking takes 45-50 minutes.
SERVING IDEAS Serve on their own with drinks or with a selection of chutneys as an appetizer.
Suitable for freezing.

CHICKEN OR TURKEY PAKORAS

This delicious recipe can be made with cooked as well as raw meat so it is an excellent and unusual way to use up left overs. Raw chicken has been used for the recipe below, which remains more succulent than cooked meat.

SERVES 6-8

⅔ cup water

1 medium-sized onion, coarsely chopped

2-3 cloves garlic, peeled and coarsely chopped

1-2 fresh green chili peppers, coarsely chopped; remove the seeds if you prefer a milder flavor

2 tbsps chopped coriander leaves

1 rounded cup besan or lentil flour/chick pea flour, sieved

1 tsp ground coriander

1 tsp ground cumin

½ tsp garam masala

½ tsp chili powder

1 tsp salt or to taste

Pinch of baking soda

12oz boneless and skinless chicken or turkey breast

Oil for deep frying

1. Put ⅓ cup water from the specified amount into a blender followed by the onion, garlic, chili peppers and coriander leaves. Blend until smooth. Alternatively, process the ingredients in a food processor without the water.

2. In a large bowl, mix the besan, coriander, cumin, garam masala, chili powder, salt and baking soda.

3. Add the processed ingredients and mix thoroughly.

4. Add the remaining water and mix well to form a thick paste.

5. Cut the chicken into pieces and gently mix into the paste until the pieces are fully coated.

6. Heat the oil over medium heat; when hot, using a spoon, put in one piece of coated chicken/turkey at a time until you have as many as the pan will hold in a single layer without overcrowding it. Make sure that each piece is fully coated with the paste.

7. Adjust heat to low and fry the pakoras for 10-15 minutes turning them over half way through. Remove the pakoras with a perforated spoon and drain on paper towels.

TIME Preparation takes 20 minutes, cooking takes 30 minutes.

SERVING IDEAS Serve with Tomato Chutney or Green Coriander Chutney. Suitable for freezing.

BOTI KABAB

Tender boneless lamb is the traditional meat used for these kababs. They are marinated in a spice-laced yogurt dressing before cooking.

SERVES 6

1½lbs boned leg of lamb
2 small cloves of garlic, peeled and
　chopped
2 tbsps chopped coriander leaves
2 tbsps lemon juice
⅓ cup thick set plain yogurt
Salt to taste
1/2 tsp ground turmeric
2 tbsps cooking oil

Grind the following 4 ingredients in a coffee or spice grinder
6 cardamons (with the skin)
1 cinnamon stick, 1-inch long
2-3 dried red chili peppers
1 tbsp coriander seeds

To garnish
Thinly sliced onion rings, separated
Crisp lettuce leaves
Wedges of cucumber

1. Wash the meat and dry with a cloth.
2. Prick all over with a sharp knife and cut into 1½-inch cubes.

3. Put the garlic, coriander leaves, lemon juice and yogurt into a blender or food processor and blend until smooth. Add the salt, turmeric and the ground ingredients.

4. Put the meat into a bowl and add the processed ingredients.

5. Mix thoroughly, cover and leave to marinate for 6-8 hours (or overnight in the refrigerator).

6. Preheat broiler to high.

7. Line the broiler pan with a piece of aluminum foil (this will reflect heat and also keep your pan clean).

8. Thread meat onto skewers leaving about ¼-inch gap between each piece.

9. Mix any remaining marinade with the oil and keep aside.

10. Place the skewers on the prepared broiler pan and cook the kababs for 2-3 minutes.

11. Turn the skewers over and broil for a further 2-3 minutes.

12. Reduce heat to medium. Brush the kababs with the oil/marinade mixture and broil for 6-8 minutes.

13. Turn the skewers over and brush the kababs with the remaining oil/marinade mixture. Broil for a further 6-8 minutes.

TIME Preparation takes 20 minutes plus time needed for marinating, cooking takes 15-20 minutes.

SERVING IDEAS Serve as an appetizer, using ingredients given for garnishing. Serve single cubes on cocktail sticks with drinks or as a side dish for a dinner party.

VARIATION Use pork tenderloin.

WATCHPOINT Do not overcook the Kababs: follow the cooking time precisely so that the Kababs remain succulent.

SEEKH KABABS

If you can't find ajwain seeds, substitute caraway seeds, which have a similar flavor. Grind them with a mortar and pestle or in a spice grinder.

MAKES 18 Kababs

Juice of half a lemon

2 tbsps chopped fresh mint or 1 tsp dried mint

3-4 tbsps chopped coriander leaves

¼ cup raw cashews

1 medium-sized onion, coarsely chopped

2 small cloves of garlic, peeled and coarsely chopped

1-2 fresh green chili peppers, finely chopped or minced; remove the seeds for milder flavor

1½lb lean ground beef or lamb

2 tsps ground coriander

2 tsps ground cumin

1 tsp ground ajwain (ajowan or carum) or ground caraway seeds

½ tsp garam masala

½ tsp Tandoori color or a few drops of red food coloring mixed with 1 tbsp tomato paste

½ tsp freshly ground black pepper

1 egg yolk

¼ tsp chili powder

1 tsp salt or to taste

4 tbsps cooking oil

Grind the following ingredients in a coffee or spice grinder

2 tbsps white or black poppy seeds

2 tbsps sesame seeds

1. Put the lemon juice, mint, coriander leaves, cashews, onion, garlic and green chili peppers in a food processor and blend to a smooth paste. Transfer the mixture to a large bowl.

2. Process the meat in 2-3 small batches until fairly smooth. Add the meat to the rest of the ingredients in the bowl.

3. Add the rest of the ingredients, except the the oil and knead the mixture until all the ingredients are mixed thoroughly and mixture is smooth.

4. Chill the mixture for 30 minutes.

5. Preheat oven to 475°F. Line a roasting pan with aluminum foil.

6. Divide the kabab mix into about 18 balls, each slightly larger than a golf ball.

7. Mold a ball onto a skewer and form into a sausage shape by gently rolling between your palms (about 4-5-inches long) and place in the prepared roasting pan. Make the rest of the kababs the same way.

8. Brush generously with the oil and place the roasting pan just below the top rung of the oven. Cook for 6-8 minutes. Remove the pan from the oven and brush the kababs liberally with the remaining oil and cook for a further 6-8 minutes.

9. Allow the kababs to cool slightly before removing them from the skewers.

TIME Preparation takes 15-20 minutes, cooking takes 35-40 minutes.

POTATO PAKORAS

The Indian love of snacks is apparent in the wide range of mouthwatering recipes created to suit different occasions. These spice-coated crunchy potato slices are easy to make and can be served in a number of different ways.

SERVES 4-6

½ cup besan (lentil flour or chick pea flour)
1 tbsp ground rice
½ tsp salt or to taste
1½ tsps ground coriander
1 tsp ground cumin
½ tsp chili powder
¼ cup water
3 medium-sized potatoes, peeled and cut into ¼-inch thick slices
Oil for deep frying

1. Mix all the dry ingredients in a large bowl.

2. Add the water and mix to thick paste.

3. Add the potatoes and mix until the potato slices are fully coated with the paste.

4. Heat the oil over medium heat in a deep pan (you can use a deep fat fryer without the basket) and put in as many of the coated potato slices as the pan will hold in a single layer.

5. Fry the pakoras until golden brown (6-8 minutes).

6. Drain on paper towels.

TIME Preparation takes 10-15 minutes, cooking takes 20 minutes.

SERVING IDEAS Serve on their own with drinks; as a side dish with any meat, fish or chicken curry; or as an appetizer with Avocado Chutney.

VARIATION Use sweet potatoes.

WATCHPOINT Do not overcrowd the pan. This will prevent the pakoras from sticking together.

Nargisi Kababs

MAKES 14 Kababs

For the filling:

2 hard-boiled eggs, shelled and coarsely chopped

1 fresh green chili pepper, finely chopped and seeded for a milder flavor

2 tbsps finely chopped or minced onion

1 tbsp finely chopped or minced coriander leaves

¼ tsp salt

1 tbsp thick set plain yogurt

2 tbsps ghee or unsalted butter

1 large onion, coarsely chopped

3-4 cloves garlic, peeled and coarsely chopped

1-inch cube of root ginger, peeled and coarsely chopped

1 tsp ground cumin

1½ tsps ground coriander

1 tsp garam masala

½ tsp chili powder

½ tsp freshly ground black pepper

¼ cup thick set plain yogurt

1 tbsp fresh mint leaves or 1 tsp dried mint

2 tbsps chopped coriander leaves

¾ tsp salt or to taste

1¼lbs fine lean ground lamb or beef

1 egg

2 tbsps besan (chick pea flour or lentil flour), sieved

1 tbsp water

⅓ cup cooking oil

1. Combine all ingredients for the filling in a bowl, mix thoroughly and keep aside.

2. Melt the ghee or butter over medium heat and fry the onion, garlic and ginger for 3-4 minutes. Adjust heat to low and add the cumin, coriander, garam masala, chili powder and pepper, stir and fry for 1-2 minutes, then remove from heat and allow to cool.

3. Put the yogurt into a food processor and add the fried ingredients, mint, coriander, salt and the meat. Blend until smooth.

4. If you are using a blender, blend the ingredients first without the mince. Transfer the blended ingredients to a mixing bowl and add the meat.

5. Knead the blended ingredients and the meat until smooth. Divide the mixture into about 14 golf ball-sized portions. Make a depression in the center of each ball and form into a cup shape. Fill with 1 heaped tsp of the egg mixture and cover the filling by pressing the edges together. Now roll it gently between the palms to form a neat ball, press the ball gently and form a round flat cake about ¾-inch thick. Make the rest of the kababs the same way.

6. Beat the egg and gradually sprinkle the besan while still beating. Add the water and beat again.

7. Heat the oil over medium heat in a wide, shallow, preferably non-stick or cast iron skillet. Dip each kabab in the batter and fry in a single layer without overcrowding the pan until they are brown on both sides (3-4 minutes each side). Drain on paper towels.

TIME Preparation takes 40-45 minutes, cooking takes 10-15 minutes.

MUSHROOM BHAJI

Although mushrooms are not widely used in India, Indian restaurants have popularised the use of mushrooms in Indian recipes. Mushroom Bhaji appears to be one of the most popular of them all.

SERVES 4

3-4 tbsps cooking oil
1 medium-sized onion, finely chopped
2-3 cloves garlic, peeled and crushed
½ tsp ground turmeric
½ tsp chili powder
1 tsp ground coriander
1 tsp ground cumin
¾ tsp salt or to taste
1 tbsp tomato paste
8oz small mushrooms

1. Heat the oil over medium heat and fry the onions until they are lightly browned.

2. Lower heat and add the garlic, turmeric, chili powder, coriander and cumin. Stir and fry the spices and add about 1 tbsp water to prevent the spices from sticking to the bottom of the pan. As soon as this water dries up, add a little more. Continue until you have fried the spices for about 5 minutes.

3. Add the salt and tomato paste, mix well and add the mushrooms. Stir until the ingredients are thoroughly mixed.

4. Sprinkle about 2 tbsps water and cover the pan. Simmer for 10 minutes.

5. The finished dish should have a little amount of sauce, but it should not be runny. If necessary take the lid off and cook quickly until the sauce is reasonably thick.

TIME Preparation takes 15 minutes, cooking takes 20 minutes.

SERVING IDEAS Serve with Plain Boiled Rice or any Indian bread accompanied by Chicken with Channa Dhal or Kofta Curry. Also excellent with Kofta Pilau.

MEAT SAMOSAS

The ever-popular Samosas make a wonderful treat on any occasion. In India,
they are a familiar sight at wedding receptions and cocktail parties.

MAKES 18 Samosas

2 tbsps cooking oil
2 medium-sized onions, finely chopped
8oz lean ground lamb or beef
3-4 cloves garlic, peeled and crushed
½-inch cube of root ginger, finely grated
½ tsp ground turmeric
2 tsps ground coriander
1½ tsps ground cumin
½-1 tsp chilli powder
½ tsp salt or to taste
½ cup warm water
1 cup frozen peas
2 tbsps flaked coconut
1 tsp garam masala
1-2 fresh green chili peppers, finely
    chopped and seeded if a milder flavor is
    preferred
2 tbsps chopped coriander leaves
1 tbsp lemon juice

1. Heat the oil over medium heat and fry the onions until they are lightly browned.

2. Add the meat, garlic and ginger. Stir and fry until all the liquid evaporates and adjust heat to low.

3. Add the turmeric, coriander, cumin, chili powder and salt. Stir and fry until meat is lightly browned.

4. Add the water and the peas, bring to the boil, cover and simmer for 25–30 minutes. If there is any liquid left, take the lid off and cook over medium heat until mixture is completely dry, stirring frequently.

5. Stir in the coconut, garam masala, green chili peppers and coriander leaves.

6. Remove from heat and add the lemon juice. Cool thoroughly before filling the pastry.

For the pastry

2 cups all purpose flour
4 tbsps ghee or butter
½ tsp salt
¼ cup warm water
Oil for deep frying

1. Add the butter and salt to the flour. Rub in well.

2. Mix a soft dough with the water adding a little more if necessary. Knead until the dough feels soft and velvety to the touch.

3. Divide the dough into 9 balls. Rotate each ball between your palms in a circular motion, then press it down to make a flat cake.

4. Roll out each flat cake into 4-inch circles

and cut into two. Use each semicircle of pastry as one envelope.

5. Moisten the straight edge with a little warm water.

6. Fold the semicircle of pastry in half to form a triangular cone.

7. Join the straight edges by pressing them hard into each other. Make sure that there are no gaps.

8. Fill these cones with the filling, leaving about ¼-inch border on the top of the cone.

9. Now moisten the top edges and press them hard together.

10. Deep fry the samosas over gentle heat until they are golden brown and drain on paper towels.

CAULIFLOWER PAKORAS

These chunky cauliflower flowerettes with a spicy coating make a versatile snack and can be served in many different ways.

SERVES 4

¾ cup besan (lentil flour or chick pea flour), sieved

1 tbsp ground rice or cream of rice

¾ tsp salt or to taste

2 tbsps ground coriander

2 tsps ground cumin

½-1 tsp chili powder

½ tsp ground turmeric

Pinch of baking soda

1 medium-sized cauliflower, cut into about 1½-inch flowerettes

⅔ cup water

Oil for deep frying

1. Mix the dry ingredients in a large bowl.

2. Add the cauliflower and water. Mix until the cauliflower is fully coated with the spiced gram flour paste. If the flowerettes are not completely covered with the batter, spread some over the uncovered areas with a spoon.

3. Heat the oil over medium heat and put in as many flowerettes as the pan will hold in a single layer. You can use a deep fat fryer without the basket.

4. Fry until the pakoras are uniformly brown (6-8 minutes per batch).

5. Drain on paper towels.

TIME Preparation takes 15 minutes, cooking takes 20 minutes.

SERVING IDEAS Serve on their own with drinks, as a side dish with almost anything or as an appetizer with Carrot & Peanut Raita.

TO FREEZE Suitable for freezing. Defrost thoroughly before reheating under a preheated medium grill for 6-8 minutes, turning them once.

WATCHPOINT Use no more than a pinch of baking soda, because any more than that will ruin the taste and appearance of the pakoras.

SPICED MIXED NUTS

These spiced nuts are delicious and irresistible.
They are roasted with a little oil and coated with spices while
still hot.

SERVES 8-10

1 cup whole almonds
1 cup raw cashews
2 tsps cooking oil
½ tsp ground coriander
½ tsp ground cumin
¼ tsp chili powder
½ tsp salt

1. In a heavy-based pan, cook the nuts over low heat until they are heated through (3-4 minutes).

2. Add 1 tsp oil, stir and mix thoroughly. Toast the nuts until they are evenly browned (10-12 minutes), stirring constantly.

3. Remove from the heat and sprinkle with the spices and salt immediately. Mix thoroughly and set aside for 10 minutes.

4. Add the remaining oil, stir and mix until the nuts are fully coated by the spices.

5. Allow to cool completely before serving.

TIME Preparation takes 5 minutes, cooking takes 15 minutes.

SERVING IDEAS Serve with pre-dinner drinks.

VARIATION Use peanuts instead of almonds.

SPICED POTATO BITES

In Indian cooking, potatoes are used very imaginatively. Here, boiled potatoes are cut into small pieces and sautéed until they are brown and then flavored with a light sprinkling of spices.

SERVES 6-8

3 or 4 medium-sized potatoes
4 tbsps cooking oil
1/2 tbsp salt or to taste
1/4 tsp garam masala
1/2 tsp ground cumin
1/2 tsp ground coriander
1/4 - 1/2 tsp chili powder

1. Boil the potatoes in their skins, cool thoroughly, peel and dice them into 1-inch cubes.

2. In a wide shallow pan, preferably a non-stick or cast iron skillet, heat the oil over medium heat. It is important to have the right pan otherwise the potatoes will stick.

3. Add the potatoes and spread them evenly around the pan. Brown the potatoes evenly, stirring them occasionally.

4. When the potatoes are brown, sprinkle over the salt, garam masala, cumin, coriander and the chili powder. Stir gently and mix until the potatoes are fully coated with the spices. Remove from the heat.

TIME Preparation takes 30 minutes to boil the potatoes plus time to cool them, cooking takes 10-12 minutes.

SERVING IDEAS Serve on cocktail sticks with drinks.

WATCHPOINT The potatoes must be allowed to cool thoroughly. Hot or warm potatoes crumble easily and therefore cannot be cut into neat pieces.

VEGETABLE SAMOSAS

As the majority of the Indian population is vegetarian, it is no wonder that the original recipe for samosas is a vegetarian one.

MAKES 18 Samosas

3 medium-sized potatoes

2 tbsps cooking oil

½ tsp black or white mustard seeds

1 tsp cumin seeds

2 dried red chili peppers, coarsely chopped

1 medium-sized onion, finely chopped

1-2 fresh green chili peppers, coarsely chopped and seeded if a milder flavor is preferred

½ tsp ground turmeric

1 tsp ground coriander

1 tsp ground cumin

1 tsp salt or to taste

1 tbsp chopped coriander leaves

1. Boil the potatoes in their skins, allow to cool thoroughly, then peel and dice them.

2. Heat the oil and add mustard seeds. As soon as they start crackling, add the cumin seeds and red chili peppers, and then the onions and green chili peppers. Fry till the onions are soft. Add the turmeric, coriander and cumin.

3. Stir quickly and add the potatoes and the salt.

4. Reduce heat to low, stir and cook until the potatoes are thoroughly mixed with the spices.

5. Remove from the heat and stir in the coriander leaves. Cool thoroughly before filling the samosas. Make the samosas as instructed in the pastry recipe given for Meat Samosas.

TIME Preparation takes about 60 minutes and cooking takes about 60 minutes.

SERVING IDEAS As for Meat Samosa

VARIATION If you can't find black mustard seeds, substitute white mustard seeds or add ½ tsp wholegrain mustard after the onions are softened.

main meals

Fish and Seafood

FISH BHOONA

SERVES 4

1½lbs steaks or fillets of any white fish
6 tbsps cooking oil

*Mix the following 4 ingredients
in a small bowl*
1 tbsp all-purpose flour
¼ tsp ground turmeric
¼ tsp chili powder
¼ tsp salt

1 large onion, coarsely chopped
½-inch cube of root ginger, peeled and
    coarsely chopped
2-4 cloves garlic, peeled and coarsely
    chopped
½ tsp ground turmeric
¼ tsp chili powder
1 tsp ground coriander
½ tsp garam masala
1 small can of tomatoes
⅔ cup warm water
⅔ cup frozen peas
1 tsp salt or to taste
1 tbsp chopped coriander leaves

1. Skin the fish, wash and dry thoroughly
on paper towels and cut the fish into
approximately 1 × 2-inch pieces.

2. Heat 2 tbsps oil from the specified
amount, in a large skillet, preferably non-
stick or cast iron, over medium heat.

3. Lightly dust the fish, one piece at a time,
in the seasoned flour and place in the hot
oil. Put in as many pieces as the pan will
hold in a single layer without overcrowding
it and adjust heat to medium-high. Fry the
fish until all the pieces are evenly browned.
This has to be done quickly in fairly hot oil
so that the fish is thoroughly sealed. Fry all
the fish this way and drain on paper towels.

4. Put the onion, ginger and garlic into a
blender or food processor and blend until
finely chopped.

5. Heat the remaining oil over medium heat
in a wide, shallow pan. Add the onion
mixture and stir. When the mixture is
heated through turn heat down to low, stir
and fry for 3-4 minutes.

6. Add the turmeric, chili powder, coriander
and garam masala and fry for 4-5 minutes,
stirring continuously. During this time, from
the can of tomatoes, add 1 tbsp juice at a
time to prevent the spices from sticking to
the bottom of the pan.

7. Now add one tomato at a time, along
with any remaining juice, breaking the
tomato with the back of the spoon. Cook
until the tomato is well incorporated into
the rest of the ingredients. Use up the rest
of the tomatoes in the same way.

8. Add the water, peas and salt. Bring to the
boil and add the fish. Cover and simmer for
5 to 6 minutes.

9. Remove from heat and sprinkle the
coriander leaves on top.

TIME Preparation takes 15-20 minutes, cooking takes 30-35 minutes.

Fish and Seafood

TANDOORI FISH

A firm-fleshed white fish is ideal for this dish; it is not necessary to use an expensive fish. The fish should be handled carefully as most white fish tends to flake during cooking.

SERVES 4

1lb fillets or steaks of any white fish
2 cloves garlic, peeled and coarsely
    chopped
¼-inch cube of root ginger, peeled and
    coarsely chopped
½ tsp salt
1 tsp ground cumin
1 tsp ground coriander
½ tsp garam masala
¼-½ tsp chili powder
¼ tsp Tandoori color or a few drops of red
    food coloring mixed with 1 tbsp tomato
    paste
Juice of half a lemon
3 tbsps water
2 tbsps cooking oil

*Mix the following ingredients
in a small bowl*
2 heaped tbsps flour
½ tsp chili powder
¼ tsp salt

1. Wash the fish and dry on absorbent paper. Cut into 1-inch squares. If using frozen fish, defrost it thoroughly and dry on paper towels before cutting it.

2. Add the salt to the ginger and garlic and crush to a smooth pulp.

3. In a small bowl, mix together the ginger/garlic pulp, cumin, coriander, garam masala, chili powder and Tandoori color or tomato paste mix. Add the lemon juice and water and mix thoroughly. Keep aside.

4. Heat the oil over medium heat in a non-stick or cast iron skillet. Dust each piece of fish in the seasoned flour and put in the hot oil in a single layer, leave plenty of room in the pan. Fry for 5 minutes, 2½ minutes each side, and drain on paper towels. Now return all the fish to the pan.

5. Hold a strainer over the pan and pour the liquid spice mixture into it. Press with the back of a metal spoon until the mixture looks dry and very coarse; discard this mixture.

6. Stir gently and cook over medium heat until the fish is fully coated with the spices and the liquid dries up. Remove from heat.

TIME Preparation takes 15 minutes, cooking takes 15-20 minutes.

SERVING IDEAS Serve garnished with shredded lettuce leaves, sliced cucumber and raw onion rings.

Fish and Seafood

MASALA MACHCHI

Masala Machchi or spicy fish is made by marinating fish in lemon juice and spices. The lemon juice gives the fish a rather smooth and velvety texture.

SERVES 4

Juice of half a lemon

1 small onion, peeled and coarsely chopped

2-3 cloves garlic, peeled and coarsely chopped

1-inch cube of root ginger, peeled and coarsely chopped

1-2 fresh green chili peppers, chopped and seeded if you like a milder flavor

3 tbsps chopped coriander leaves

1 tsp salt or to taste

1lb fillets of any white fish

⅓ cup oil for shallow frying

To coat the fish

3 tbsps plain flour

1 egg, beaten

¼ tsp salt

¼ tsp chili powder

1. Put the lemon juice, onion, garlic, ginger, green chili peppers, coriander leaves and 1 tsp salt into a food processor and blend until smooth.

2. Wash the fish gently and pat dry with paper towels. If you are using frozen fish, defrost thoroughly and then dry as for fresh fish.

3. Cut the fish into 1½ × 1-inch pieces. Put a light coating of the spice paste on all sides of each piece of fish, cover the container and leave to marinate in a cool place for 2-3 hours, or overnight in the refrigerator.

4. Mix the flour with the salt and chili powder. Dust each piece of fish lightly with this, then dip in the beaten egg. Shallow fry in a single layer over medium heat until brown on both sides (2-3 minutes on each side). Drain on paper towels. Alternatively, deep fry the fish until golden brown and drain on paper towels.

TIME Preparation takes 15-20 minutes, cooking takes 12-15 minutes.

SERVING IDEAS Serve with Bhindi (Okra) Raita or Eggplant Raita. Can be served as a side dish with rice and Tarka Dhal or Saagwalla Dahl.

Fish and Seafood

SPICED SARDINES

If fresh sardines are not available use any other small, whole fish. The recipe couldn't be easier or more delicious.

SERVES 4

8 fresh sardines (about 1½lb)

1 tsp salt or to taste

3-4 cloves garlic, peeled and coarsely chopped

Juice of half a lemon

½ tsp ground turmeric

½-1 tsp chili powder

3 heaped tbsps plain flour

⅓ cup cooking oil

1. Scale and clean the fish, if necesssary. Wash gently in cold water and dry on paper towels.

2. Add the salt to the garlic and crush to a smooth pulp.

3. Mix all the ingredients together, except the fish, flour and oil, in a small bowl.

4. Put the fish in a wide shallow dish and pour the marinade over. Spread it gently on both sides of the fish, cover and refrigerate for 2-4 hours.

5. Heat the oil over medium heat. Dip each fish in the flour and coat it thoroughly. Fry until golden brown on both sides (2-3 minutes each side). Drain on paper towels.

TIME Preparation takes 20 minutes plus 2-4 hours to marinate, cooking takes 6-8 minutes

SERVING IDEAS Serve as an appetizer with Avocado Chutney and sliced cucumber.

Fish and Seafood

FISH ROE SCRAMBLE

Fish roe makes a very nutritious dish and a few fairly standard ingredients transform the taste dramatically. If fresh roe is not available, substitute canned roe and cut the cooking time in half.

SERVES 4

8oz fresh fish roe

2 tbsps cooking oil

1 medium-sized onion, finely chopped

1 fresh green chili pepper, finely chopped

2 tbsps ground coriander

½ tsp ground turmeric

½ tsp salt or to taste

1. Chop the cod roe coarsely.

2. Heat the oil over medium heat in a non-stick or cast iron skillet and fry the onion and the green chili pepper until the onion is soft but not brown.

3. Add the coriander and turmeric, stir and fry for 1 minute.

4. Add the cod roe and salt, stir and fry for 3-4 minutes, breaking up the pieces with the spoon.

5. Adjust heat to low and let it cook until it begins to brown (6-8 minutes), stirring occasionally.

6. Remove from the heat and serve.

TIME Preparation takes 10-15 minutes, cooking takes 12-15 minutes.

SERVING IDEAS Serve with Plain Boiled Rice, Tarka Dhal and/or Boti Kabab.

Fish and Seafood

FISH SHAHJAHANI

A rich, but easy to prepare fish dish which is named after the Mughal Emperor Shahjahan, who was noted for his love of good food.

SERVES 4

1½lbs fillets of any white fish

¾ cup roasted cashews

½ cup cream

4 tbsps unsalted butter

1 large onion, finely sliced

2-inch piece of cinnamon stick, broken up

4 cardamoms, split open on the top

2 whole cloves

1-2 fresh green chili peppers, sliced lengthwise; seeded if a milder flavor is preferred

1 tsp ground turmeric

¾ cup warm water

1 tsp salt or to taste

1 tbsp lemon juice

1. Rinse the fish gently in cold water, dry on paper towels and cut into 1 × 2-inch pieces.

2. Put the cashews and the cream in a blender and blend to a reasonably fine mixture.

3. In a skillet melt the butter over medium heat and fry onions, cinnamon, cardamom, cloves and green chili peppers until the onions are lightly browned (6-8 minutes). Stir in the turmeric.

4. Add the water and salt and arrange the fish in a single layer. Bring to the boil, cover the pan and simmer for 2-3 minutes.

5. Now add the cashew/cream mixture and stir gently until the pieces of fish are well coated. Cover the pan again and simmer for a further 2-3 minutes.

6. Remove from heat and gently stir in the lemon juice.

TIME Preparation takes 15 minutes, cooking takes 15-20 minutes.

SERVING IDEAS To appreciate the wonderful flavor of this dish fully, the rice served with it should not be too highly flavored. Choose a mild recipe such as Cardamom Rice or Fried Brown Rice. Serve Green Beans with Garlic Butter as a side dish.

VARIATION Add potatoes which have been boiled in their skins, peeled and diced

WATCHPOINT It is important to use a wide shallow skillet so that the fish can be arranged in a single layer to prevent them from breaking up during cooking.

Fish and Seafood

BENGAL FISH CURRY

The abundance of fish in the Bay of Bengal has enabled the people of this north eastern part of India to develop many delicious dishes using fish. In the recipe below, the fish is cooked entirely in plain yogurt which, with the addition of a little lentil flour, gives it an unusual touch.

SERVES 4

1½lbs firm fleshed fish such as river trout, or catfish, skinned
1 tsp ground turmeric
1¼ tsps salt or to taste
5 tbsps cooking oil
1 large onion, finely chopped
¼-in cube of root ginger – peeled and finely chopped or grated
1 tbsp ground coriander
½-1 tsp chili powder
1 tsp paprika
1¼ cups thick set plain yogurt
4-6 whole fresh green chili peppers
1-2 cloves of garlic, peeled and crushed
1 tbsp besan (lentil or chick pea flour)
2 tbsps chopped coriander leaves (optional)

1. Clean and wash the fish and pat dry.

2. Cut each fish in to 1½-inch pieces.

3. Gently rub into the fish ¼ tsp turmeric and ¼ tsp salt from the specified amount and put it aside for 15-20 minutes.

4. Meanwhile, heat the oil over medium heat; use a pan wide enough to hold the fish in a single layer and fry onion and ginger until the onions are lightly browned (6-7 minutes), stirring frequently.

5. Add coriander, remaining turmeric, chili powder and the paprika – adjust heat to low and fry for 1-2 minutes, stirring continuously.

6. Beat the yogurt with a fork until smooth and add to the onion and spice mixture, adjust heat to medium, add the green chili peppers, the remaining salt and the garlic. Stir and mix well.

7. Arrange the pieces of fish in this liquid in a single layer and bring to the boil. Cover and cook over low heat for 5-6 minutes.

8. Blend the flour with a little water to make a pouring consistency. Strain this over the fish curry, stir gently, and mix. Cover and cook for 2-3 minutes.

9. Remove from heat and gently mix in half the coriander leaves.

10. Transfer the fish curry to a serving dish and garnish with the remaining coriander leaves (if used).

TIME Preparation takes 20-25 minutes, cooking takes 20 minutes.

SERVING IDEAS Serve with plain boiled rice and Cabbage with Lentil Flour. For a dinner party or special occasion, serve with Fried Brown Rice and Spiced Green Beans. Carrot & Mooli Salad makes an interesting addition to the menu.

Fish and Seafood

SHRIMP CHILI MASALA

This is a delicate but richly flavored dish. In India, only fresh and juicy large shrimps will do, but standard sized shrimps can be used, too.

SERVES 4

⅓ cup unsalted butter

6 green cardamoms, split open on the top

1-inch cube of root ginger, peeled and finely grated

3-4 cloves garlic, peeled and crushed

1 tbsp ground coriander

½ tsp ground turmeric

1lb raw shrimps

⅔ cup plain yogurt

⅓ cup water

1 tsp sugar

1 tsp salt or to taste

¼ cup ground almonds

4-6 whole fresh green chili peppers

1 small onion, finely chopped

2 fresh green chili peppers, seeded and minced

½ tsp garam masala

1 tbsp chopped coriander leaves

1. Melt ⅔ of the butter from the specified amount over gentle heat and add the whole cardamoms, fry for 30 seconds and add the ginger and garlic. Stir and cook for 1 minute, then add the ground coriander and turmeric. Stir and fry for 30 seconds.

2. Add the shrimps, turn the heat up to medium and cook for 5-6 minutes, stirring frequently.

3. Beat the yogurt until smooth, gradually add the water and beat until well blended. Add this mixture to the shrimps, stir in the sugar and the salt, cover the pan and simmer for 5-6 minutes.

4. Add the ground almonds and the whole green chili peppers and cook, uncovered, for 5 minutes.

5. Meanwhile, fry the onions in the remaining butter until they are just soft, but not brown. Add the minced chili peppers and the garam masala; stir and fry for a further 1-2 minutes. Stir this mixture into the shrimps along with any butter left in the pan. Remove the pan from the heat.

6. Place in a serving dish and garnish with the coriander leaves or more sliced chili peppers.

TIME Preparation takes 15 minutes, cooking takes 20-25 minutes.

SERVING IDEAS Serve with Mushroom Pilau or Fried Brown Rice. Green Beans in Garlic Butter or Spiced Green Beans are ideal as a side dish.

Fish and Seafood

SMOKED MACKEREL SALAD

As smoked fish is not readily available in India, the smoking is usually done at home. You can use kippered herrings if you can't find smoked mackerel.

SERVES 4

8oz smoked mackerel
¼ cup finely chopped onions
1 fresh green chili pepper, seeded and
    diced
2 tbsps finely chopped coriander leaves
1½ tbsps lemon juice

1. Remove any skin and bones from the fish and mash it with a fork.

2. Add all ingredients and mix thoroughly. Cover the container and refrigerate for 2-3 hours before serving.

TIME Preparation takes 10 minutes.

SERVING IDEAS Serve garnished with Tarka Dhal and Fried Brown Rice or
on small crackers with drinks.
Suitable for freezing.

Vegetarian Dishes

MIXED VEGETABLE CURRY

A variety of seasonal vegetables are cooked together in a sauce flavored by ground spices, onions and tomatoes. Whole green chili peppers are added towards the end to enhance the flavor of the dish and also to retain their fresh green color.

SERVES 4-6

4-5 tbsps cooking oil
1 large onion, finely chopped
½-inch cube of root ginger, peeled and
   finely sliced
1 tsp ground turmeric
1 tsp ground coriander
1 tsp ground cumin
1 tsp paprika
4 small ripe tomatoes, skinned and
   chopped or a small can of tomatoes with
   the juice
2 small potatoes, peeled and diced
½ cup sliced green beans
¾ cup carrots, scraped and sliced
½ cup peas, shelled weight
Scant 2 cups warm water
2-4 whole fresh green chili peppers
1 tsp garam masala
1 tsp salt or to taste
1 tbsp chopped coriander leaves

1. Heat the oil over medium heat and fry the onion until lightly browned. (6-7 minutes).

2. Add the ginger and fry for 30 seconds.

3. Adjust heat to low and add the turmeric, coriander, cumin and paprika. Stir and mix well.

4. Add half the tomatoes and fry for 2 minutes, stirring continuously.

5. Add all the vegetables and the water. Stir and mix well. Bring to the boil, cover and simmer until vegetables are tender (15-20 minutes).

6. Add the remaining tomatoes and the chili peppers. Cover and simmer for 5-6 minutes.

7. Add the garam masala and salt, mix well. Stir in half the coriander leaves and remove from heat.

8. Put the vegetable curry into a serving dish and sprinkle the remaining coriander leaves on top.

TIME Preparation takes 25-30 minutes, cooking takes 30 minutes.

SERVING IDEAS Serve with Tandoori Roti or Naan and Kababs, Masala Machchi or Tandoori Fish. Can also be served with Meat Biriani.

TO FREEZE Suitable for freezing, but omit the potatoes. Add pre-boiled diced potatoes during reheating.

WATCHPOINT Frozen peas and beans may be used for convenience, but the cooking time should be adjusted accordingly. Cook the fresh vegetables first and follow cooking time for frozen vegetables as per instructions on pack.

Vegetarian Dishes

EGG & POTATO DUM

Hard-cooked curried eggs are very popular in the northeastern part of India. Here, the eggs are cooked with potatoes and they are both fried first until they form a light crust. Slow cooking, without any loss of steam, is the secret of the success of this dish.

SERVES 4-6

6 hard-boiled eggs

5 tbsps cooking oil

3 medium-sized potatoes, peeled and quartered

⅛ tsp each of chili powder and ground turmeric, mixed together

1 large onion, finely chopped

½-inch cube of root ginger, peeled and grated

1 cinnamon stick, 2-inch long; broken up into 2-3 pieces

2 black or green cardamoms, split open on the top

4 whole cloves

1 fresh green chili pepper, chopped

1 small can of tomatoes

½ tsp ground turmeric

2 tsps ground coriander

1 tsp ground fennel

¼-½ tsp chili powder (optional)

1 tsp salt or to taste

1 cup warm water

1 tbsp chopped coriander leaves

1. Shell the eggs and make 4 slits lengthwise on each egg leaving about ½-inch gap on either end.

2. Heat the oil over medium heat in a cast iron or non-stick skillet (enamel or steel pans will cause the eggs and the potatoes to stick). Fry the potatoes until they are well browned on all sides (about 10 minutes). Remove them with a slotted spoon and keep aside.

3. Remove the pan from heat and stir in the turmeric and chili mixture. Place the pan back on heat and fry the whole eggs until they are well browned. Remove them with a slotted spoon and set aside.

4. In the same oil, fry the onions, ginger, cinnamon, cardamom, cloves and green chili pepper until the onions are lightly browned (6-7 minutes).

5. Add half the tomatoes, stir and fry until the tomatoes break up (2-3 minutes).

6. Add the turmeric, ground coriander, fennel and chili powder (if used); stir and fry for 3-4 minutes.

7. Add the rest of the tomatoes and fry for 4-5 minutes, stirring frequently.

8. Add the potatoes, salt and water, bring to the boil, cover the pan tightly and simmer until the potatoes are tender, stirring occasionally.

9. Now add the eggs and simmer, uncovered for 5-6 minutes, stirring once or twice.

10. Stir in the coriander leaves and remove from heat.

TIME Preparation takes 15 minutes, cooking takes 35-40 minutes.

Classic Chicken Dishes

TANDOORI CHICKEN

The Tandoor, because of its fierce but even distribution of heat, enables meat to cook quickly, forming a light crust on the outside but leaving the inside moist and succulent.
It is possible to achieve perfectly satisfactory results by using a conventional gas or electric oven at the highest temperature setting, though the distinctive flavor of clay-cooked chicken will be missing.

SERVES 4-6

2½lbs chicken legs or breasts or a
    combination of the two
1 tsp salt or to taste
Juice of half a lemon
½-inch cube of root ginger, peeled and
    coarsely chopped
2-3 small cloves of garlic, peeled and
    coarsely chopped
1 fresh green chili pepper, coarsely
    chopped and seeded for a milder flavor
2 tbsps chopped coriander leaves
⅓ cup thick set plain yogurt
1 tsp ground coriander
½ tsp ground cumin
1 tsp garam masala
¼ tsp freshly ground black pepper
½ tsp Tandoori color, or a few drops of red
    food coloring mixed with 1 tbsp tomato
    paste.

1. Remove skin from the chicken and cut each piece into two. With a sharp knife, make 2-3 slits in each piece. Rub salt and lemon juice into the chicken pieces and set aside for half an hour.

2. Meanwhile, put the ginger, garlic, green chillies, coriander leaves and the yogurt into a food processor and blend until smooth. Add the rest of the ingredients and blend again.

3. Pour and spread the marinade all over the chicken, especially into the slits. Cover the container with plastic wrap and leave to marinate for 6-8 hours or overnight in the refrigerator.

4. Preheat oven to 475°F. Line a roasting pan with aluminum foil (this will help to maintain the high level of heat required to cook the chicken) and arrange the chicken pieces in it. Place the roasting tin in the center of the oven and bake for 25-30 minutes, turning the pieces over carefully as they brown and basting with juice in the roasting pan as well as any remaining marinade.

5. Remove from the oven, lift each piece with a pair of tongs and shake off any excess liquid.

TIME Preparation takes 20-25 minutes, cooking takes 25-30 minutes.

SERVING IDEAS Serve as an appetizer with lettuce, cucumber, tomatoes and sliced raw onions; or as a side dish with Plain Pillau, Mushroom Bhaji and Mint & Onion Raita.
Suitable for freezing.

Classic Chicken Dishes

MURGHI NAWABI

This is a classic example of the popular Mughal cuisine which is noted for its delicate flavorings and rich smooth sauces. The chicken is marinated in yogurt and turmeric and simmered in delicately flavored coconut sauce.

SERVES 4-6

2¼lbs chicken, skinned and jointed

⅔ cup thick set plain yogurt

½ tsp ground turmeric

3-4 cloves garlic, peeled and coarsely chopped

1-inch cube of root ginger, peeled and coarsely chopped

4-6 dried red chili peppers

4 tbsps ghee or unsalted butter

2 large onions, finely sliced

1 tsp caraway seeds

1 tsp garam masala

1¼ tsps salt or to taste

1 cup warm water

⅓ cup cold water

1 cup finely grated fresh coconut

½ cup raw cashews

2 hard-boiled eggs, sliced

¼ tsp paprika

---

1. Cut each chicken joint into two pieces (separate leg from thigh and cut each breast into two pieces). Wash the chicken and dry on paper towels.

2. Beat the yogurt and turmeric powder together until smooth. Add to the chicken and mix thoroughly, cover the container and leave to marinate for 4-6 hours or overnight in the refrigerator.

3. Put the garlic, ginger and red chili peppers in a blender or food processor with just enough water to make blending easy. Blend until the ingredients are smooth. Alternatively, crush the garlic and ginger and finely chop the chili peppers.

4. Melt the ghee or butter over medium heat and fry the onions until they are brown (8-10 minutes). Remove from the heat and press the onions against the side of the pan to squeeze out excess fat. Transfer the onions onto a plate and set aside.

5. Place the pan back on heat and fry the caraway seeds and garam masala for 30 seconds. Add the blended ingredients. Stir briskly and add the chicken, fried onions and salt. Fry the chicken for 5-6 minutes, stirring frequently and lowering heat as the chicken is heated through. If there is any yogurt marinade left in the container add this to the chicken.

6. Add the warm water and the coconut. Bring to the boil, cover the pan and simmer until the chicken is tender and the sauce is thick (30-35 minutes). Stir occasionally during this time.

7. Meanwhile, put the cashews into a blender and add the cold water and blend until smooth. Add the cashew paste to the chicken during the last 5 minutes of cooking time. Simmer uncovered for 4-5 minutes, stirring frequently.

8. Put the chicken into a serving dish and garnish with the sliced eggs. Sprinkle the paprika on top.

Classic Chicken Dishes

CHICKEN CHAAT

Recipes do not have to be elaborate to be tasty, and Chicken Chaat is a perfect example. Cubes of chicken meat, stir-fried with a light coating of spices look impressive with a crisp salad and taste superb.

SERVES 4

1½lbs chicken breasts, skinned and boned

1 tsp salt or to taste

2-3 cloves garlic, peeled and coarsely chopped

2 tbsps cooking oil

1½ tsps ground coriander

¼ tsp ground turmeric

¼-½ tsp chili powder

1½ tbsps lemon juice

2 tbsps finely chopped coriander leaves

1. Wash the chicken and dry on paper towels. Cut into 1-inch cubes.

2. Add the salt to the garlic and crush to a smooth pulp.

3. Heat the oil in a frying pan, preferably non-stick or cast iron, over medium heat.

4. Add the garlic and fry until it is lightly browned.

5. Add the chicken and fry for 6-7 minutes, stirring constantly.

6. Add the ground coriander, turmeric and chili powder. Fry for 3-4 minutes, stirring frequently. Remove from heat and stir in the lemon juice and coriander leaves.

TIME Preparation takes 15 minutes, cooking takes 12-15 minutes.

SERVING IDEAS Serve as an appetizer garnished with crispy lettuce leaves, sliced cucumber, raw sliced onion and wedges of lemon or with a selection of chutneys. Chicken Chaat can also be served with drinks on cocktail sticks, hot or cold.
Suitable for freezing.

Classic Chicken Dishes

SABJI MASALA MURGH

This chicken dish is wonderful when time may be too short to cook a separate vegetable dish, because a selection of vegetables are added at different stages. Frozen vegetables are used in this recipe; if using fresh vegetables, the cooking time should be adjusted accordingly.

SERVES 4-6

2¼lbs chicken pieces
Scant 1 cup water
¾ cup roasted cashews
4 tbsps ghee or unsalted butter
1-inch cube of root ginger, peeled and finely grated
4-6 cloves garlic, peeled and finely chopped

Grind the following 4 ingredients in a spice or coffee grinder
¼ tsp ground nutmeg
6 green cardamoms with the skin
1 tsp caraway seeds
4-6 dried red chili peppers

1¼ tsps salt or to taste
6 whole baby carrots
⅓ cup frozen peas
⅓ cup frozen corn
4 green onions, coarsely chopped
1 small green pepper, seeded and finely shredded

1. Skin the chicken and separate legs from thighs; wash and pat dry.

2. Put half of the water from the specified amount into a blender and add the cashews. Blend to a smooth paste.

3. Melt the ghee or butter over medium heat and fry the ginger and garlic for 1 minute.

4. Adjust heat to low and add the ground ingredients, stir and fry for 1 minute.

5. Add the chicken, adjust heat to medium-high and fry the chicken until it changes color (5-6 minutes).

6. Add the cashew paste, stir and mix thoroughly. Rinse out the blender container with the remaining water and add to the chicken.

7. Add the salt, mix well, cover the pan and cook over low heat for 15 minutes, stirring occasionally.

8. Add the carrots, stir and mix; cover and cook for a further 15 minutes.

9. Add the peas and the corn, mix well, cover the pan and cook over medium heat for 5 minutes.

10. Reserve half the green onions and add the rest to the chicken along with the green pepper. Cook, uncovered, for 5-6 minutes, stirring frequently. Remove from the heat.

11. Put the chicken in a serving dish and garnish with the reserved green onions.

TIME Preparation takes 20-25 minutes, cooking takes 45-50 minutes.

SERVING IDEAS Serve with Plain Fried Rice or Cardamom Rice.

Classic Chicken Dishes

CHICKEN KOHLAPURI

This delicious chicken dish comes from Kohlapur in southern India. The original recipe has a large amount of chili peppers as people in this part of India prefer a very hot flavor. For this recipe, however, the quantity has been reduced.

SERVES 4-6

2½lbs chicken pieces, skinned

1 large onion, coarsely chopped

3-4 cloves garlic, peeled and coarsely chopped

1-inch cube of root ginger, peeled and coarsely chopped

6 tbsps cooking oil

1 tsp ground turmeric

2 tsps ground coriander

1½ tsps ground cumin

1-1¼ tsps chili powder

1 small can of tomatoes

1¼ tsps salt or to taste

¾ cup water

4-6 whole green chili peppers

1 tsp garam masala

2 tbsps chopped coriander leaves

1. Cut each chicken piece in two (separate legs from thighs or cut breast into 2-3 pieces); wash and dry on paper towels.

2. Place the onion, garlic and ginger in a food processor or blender and blend to a smooth purée. You may need to add a little water if you are using a blender.

3. Heat the oil over medium heat and add the puréed ingredients. Stir and fry for 5-6 minutes.

4. Add turmeric, ground coriander, cumin and chili powder; adjust heat to low and fry for 4-5 minutes stirring frequently.

5. Add half the tomatoes, stir and cook for 2-3 minutes.

6. Now add the chicken, stir and cook until chicken changes color (4-5 minutes), then add the rest of the tomatoes, along with all the juice.

7. Add salt and water, bring to the boil, cover and simmer until the chicken is tender. Stir occasionally to ensure that the thickened sauce does not stick to the bottom of the pan.

8. Add the whole green chili peppers and garam masala, cover and simmer for 5 minutes.

9. Remove the pan from heat and stir in the coriander leaves.

TIME Preparation takes 15-20 minutes, cooking takes 55 minutes.

SERVING IDEAS Serve with Plain Boiled Rice and Mixed Vegetable Bhaji.
Suitable for freezing.

WATCHPOINT In stage 3, it is important to fry the ingredients for the specified time so that the raw smell of the onions, ginger and garlic can be eliminated before adding the rest of the ingredients.

Classic Chicken Dishes

CHICKEN WITH CHANNA DHAL

*Channa dhal has a distinctive flavor which goes particularly well with chicken.
As channa dhal is difficult to find, yellow split peas, which are similar, can
be used.*

SERVES 6-8

---

1 cup/8oz channa chal or yellow split peas
2¼lbs chicken pieces

*Make a paste of the following 6 ingredients
by adding ¼ cup water*
1 tbsp ground coriander
1 tsp ground turmeric
½ tsp cayenne or chili powder
½ tsp freshly ground black pepper
1 tsp ground cinnamon
½ tsp ground nutmeg

2 tbsps cooking oil
1-inch cube of root ginger, peeled and
  grated
3-4 cloves garlic, peeled and crushed
1 fresh green chili pepper, finely chopped
1¼ tsps salt or to taste
Scant 2 cups warm water
3 tbsps ghee or unsalted butter
1 large onion, finely sliced
2 tbsps chopped coriander leaves
1 medium-sized ripe tomato, sliced

1. Clean and wash the channa dhal or the split peas and soak them in plenty of cold water for about 2 hours. Drain well.

2. Cut each chicken piece into two, separating leg from thigh. Wash and pat dry.

3. In a heavy-based pan, heat the oil gently over low heat and fry the ginger, garlic and green chili pepper for 1 minute.

4. Add the spice paste, stir and fry for 2-3 minutes.

5. Add the chicken, adjust heat to medium-high, stir and fry the chicken until it changes color (3-4 minutes).

6. Add the dhal or split peas, stir and fry for a further 3-4 minutes.

7. Stir in the salt and add the water. Bring to the boil, cover the pan and simmer until the chicken and the dhal or split peas are tender (35-40 minutes).

8. Meanwhile, in a separate pan, melt the ghee or butter over medium heat and fry the onions until they are golden brown (8-10 minutes), stirring frequently.

9. Add the onions to the chicken along with any remaining ghee in the pan. Add half the coriander leaves and stir until all the ingredients are mixed thoroughly. Cover the pan and simmer for 10 minutes.

10. Put the chicken in a serving dish and garnish with the tomatoes and the remaining coriander leaves.

TIME Preparation takes 25 minutes plus time needed to soak the dhal or
split peas, cooking takes 55 minutes.

Classic Chicken Dishes

CHICKEN KORMA

Korma is a classic north Indian dish and there are many variations, some of which are quite elaborate. The recipe below, though simple and prepared with readily available ingredients, has all the characteristic features of this classic dish.

SERVES 4-6

2½lbs chicken pieces, skin removed

1-inch cube of root ginger, finely grated

⅔ cup thick set plain yogurt

1 small onion, coarsely chopped

3-4 dried red chili peppers

2-4 cloves garlic, peeled and coarsely chopped

5 tbsps cooking oil plus 2 tbsps extra oil

2 large onions, finely sliced

1 tbsp ground coriander

½ tsp powdered black pepper

1 tsp garam masala

1 tsp ground turmeric

1 cup warm water (reduce quantity if using boneless chicken)

⅓ cup finely grated fresh coconut

1¼ tsps salt or to taste

2 heaped tbsps ground almonds

Juice of ½ a lemon

---

1. Cut each chicken piece into half, separating leg from thigh and cutting each breast into two.

2. Mix with ginger and yogurt, cover and leave to marinate in a cool place for 2-4 hours or in the refrigerator overnight.

3. Place the chopped onion, red chili peppers and garlic in a blender or food processor and purée to a smooth paste. You may need to add a little water if you are using a blender.

4. Heat the 5 tbsps oil over medium heat and fry the sliced onions till they are golden brown. Remove the pan from the heat and using a slotted spoon, transfer the onions to another dish, Leave any remaining oil in the pan.

5. Place the pan in which the onions have been fried, over medium heat and add the other 2 tbsps cooking oil.

6. When hot, add the ground coriander, powdered pepper, garam masala and turmeric, stir rapidly (take the pan off the heat if the oil is too hot) and add the chicken along with the marinade. Adjust the heat to medium-high and fry the chicken for about 10 minutes, stirring frequently.

7. Add the blended spices and continue to fry for 6-8 minutes on low heat.

8. Add the water and the coconut and bring to the boil. Stir until coconut is soft. Add fried onion slices and salt.

9. Reduce heat to low, cover the pan and simmer until the chicken is tender (25-30 minutes). Sprinkle the ground almonds and mix well. Remove from heat and add the lemon juice.

TIME Preparation takes 15 minutes plus time needed to marinate, cooking takes 55 minutes.

SERVING IDEAS Serve with Pilau Rice or Mushroom Pilau and Carrot & Peanut Raita.
Suitable for freezing.

Classic Chicken Dishes

CHICKEN DO-PIAZA

A fairly easy dish to prepare in which more than the usual quantity of onions are used. The name itself suggests the quantity of onions required, Do means twice and Piaz means onion. The literal translation would, therefore, be 'chicken with twice the amount of onions'.

SERVES 4-6

2½lbs chicken pieces, skin removed

1 large onion, coarsely chopped

1-inch cube of root ginger, peeled and coarsely chopped

3-4 cloves garlic, peeled and coarsely chopped

4 tbsps cooking oil

1 tsp ground turmeric

1 tsp ground coriander

1 tsp ground cumin

¼-½ tsp chili powder

1 small can of tomatoes

¾ cup warm water

2 cinnamon sticks, each 2-inches long; broken up

4 cardamoms, split open on the top

4 whole cloves

2 dried bay leaves, crumpled

1¼ tsp salt or to taste

2 level tbsps ghee or unsalted butter

1 large onion, finely sliced

1 tbsp chopped coriander leaves (optional)

---

1. Cut each chicken breast into 3 pieces. If you are using legs, separate leg from thigh.

Wash and dry on paper towels.

2. Place the chopped onion, ginger and garlic in a blender or food processor and purée to a smooth paste, add a little water if necessary, to facilitate blade movement.

3. Heat the oil over medium heat and add the blended ingredients. Stir and fry for 4-5 minutes.

4. Add turmeric, coriander, cumin and chilli powder. Fry for 4-5 minutes stirring frequently. During this time, from the can of tomatoes, add 1 tbsp juice at a time to prevent the spices from sticking to the pan. When you have used up all the tomato juice, add the chicken and fry it over medium-high heat until the chicken has changed color.

5. Add the water, cinnamon, cardomom, cloves, bay leaves, salt and the whole tomatoes. Bring to the boil, cover and simmer until the chicken is tender and the sauce is fairly thick (about 25 minutes). Cook uncovered, if necessary, to thicken the sauce.

6. Heat the ghee or butter and fry the sliced onion for 5 minutes. Add the onions along with the ghee to the chicken. Remove from heat and stir in the coriander leaves.

TIME Preparation takes 15 minutes, cooking takes 45 minutes.

SERVING IDEAS Serve with Naan or Tandoori Roti and Potato Raita or with Plain Boiled Rice and Potatoes with Garlic & Chillies.
Suitable for freezing.

VARIATION Use lamb, but lengthen cooking time.

Classic Chicken Dishes

Chicken with Whole Spices

This recipe is the answer to a good, tasty curry in a hurry! With this curry on the menu, you can present a whole meal in approximately one hour.

SERVES 4-6

1¼ lbs chicken pieces, skinned

4 tbsps cooking oil

1 tsp cumin seeds

1 large onion, finely chopped

½-inch cube of root ginger, peeled and finely chopped

2-4 cloves garlic, peeled and crushed or finely chopped

2-3 dried red chili peppers, whole

2 cinnamon sticks, 2-inches long each, broken up

2 cardamoms, split open on the top

4 whole cloves

10 whole allspice berries

½ tsp ground turmeric

1 tsp paprika

⅔ cup warm water

1¼ tsp salt or to taste

2 ripe tomatoes, skinned and chopped

2 fresh green chili peppers, whole

1 tbsp ground almond

2 tbsps chopped coriander leaves (optional)

1. Cut each chicken piece in two; separate leg from thigh and cut each breast in two.

2. Heat the oil over medium heat and fry the cumin seeds until they pop, then add the onions, ginger, garlic and red chili peppers. Fry until the onions are soft but not brown, stirring frequently.

3. Add the cinnamon, cardamom, cloves and allspice, stir and fry for 30 seconds.

4. Stir in the turmeric and paprika and immediately follow with the chicken. Adjust heat to medium-high and fry the chicken until it changes color (5-6 minutes), stirring frequently.

5. Add the water and salt, bring to the boil, cover the pan and simmer until the chicken is tender (about 30 minutes).

6. Add the tomatoes, green chili peppers and the ground almonds. Stir and mix well, cover the pan and simmer for a further 6-8 minutes.

7. Stir in half the coriander leaves and remove the pan from heat.

8. Transfer the chicken into a serving dish and garnish with the remaining coriander leaves, (if used).

TIME Preparation takes 15-20 minutes, cooking takes 50 minutes.

SERVING IDEAS Serve with Plain Boiled or Plain Fried Rice, Cucumber Raita and/or Cauliflower Masala.
Suitable for freezing.

VARIATION Add peeled and diced potatoes about 20 minutes before completion of cooking time.

Classic Chicken Dishes

DAHI MURGHI

Dahi Murghi or chicken in yogurt needs little effort to cook and is simply delicious. The chicken is marinated in a yogurt-laced mixture and simmered until tender. Its simple method of cooking means that it can easily be fitted into a busy lifestyle.

SERVES 4-6

2¼lbs chicken pieces, skinned

⅔ cup thick set plain yogurt

3-4 cloves garlic, peeled and coarsely chopped

1-inch cube of root ginger, peeled and coarsely chopped

2-3 dried red chili peppers

½ tsp ground turmeric

1 tbsp ground coriander

4 tbsps cooking oil

1 large onion, finely sliced

2-4 fresh green chili peppers, whole

1 tsp salt or to taste

½ tsp garam masala

2 tbsps chopped coriander leaves

1. Cut each chicken piece into two, separate leg from thigh and cut each breast into two pieces. Wash the chicken and dry on paper towels.

2. Put the yogurt, garlic, ginger, dried red chili peppers, turmeric and ground coriander in a blender and blend until smooth.

3. Put the chicken in a large mixing bowl and pour the marinade over. Mix thoroughly, cover the container and leave to marinate for 6-8 hours, or overnight in the refrigerator.

4. Put the chicken into a heavy-based pan with a lid and place over medium heat, stirring occasionally until the chicken is heated through. Cover the pan and simmer gently until the chicken is tender (about 25-30 minutes). Remove the pan from heat.

5. Heat the oil over medium heat in a wide shallow pan and brown the onions.

6. Add the chicken and cook uncovered for 5-6 minutes stirring frequently.

7. Add the whole green chili peppers, salt and garam masala and cook for a further 3-4 minutes.

8. Remove the pan from the heat and stir in half the coriander leaves.

9. Put the chicken into a serving dish and sprinkle the remaining coriander leaves on top.

TIME Preparation takes 15 minutes plus time needed to marinate, cooking takes 30-35 minutes.

SERVING IDEAS Serve with Chapattis, Rotis or Cardamom Rice and a side dish such as Gobi Aloo or Spicy Channa Dhal.
Suitable for freezing.

WATCHPOINT Reduce cooking time if boneless chicken is used.

Classic Chicken Dishes

CHICKEN TIKKA MASALA

The delicate flavor of chicken smothered in almond and cream sauce makes this a wonderful choice for a dinner party or a special occasion menu.

SERVES 4

1lb Chicken Tikka (see separate recipe)

½-inch cube of root ginger, peeled and coarsely chopped

2 cloves garlic, peeled and coarsely chopped

1 tsp salt or to taste

4 tbsps unsalted butter

1 small onion, finely chopped

¼ tsp ground turmeric

½ tsp ground cumin

½ tsp ground coriander

½ tsp garam masala

¼-½ tsp chili powder

½ cup liquid, made up of the reserved juices from the precooked Chicken Tikka and warm water

1¼ cups double cream

2 heaped tbsps ground almonds

1. Mix together the ginger, garlic and ½ tsp salt from the specified amount and crush to a pulp. Keep the remaining salt aside for later use.

2. Melt the butter gently and fry the onions for 2-3 minutes.

3. Add the ginger/garlic paste and cook for 1 minute.

4. Stir in the turmeric and then the cumin, coriander, garam masala and chili powder. Stir and cook for 2 minutes.

5. Add the liquid and stir gently.

6. Gradually add the cream and stir.

7. Add the remaining salt and simmer for 5 minutes and then add the chicken. Adjust heat to low, cover and cook for 10 minutes.

8. Stir in the ground almonds and simmer for 5-6 minutes.

9. Remove from heat.

TIME Preparation takes 10 minutes plus time needed to marinate the tikka, cooking takes 25 minutes plus time needed to cook the tikka.

SERVING IDEAS Serve with Saffron Rice and Spiced Green Beans. Suitable for freezing. Defrost thoroughly before reheating. Reheat gently in a covered pan; do not boil.

Classic Chicken Dishes

MURGHI JHAL FREZI

This delicious and relatively easy dish to cook, with thick spice paste clinging to the pieces of chicken, makes it an irresistible choice for entertaining.

SERVES 4-6

2¼lbs chicken pieces

3 large onions, finely chopped

¾ cup water

1-inch cube of root ginger, peeled and grated

2-4 cloves garlic, peeled and crushed

1 tsp ground coriander

1 tsp ground cumin

1 tsp ground ajwain or caraway

½ tsp ground turmeric

½ chili powder

2 cinnamon sticks, 2-inch long each, broken up

2 cardamoms, split open on the top

4 whole cloves

5 tbsps cooking oil

1¼ tsp salt or to taste

1 tbsp tomato paste

1-2 fresh green chili peppers, sliced lengthwise, seeded for a milder flavor

2 tbsps chopped coriander leaves

1. Skin and cut each joint into two, separate leg from thigh and cut each breast into two pieces, wash and dry on paper towels.

2. Put the chicken in a saucepan, add half the chopped onions, water, ginger, garlic, coriander, cumin, ajwain, turmeric, chili powder, cinnamon, cardamom and cloves. Bring to the boil, stir and mix thoroughly. Cover and simmer for 20-25 minutes.

3. In a separate pan, heat the oil over medium heat and fry the rest of the onions until they are golden brown.

4. Remove each piece of chicken with a pair of tongs and add to the onions. Fry over medium heat until the chicken is brown (about 5 minutes).

5. Now add half the spiced liquid in which the chicken was cooked, stir and fry for 4-5 minutes. Add the rest of the liquid and fry for a further 4-5 minutes.

6. Add salt, tomato paste, green chili peppers and coriander leaves, stir and fry on low heat for 5-6 minutes. Remove from heat.

TIME Preparation takes 20-25 minutes, cooking takes 45-50 minutes.

SERVING IDEAS Serve with Chapattis, Puris or Parathas; or with Plain Boiled Rice and Tarka Dhal.
Suitable for freezing.

VARIATION Use lean pork instead of chicken.

WATCHPOINT Reduce the cooking time for boneless chicken and in stage 5, fry the chicken for a little longer to reach the paste-like consistency required.

Classic Chicken Dishes

CORIANDER CHICKEN

Coriander Chicken is quick and easy to make, it tastes wonderful and looks very impressive – a perfect choice for any dinner party menu.

SERVES 4-6

2¼lbs chicken joints, skinned
2-4 cloves garlic, peeled and crushed
⅔ cup thick set plain yogurt
5 tbsps cooking oil
1 large onion, finely sliced
2 tbsps ground coriander
½ tsp ground black pepper
1 tsp ground mixed spice
½ tsp ground turmeric
½ tsp cayenne pepper or chili powder
½ cup warm water
1 tsp salt or to taste
¼ cup ground almonds
2 hard-boiled eggs, sliced
¼ tsp paprika

1. Cut each chicken piece into two, mix thoroughly with the crushed garlic and the yogurt. Cover the container and leave to marinate in a cool place for 2-4 hours or overnight in the refrigerator.

2. Heat the oil over medium heat and fry the onions until they are golden brown (6-8 minutes). Remove with a slotted spoon and set aside.

3. In the same oil, fry the coriander, ground pepper, ground mixed spice and turmeric for 15 seconds and add the chicken along with all the marinade in the container.

4. Adjust heat to medium-high and fry the chicken until it changes color (5-6 minutes).

5. Adjust the cayenne or chili powder, water, salt, and the fried onion slices. Bring to the boil, cover the pan and simmer until the chicken is tender (about 30 minutes).

6. Stir in the ground almonds and remove from heat.

TIME Preparation takes 20 minutes plus time needed for marinating, cooking takes 45-50 minutes.

SERVING IDEAS Serve with Pilau Rice or Mushroom Pilau.
Suitable for freezing.

WATCHPOINT Reduce cooking time if boneless chicken is used.

Classic Chicken Dishes

CHICKEN DHANSAK

Dhansak is a combination of dried split peas, lentils and meat or chicken.

SERVES 6-8

2¼lbs chicken pieces, skinned

1 tsp salt or to taste

1-inch cube of root ginger, peeled and coarsely chopped

4-6 cloves garlic, peeled and chopped

Grind the following 10 ingredients in a spice or coffee grinder

1 tsp coriander seeds

1 tsp cumin seeds

1 tsp fennel seeds

4 cardamoms

1 cinnamon stick, 2-inches long, broken up

4-6 dried red chili peppers

10 black peppercorns

2 bay leaves

¼ tsp fenugreek seeds

½ tsp black or white mustard seeds

2 tbsps ghee or unsalted butter

½ cup warm water

For the dhal

⅓ cup toor dhal (yellow split peas)

⅓ cup masoor dhal (red split lentils)

5 tbsps cooking oil

1 large onion, finely chopped

1 tsp ground turmeric

1 tsp garam masala

2½ cups warm water

1 tsp salt or to taste

1 tsp tamarind concentrate or 1½ tbsp lemon juice

1 tbsp chopped coriander leaves, optional

---

1. Wash and dry the chicken pieces and cut each into two.

2. Add the salt to the ginger and garlic and crush to a pulp.

3. Make a paste of the ground ingredients and the ginger/garlic pulp by adding 6 tbsps water. Pour this mixture over the chicken and mix to coat thoroughly. Cover and set aside for 4-6 hours or overnight in the refrigerator.

4. Melt the ghee or butter over medium heat and fry chicken for 6-8 minutes, stirring frequently. Add the water, bring to the boil, cover and simmer for 20 minutes. Stir several times.

5. Meanwhile, mix together the split peas and lentils, wash and drain well.

6. Heat the oil over medium flame and fry onions for 5 minutes, stirring frequently. Add turmeric and garam masala, stir and fry for 1 minute. Add the pulses, adjust heat to low and fry for 5 minutes, stirring frequently. Add the water and salt, bring to the boil, cover and simmer for 30 minutes until soft, stirring occasionally. Remove from heat.

7. Using a metal spoon, push some of the cooked pulses through a strainer until there is a very dry and coarse mixture left. Discard the coarse mixture and sieve the rest the same way.

8. Pour the sieved pulses over the chicken, cover and place the pan over medium heat. Bring to the boil, reduce heat and simmer for 20-25 minutes. Stir occasionally during the first half of the cooking time, but more frequently during the latter half, to ensure that the mixture does not stick to the bottom of the pan.

9. Dissolve the tamarind pulp in 3 tbsps boiling water. Add this to the chicken/dhal mixture, stir and mix thoroughly. Cover and simmer for 5 minutes. Stir in the coriander leaves and remove from heat. If using lemon juice, simply add this at the end of the cooking time.

Classic Chicken Dishes

MURGHI AUR PALAK

Murghi aur Palak is a delicious combination of chicken and spinach with fennel, coriander and chili peppers.

SERVES 4-6

2¼lbs chicken quarters, skinned

4 tbsps cooking oil

2 medium-sized onions, finely chopped

1-inch cube of root ginger, peeled and finely grated

2-3 cloves garlic, peeled and crushed

Make a paste of the following 4 ingredients by adding 3 tbsps water

1 tsp ground turmeric

1 tsp ground fennel

1 tsp ground coriander

½ tsp chili powder

1½ tsps salt or to taste

⅓ cup warm water

1 heaped tbsp ghee or unsalted butter

1-2 cloves garlic, peeled and finely chopped

6-8 curry leaves (or ½ tbsp mild curry powder)

½ tsp cumin seeds

½ tsp fennel seeds

1-2 dried red chili peppers, coarsely chopped

1lb fresh or 8oz frozen leaf spinach, (defrosted and drained) coarsely chopped

4 tbsps plain yogurt

½ tsp garam masala

1. Cut each chicken quarter into half, separating leg from thigh and cutting each breast into two, lengthwise.

2. Heat the oil over medium heat and fry the onions, ginger and garlic until the onions are lightly browned (6-8 minutes).

3. Adjust heat to low and add the spice paste, stir and fry for 4-5 minutes. Rinse out the bowl with 2 tbsps water and add to the spice mixture. Stir and fry for a further 2-3 minutes.

4. Add the chicken and adjust heat to medium-high. Stir and fry until chicken changes color (about 3-4 minutes). Add 1 tsp salt and the water, bring to the boil, cover the pan and simmer for 15 minutes; stir once or twice during this time.

5. In a separate pan, melt ghee or butter over medium heat and add garlic and curry leaves or powder followed by cumin, fennel and red chili peppers, stirring briskly. Wash fresh spinach thoroughly, remove any hard stalks and add the spinach and the remaining salt. Stir and fry for 5-6 minutes and mix spinach and chicken together, bring to the boil, cover the pan and simmer for 20 minutes, stirring occasionally.

6. Mix yogurt and garam masala together and beat until the yogurt is smooth. Add to the chicken/spinach mixture – stir and mix thoroughly. Cook uncovered for 6-8 minutes over medium heat, stirring frequently.

TIME Preparation takes 25-30 minutes, cooking takes 50-55 minutes.

SERVING IDEAS Serve with Fried Brown Rice and Potato Raita.

TO FREEZE Suitable for freezing, if fresh spinach is used.

VARIATION Use lamb, but replace fennel with cumin, both whole and ground.

Classic Chicken Dishes

MURGHI AUR ALOO

This recipe is a fine example of the Persian influence in Indian cooking. Chicken and potatoes are cooked with saffron and a generous amount of fresh coriander.

SERVES 4-6

2¼lbs chicken pieces, skinned

1½ tsps salt or to taste

1-inch cube of root ginger, peeled and coarsely chopped

4-6 cloves garlic, peeled and coarsely chopped

Grind the following ingredients in a coffee grinder

2 tsps cumin seeds

4-6 dried red chili peppers

2 black cardamoms; the inner seeds only or 4 green cardamoms with the skin

6 whole cloves

2 cinnamon sticks, each 2-inches long; broken up into 2-3 pieces

6 black peppercorns

Grind the following 2 ingredients separately

1 tbsp white or black poppy seeds

10 raw cashews

4 tbsps cold water

4 tbsps ghee or unsalted butter

2 tbsps fresh coriander leaves and stalks, finely chopped

1-2 fresh green chili peppers, cut into halves lengthwise; seed them if a milder flavor is preferred

½ tsp ground turmeric

1¼ cups warm water

½ tsp saffron strands

3 medium-sized potatotes, peeled and quartered

⅔ cup sour cream

2-3 hard-boiled eggs, cut into quarters lengthwise

1. Wash the chicken and dry on paper towels. Cut each piece into two; separate leg from thigh and cut each breast into two pieces.

2. Add the salt to the ginger and garlic and crush them to a pulp.

3. Convert the ground ingredients, including the poppy seeds and the cashews, into a thick paste by adding the cold water. Break up any lumps with the back of a spoon and then set aside.

4. Melt the ghee or butter over low heat and add the ginger/garlic paste. Cook for 2-3 minutes stirring continuously.

5. Add the spice paste, stir and fry for 2-3 minutes.

6. Add chicken and adjust heat to medium-high. Fry the chicken until it changes color (5-6 minutes).

7. Add the coriander leaves, green chili peppers and turmeric, stir and fry for a further 2-3 minutes.

8. Add the water, bring to the boil and add the saffron strands. Cover and simmer for 15 minutes.

9. Add the potatoes and cook for a further 20 minutes or until the chicken and the potatoes are tender and the gravy is fairly thick.

10. Beat the sour cream until smooth and stir into the chicken. Cook uncovered for 6-8 minutes stirring frequently. Remove from the heat.

11. Arrange the chicken curry in a serving dish and garnish with the quarters of hard-boiled eggs.

Classic Chicken Dishes

MAKKHANI MURGHI

Makkhani Murghi, or Chicken in a Butter Sauce, is rich, delicious and irresistible! Not for the calorie or cholesterol conscious, it makes a fantastic special occasion treat.

SERVES 6-8

2¼lbs chicken breasts, skinned and boned

1¼ tsps salt or to taste

1-inch cube of root ginger, peeled and coarsely chopped

4-6 cloves garlic, peeled and coarsely chopped

⅔ cup thick set plain yogurt

Juice of 1 lemon

Grind the following 5 ingredients in a spice or coffee grinder

1 cinnamon stick, 2-inches long; broken up

8 cardamoms with the skin

6 whole cloves

8-10 red chili peppers

6-8 white peppercorns

2 tbsps cooking oil

2 tbsps tomato paste

2 sticks of butter

14oz can of tomatoes

2 cinnamon sticks, each 2-inches long; broken up

⅔ cup cream

1. Wash and dry the chicken and cut into 4 × 2-inch strips.

2. Add the salt to the ginger and garlic and crush to a smooth pulp.

3. Combine the yogurt, lemon juice and the ground spices and beat until the mixture is smooth. Marinate the chicken in this mixture, cover the container and leave it in a cool place for 2-4 hours or overnight in the refrigerator.

4. Heat the oil over medium heat and add the ginger/garlic pulp, stir and fry for 1 minute. Add the chicken and stir and fry for 10 minutes.

5. Add the tomato paste and butter, cook on low heat, uncovered, for 10 minutes. Remove the pan from the heat, cover and keep aside.

6. Put the tomatoes and the cinnamon sticks in a separate pan, bring to the boil, cover and simmer for 10 minutes. Remove the lid and adjust heat to medium; cook uncovered until the liquid is reduced to half its original volume (6-8 minutes). Remove the pan from the heat and allow the tomato mixture to cool slightly.

7. Sieve the cooked tomatoes, discard the cinnamon sticks. Add the sieved tomatoes to the chicken and place the pan over medium heat. Bring the liquid to the boil, reduce heat to low and cook, uncovered, for 5-6 minutes.

8. Add the cream, stir and mix well, and simmer uncovered for about 5 minutes. Remove from the heat.

TIME Preparation takes 20-25 minutes plus time needed for marinating, cooking takes 40-45 minutes.

SERVING IDEAS Serve with Naan or Tandoori Roti or Plain Boiled Rice.

TO FREEZE Suitable for freezing, but reheat over very gentle heat. Simmer uncovered until heated through; do not boil.

Classic Chicken Dishes

MURGHI BADAMI

Murghi Badami is a richer version of Chicken Korma, where the chicken is cooked entirely in plain yogurt and cream. No water is added to the chicken and the result is a thick and silky sauce with a delightful taste.

SERVES 4-6

2¼lbs chicken pieces, skinned
1 tsp salt or to taste
1-inch cube of root ginger, peeled and chopped
3-4 cloves garlic, peeled and chopped
1 tsp freshly ground black pepper
1 tbsp lemon juice
1¼ cups thick set plain yogurt
4 tbsps ghee or unsalted butter
2 medium-sized onions, finely sliced
6 cardamoms, split open on the top
1 tbsp ground coriander
1 tsp ground turmeric
⅔ cup cream
¼-½ tsp chili powder
½ cup flaked almonds
1 heaped tbsp ground almonds

---

1. Cut each chicken piece into two – separating leg from thigh and cutting each breast into two pieces. Wash the chicken and dry with paper towels. Make small incisions on both sides of the pieces of chicken with a sharp knife. This is to allow the spices to penetrate deep inside.

2. Add the salt to the ginger and garlic and crush to a fine pulp. Mix with the pepper and lemon juice. Rub this mixture into the chicken, cover it and keep aside for 30 minutes-1 hour.

3. Beat the yogurt until smooth and set aside.

4. Melt the ghee or butter over medium heat and fry the onions until well browned (10-12 minutes). Remove pan from heat and squeeze out excess fat by pressing the onions to the side of the pan. Transfer the onions to a plate.

5. Return pan to heat and add cardamoms and coriander, stir and fry for 30 seconds. Add the chicken, adjust heat to medium-high and fry the chicken until it changes colour (5-6 minutes) stirring continuously.

6. Stir in the turmeric and the yogurt and simmer; cover the pan and cook for 15 minutes, stirring occasionally.

7. Reserve 2 tbsps of the fried onions and add the rest to the chicken along with the cream, chili powder and the almonds, stir and mix well. Cover and simmer for a further 15-20 minutes stirring occasionally.

8. Sprinkle the round almonds and mix well, cover and simmer for 6-8 minutes. Remove from the heat.

9. Put the chicken in a serving dish and garnish with the remaining fried onions.

TIME Preparation takes 25-30 minutes plus time needed for marinating, cooking takes 55-60 minutes.

SERVING IDEAS Serve with any Indian bread, Saffron Rice or Pilau Rice.

Classic Chicken Dishes

MURGH DILKUSH

Chicken is still regarded as a bit special in India as it is more expensive than other meats. This is a wonderfully aromatic chicken dish which is ideally suited for a special occasion.

SERVES 6-8

2½lbs chicken pieces, skin removed

4 tbsps ghee or unsalted butter

2 medium-sized onions, finely chopped

1-inch cube of root ginger, peeled and coarsely chopped

4-6 cloves garlic, peeled and coarsely chopped

⅔ cup thick set plain yogurt

Roast the following ingredients gently over low heat until the spices release their aroma, cool and grind in a spice or coffee grinder.

2-inch piece cinnamon stick, broken up

6 green cardamoms, skin left on

6 whole cloves

1 tsp cumin seeds

2-3 dried red chili peppers

1 tbsp channa dhal or yellow split peas

Similarly, roast the following 2 ingredients until they are lightly browned, cool and grind separately from the above ingredients, in a spice or coffee grinder.

¼ cup raw cashews

1 tbsp white or black poppy seeds

1 tsp garam masala

⅔ cup warm water

1¼ tsps salt or to taste

2 tbsps fresh coriander leaves, finely chopped

1 tbsp fresh mint leaves, finely chopped or 1 tsp dried mint

1-2 fresh green chili peppers, seeded and coarsely chopped

1. Cut each chicken piece into two (separate leg from thigh and cut each breast into two).

2. Melt 2 tbsps ghee, from the specified amount, over medium heat and fry the onions, ginger and garlic for 4-5 minutes. Squeeze out excess ghee by pressing the onion mixture onto the side of the pan. Transfer them to another plate. Allow to cool slightly.

3. Put the yogurt into a blender or food processor and add all the roasted and ground ingredients and the fried onions. Blend until smooth.

4. Rub this marinade into the chicken and pour over any remaining marinade – mix thoroughly and leave to marinate for 4-6 hours or overnight in the refrigerator.

5. Melt the remaining 2 tbsps ghee over low heat and add the garam masala, stir and fry for 30 seconds.

6. Add the marinated chicken, adjust heat to medium-high and fry for 5-6 minutes, stirring frequently.

7. Add the water and salt, bring to the boil, cover and simmer until the chicken is tender (35-40 minutes).

8. Adjust heat to medium, add the fresh coriander, mint and green chili peppers – stir and fry for 5 minutes and remove from heat.

Classic Chicken Dishes

MURGH MUSALLAM

SERVES 4-6

4 poussins or Cornish game hens

Grind together the following 5 ingredients

2 tbsps white or black poppy seeds

2 tbsps sesame seeds

10 black peppercorns

4 cardamoms

2-4 dried red chili peppers

⅔ cup thick set plain yogurt

2½ tsps salt or to taste

½ tsp ground turmeric

1 tbsp ground coriander

⅓ cup ghee or unsalted butter

2 medium-sized onions, finely sliced

2-3 cloves garlic, peeled and finely
   chopped

2 cinnamon sticks, 2-inches each;
   broken up

6 cardamoms, split open on the top

4 whole cloves

1¼ cups basmati rice, washed and soaked
   in cold water for 30 minutes

2½ cups water

½ tsp saffron strands

2 tbsps ghee or unsalted butter

1 medium-sized onion, finely chopped

2-4 cloves garlic, peeled and crushed

1. Remove the skin and the giblets from the poussins. With a sharp knife, make several slits all over each (do not forget the thighs and the back).
2. Mix the ground ingredients with the yogurt and add 1 tsp salt, turmeric and coriander. Rub half of this mixture in, making sure that the spices are rubbed deep into the slits. Put the poussins in a deep container, cover and set aside for 1 hour.

3. Meanwhile cook the pilau rice. Melt the ⅓ cup ghee or butter over medium heat and fry the sliced onions, chopped garlic, cinnamon, cardamom and cloves, until the onions are lightly browned (6-7 minutes).
4. Add the rice, stir and fry until all the moisture evaporates (4-5 minutes). Add the remaining salt, water and saffron strands. Bring to the boil, cover the pan and simmer until the rice has absorbed all the water (12-14 minutes). Do not lift the lid or stir the rice during cooking. Remove the pan from the heat and leave it undisturbed for about 10 minutes.
5. Using a metal spoon, carefully transfer about a quarter of the cooked rice to a plate and allow it to cool. Keep the remaining rice covered.
6. Stuff each poussin with as much of the cooled pilau rice as the stomach cavity will hold. Truss it up as for roasting, so that the rice stays intact while the poussins are being braised.
7. Melt the 2 tbsps ghee or butter in a deep cast iron or nonstick pan. Add the chopped onions and the crushed garlic, stir and fry for 2-3 minutes.
8. Place the poussins on the bed of onions, on their backs, along with any marinade left in the container, but not the other half of the marinade which has been reserved. Cover the pan and cook for 10 minutes; turn the poussins over, breast side down, cover and cook for a further 10 minutes.
9. Turn them on their backs again and spread the reserved marinade evenly on each. Cover the pan and cook for 30 minutes turning poussins over every 10 minutes.
10. Transfer to a serving dish and spread a little sauce evenly over the breast. Spoon the remaining sauce round the poussins.
11. Serve the remaining pilau rice separately.

Classic Chicken Dishes

CHICKEN LIVER MASALA

*Curried liver is quite a popular item in India, particularly with Muslims.
This recipe is made more interesting by adding diced potatoes and
frozen peas.*

SERVES 4

1lb chicken livers

4 tbsps cooking oil

1 large onion, finely chopped

1 cinnamon stick, 2-inches long, broken up

2 medium-sized potatoes, peeled and diced

1¼ tsps salt or to taste

⅓ cup warm water

3-4 cloves garlic, peeled and crushed

*Make a paste of the following 4 ingredients
by adding 2 tsps water*

2 tsps ground coriander

1 tsp ground cumin

1 tsp ground turmeric

½ tsp chilli powder

1 small can of tomatoes

½ cup frozen peas

2-3 fresh green chili peppers, whole

½ tsp garam masala

---

1. Clean the livers, remove all skin and gristle and cut into ½-inch pieces.

2. Heat 2 tbsps oil over medium heat and fry the onions and cinnamon stick until the onions are soft.

3. Add the potatoes and ¼ tsp salt and stir

fry vegetables and cinnamon for about 2 minutes.

4. Add the water, cover the pan and simmer until the potatoes are tender.

5. Meanwhile, heat the remaining oil over medium heat in a heavy-based skillet. A nonstick or cast iron one is ideal as the livers need to be stir-fried over high heat.

6. Add the garlic and stir fry for 30 seconds.

7. Add the spice paste, reduce heat to low, and stir and fry for about 2 minutes.

8. Add half the tomatoes, along with some of the juice, stir and cook for a further 2-3 minutes, breaking the tomatoes with the spoon.

9. When the mixture is fairly dry, add the livers and adjust heat to medium-high. Stir-fry the liver for 3-4 minutes.

10. Add the remaining tomatoes and the juice, stir and fry for 5-6 minutes.

11. Cover the pan and simmer for 6-8 minutes.

12. Add the potatoes, peas, chili peppers and the remaining salt and cook for 1-2 minutes. Adjust heat to medium and cook, uncovered, for a further 4-5 minutes.

13. Stir in the garam masala and remove from heat.

TIME Preparation takes 20-25 minutes, cooking takes 36-40 minutes.

SERVING IDEAS Serve with Plain Fried Rice or Chapattis or Rotis and
Saagwalla Dhal.

Classic Chicken Dishes

CHICKEN LIVERS WITH SPINACH

An unusual and interesting combination which is high in vitamins and iron. Be careful while browning the livers, as they tend to pop in hot oil.

SERVES 4-6

1lb chicken livers

1¼ tsps salt or to taste

2-3 cloves garlic, peeled

6oz pack frozen leaf spinach (defrosted and drained), or 12oz fresh spinach coarsely chopped

5 tbsps cooking oil

1 tsp ground turmeric

1½ tsps ground coriander

1 tsp ground cumin

¼-½ tsp chili powder

¼ tsp black or white mustard seeds

1 tsp cumin seeds

1 large onion, finely sliced

½ tsp garam masala

½ a small red pepper, white pith and seeds removed and cut into thin strips

1. Clean the livers, remove skin and gristle and cut into 1-inch pieces. Wash and drain thoroughly, and dry on paper towels.

2. Add the salt to the garlic and crush to a pulp, using a spoon or pestle and mortar.

3. Heat 2 tbsps oil over medium heat, when the oil is smoking hot, put in the chicken livers, spread them out quickly and cover the pan. Cook for 6-8 minutes, stir once or twice. Remove the lid and cook further to dry off any excess liquid.

4. Add the garlic pulp, lower heat and stir fry the garlic for 2-3 minutes.

5. Add the turmeric, coriander, cumin and chili powder; stir and mix well. Let the liver cook, uncovered, over low heat for 4-5 minutes, stirring occasionally.

6. In a separate pan, heat the remaining oil over medium heat and add the mustard seeds. As soon as they pop, add the cumin seeds followed by the onions. Stir and fry the onions until they are golden brown (6-8 minutes).

7. Add the garam masala and the red pepper and stir fry for 1-2 minutes.

8. Add the spinach, adjust heat to medium-high and stir fry the spinach for 2-3 minutes.

9. Add the spinach to the liver along with any juices/oil left in the pan. Adjust heat to low, stir and fry the spinach and the livers for 1-2 minutes. Cook, uncovered, for 6-8 minutes more, stirring occasionally. Remove from heat.

TIME Preparation takes 15-20 minutes, cooking takes 35-40 minutes.

SERVING IDEAS Serve with Puris, Loochis or Plain Boiled Rice and Spicy Channa Dhal.
Suitable for freezing.

Classic Chicken Dishes

TANDOORI CHICKEN MASALA

The word masala means a combination of spices. In this recipe the chicken is simmered gently in a smooth velvety sauce flavored with saffron, ground cardamom and cinnamon.

SERVES 4-6

2¼lbs cooked Tandoori Chicken (see separate recipe)

4 tbsps ghee or unsalted butter

1 large onion, finely chopped

½-inch cube of root ginger, peeled and crushed

2 cloves garlic, peeled and crushed

1 tsp ground cardamom

1 tsp ground cinnamon

¼ tsp chili powder

1 tsp salt or to taste

⅔ cup sour cream

1 cup warm stock; (made up of the reserved cooking liquid and warm water)

4 level tbsps ground almonds

2 tbsps milk

½ tsp saffron strands

¼ cup toasted sliced almonds

---

1. Heat the ghee or butter over low heat and fry the onions until they are just soft, but not brown.

2. Add the ginger and garlic and fry for two minutes, stirring constantly.

3. Add the cardamom, cinnamon, chili powder and salt and fry for 1 minute, stirring constantly.

4. Beat the sour cream with a fork until smooth, add half the stock while still beating. Add this mixture to the onions and bring the liquid to a slow simmer.

5. Add the remaining stock, cover the pan and simmer for 10 minutes.

6. Sprinkle the ground almonds evenly, stir and mix well and remove the pan from heat.

7. Heat the milk and soak the saffron strands in it for 10-15 minutes.

8. Arrange the tandoori chicken in a wide shallow pan. Hold a strainer over the pan and pour the sauce into it. Press with the back of a metal spoon to extract as much of the spiced mixture as possible as the onion pulp is necessary to add to the thickness of the sauce. Alternatively, process the mixture until smooth and then pour over the chicken.

9. Sprinkle the saffron milk and all the saffron strands evenly over the chicken.

10. Place the pan back over gentle heat and bring the liquid to the boiling point. Cover the pan and simmer for 10 minutes, turning the chicken once or twice.

11. Put the chicken in a serving dish and garnish with the toasted almonds.

TIME Preparation takes 25-30 minutes plus time needed for marinating, cooking takes 25-30 minutes for the chicken and 20-25 minutes for the sauce.

SERVING IDEAS Serve with Pilau Rice and Mixed Vegetable Bhaji or Bhindi (Okra) with Coconut and/or Carrot & Peanut Raita.

Classic Meat Dishes

CAULIFLOWER SURPRISE

An imaginative way to serve cauliflower and another welcome variation on ground beef or lamb.

SERVES 4

---

1 medium-sized cauliflower

4 tbsps cooking oil

1 tsp cumin seeds

1 large onion, finely chopped

1-inch cube of root ginger, peeled and grated

3-4 cloves garlic, peeled and crushed

1lb lean ground lamb or beef

1 tsp ground turmeric

1 tbsp ground coriander

1 tsp ground cinnamon

1 tsp ground cardamom

½ tsp chili powder

1 small can of tomatoes, drained

1 tsp salt or to taste

¼ tsp black or white mustard seeds

½ tsp cumin seeds

8-10 curry leaves or 2 tsps mild curry powder

To garnish

2 small tomatoes, quartered

1 tbsp chopped coriander leaves

---

1. Blanch the cauliflower in boiling salted water, then drain and cool.

2. Heat 3 tbsps oil over medium heat and add the cumin seeds; as soon as the seeds start popping, add the onion and fry for 3-4 minutes, stirring frequently.

3. Add the ginger and garlic, stir and fry for 1 minute.

4. Add the ground meat, adjust heat to medium-high, stir and fry the meat until it breaks up finely and all the liquid evaporates.

5. Adjust heat to low and add the turmeric, coriander, cinnamon, cardamom and chili powder. Stir and fry until the spices are well-blended (3-4 minutes).

6. Add the tomatoes and salt, stir and cook for 1-2 minutes. Cover the pan and simmer for 10-15 minutes. Remove the pan from heat and allow the mixture to cool.

7. Place the cauliflower on a chopping board, stem side up. Fill all the spaces between the stems with the cooked meat; this should be as tightly packed as possible.

8. Turn the cauliflower over and gently pull the florets apart and fill with as much meat as possible.

9. Heat the remaining oil over medium heat and add the mustard seeds. As soon as the seeds pop, add the cumin and the curry leaves.

10. Place the cauliflower in the seasoned oil, the right way up, and let it cook, uncovered for 2-3 minutes. Turn it over and cook the other side for 2-3 minutes.

11. Turn the cauliflower over again and arrange the remaining meat round it. Cover the pan and adjust heat to the minimum setting. Cook for 10-15 minutes or until the cauliflower is tender.

12. Put the cauliflower on a serving dish and spread some of the meat on it and arrange any remaining meat round it. Garnish with the tomatoes and the coriander leaves.

TIME Preparation takes 20 minutes plus cooling time, cooking takes 55-60 minutes.

Classic Meat Dishes

ROGAN JOSH

Rogan Josh finds its origin in Kashmir, the northern-most state in India. In the recipe below, more than the usual quantity of spices are used, but these are toned down by using a large quantity of tomatoes and a little double cream.

SERVES 4-6

3 tbsps ghee or unsalted butter

2¼lbs leg of lamb, without bones, cut into 1½-inch cubes

1 tbsp ground cumin

1 tbsp ground coriander

1 tsp ground turmeric

1 tsp chili powder

1-inch cube of root ginger, peeled and grated

2-4 cloves garlic, peeled and crushed

1 large onion, finely sliced

14oz tin of tomatoes

1 tbsp tomato paste

½cup warm water

1/¼ tsps salt or to taste

⅓ cup heavy cream

2 tsps garam masala

2 tbsps chopped coriander leaves

1. Melt 2 tbsps ghee or butter, from the specified amount, over medium heat and fry the meat in 2-3 batches until it changes color. Remove each batch with a slotted spoon and set aside.

2. Lower heat and add the cumin, coriander, turmeric, chili powder, ginger and garlic. Stir and fry for 30 seconds.

3. Adjust heat to medium and add the meat along with the ghee and juices in the pan. Stir and fry for 3-4 minutes and add the onions. Fry for 5-6 minutes stirring frequently.

4. Now add the tomatoes and tomato paste – stir and cook for 2-3 minutes.

5. Add the water and salt, bring to the boil, cover and simmer until the meat is tender (about 60 minutes).

6. Stir in the cream and remove from heat.

7. In a separate pan melt the remaining ghee over medium heat and add the garam masala, stir briskly and add to the meat.

8. Transfer a little sauce to the pan in which the garam masala was fried – stir thoroughly to ensure that any remaining garam masala and ghee mixture is fully incorporated and add this to the meat. Mix well.

9. Stir in the coriander leaves.

TIME Preparation takes 20 minutes, cooking takes 1 hour 30 minutes.

SERVING IDEAS Serve with plain boiled rice or plain fried rice and Cabbage with Cinnamon. If you are entertaining, add Naan or Tandoori Roti and Aubergine Raita.

TO FREEZE Freeze before adding cream, garam masala and coriander leaves. Defrost thoroughly before reheating. Bring to the boil, add the cream and remove from heat. Add garam masala and coriander leaves.

VARIATION Use braising steak, but increase cooking time.

Classic Meat Dishes

SIKANDARI RAAN

SERVES 6-8

3-½-4lbs leg of lamb

Put the following ingredients into a food processor or blender and purée until smooth

1¼ cups thick set plain yogurt

1-inch cube of root ginger, peeled and
    coarsely chopped

4-6 cloves garlic, peeled and coarsely
    chopped

1 medium-sized onion, coarsely chopped

1 fresh green chili pepper

2 tbsps fresh mint or 1 tsp dried mint

Add the following ingredients and blend for a few seconds longer

1 tbsp ground coriander

1 tsp ground cumin

1 tsp garam masala

1 tsp ground turmeric

1¼ tsps salt or to taste

Grind the following 3 ingredients in a spice or coffee grinder

2 tbsps white or black poppy seeds

1 tbsp sesame seeds

2 tbsps flaked coconut

2 tbsps ghee or unsalted butter

4 medium-sized potatoes, peeled and
    halved

Purée to a smooth paste

⅔ cup thick set plain yogurt

½ cup raw cashews

¼ cup seedless raisins, soaked in a little
    warm water for 30 minutes

1. Remove as much fat as possible from the meat and lay it flat on a board. Make deep incisions from top to bottom at about ¼ -inch intervals. These incisions should be as deep as possible, almost down to the bone. Turn the leg over and repeat the process.

2. Mix the yogurt-based mixture with the ground spices. Rub this marinade into each incision, and then fill the incisions with it. Rub the remaining marinade all over the surface of the leg of lamb on both sides. Place in a covered container and leave to marinate in the refrigerator for 48 hours. Turn it over about every 12 hours.

3. Preheat the oven to 450°F. Place the leg of lamb on a roasting tin, melt the ghee or butter and pour it over the meat. Cover the meat with aluminum foil or use a covered roasting pan and cook in the center of the oven for 20 minutes. Reduce heat to 375°F and cook for 30 minutes. Now add the potatoes and spoon some of the spiced liquid over them as well as over the meat. Cover and cook for a further 35-40 minutes, basting the meat and the potatoes occasionally.

4. Now pour the nut mixture over the meat, cover and return the meat to the oven for about 30 minutes, basting the meat and the potatoes as before.

5. Transfer the meat onto a serving dish and arrange the potatoes around it. Spoon any remaining liquid over the meat and the potatoes. The meat is served cut into chunky pieces rather than thin slices.

TIME Preparation takes 25-30 minutes plus time needed for marinating,
cooking takes 1 hour 45 minutes – 2 hours.

Classic Meat Dishes

KOFTA (MEATBALL) CURRY

Koftas are popular throughout India, and they are made using fine lean ground lamb which is blended with herbs and spices.

SERVES 4

For the koftas

1lb lean ground lamb

2 cloves garlic, peeled and chopped

½-inch cube of root ginger, peeled and coarsely chopped

1 small onion, coarsely chopped

¼ cup water

1 fresh green chili pepper, seeded and chopped

2 tbsps chopped coriander leaves

1 tbsp fresh mint leaves, chopped

1 tsp salt or to taste

For the sauce

5 tbsps cooking oil

2 medium-sized onions, finely chopped

½-inch cube of root ginger, peeled and grated

2 cloves garlic, peeled and crushed

2 tsps ground coriander

1½ tsps ground cumin

½ tsp ground turmeric

¼-½ tsp chili powder

1 small can of tomatoes

⅔ cup warm water

½ tsp salt or to taste

2 cardamom pods, opened

4 whole cloves

2-inch piece of cinnamon stick, broken up

2 bay leaves, crumpled

2 tbsps thick set plain yogurt

2 tbsps ground almonds

1 tbsp chopped coriander leaves

1. Put half the lamb, all the garlic, ginger, onion and the water into a saucepan and place over medium heat. Stir until the mince is heated through.

2. Cover and simmer until all liquid evaporates (30-35 minutes) then cook uncovered if necessary, to dry out excess liquid.

3. Combine the cooked lamb with the rest of the ingredients, including the raw lamb.

4. Put the mixture into a food processor or blender and blend until smooth. Chill the mixture for 30 minutes.

5. Divide the mixture into approximately 20 balls, each slightly bigger than a walnut.

6. Rotate each ball between your palms to make neat round koftas.

7. Heat the oil for the sauce over medium heat and fry the onions until they are just soft.

8. Add the ginger and garlic and fry for 1 minute.

9. Add the coriander, cumin, turmeric and chili powder and stir quickly.

10. Add one tomato at a time, along with a little juice to the spice mixture, stirring until mixture begins to look dry.

11. Now add the water, salt, cardamom, cloves, cinnamon and the bay leaves.

12. Stir once and add the koftas. Bring to the boil, cover and simmer for 5 minutes.

13. Beat the yogurt with a fork until smooth, add the ground almonds and beat again – stir GENTLY into the curry. Cover and simmer until the koftas are firm.

14. Stir the curry GENTLY, cover again, and simmer for a further 10-15 minutes, stirring occasionally to ensure that the thickened sauce does not stick to the pan.

15. Stir in half the coriander leaves and remove from heat.

Classic Meat Dishes

KHEEMA-SALI-MATTAR

This superb dish is another contribution from the ancient Persians, who settled in India and have come to be known as the Parsis.

SERVES 4-6

5 tbsps cooking oil

1 tsp cumin seeds

1 large onion, finely chopped

½-inch cube of root ginger, peeled and finely grated

3-4 cloves garlic, peeled and crushed

½ tsp ground turmeric

1 tsp ground cinnamon

½ tsp ground nutmeg

1 tsp ground mixed spice

2 tsps ground coriander

½ tsp chili powder

1lb lean coarse ground lamb or beef

1 small can of tomatoes

1 tsp salt or to taste

⅔ cup warm water

2 tbsps plain yogurt

1 cup frozen peas or shelled fresh peas, boiled until tender

2 tbsps chopped coriander leaves

2 tbsps ghee or unsalted butter

2 potatoes, peeled and cut into matchstick strips

¼ tsp salt

¼ tsp chili powder

1. Heat the oil over medium heat and fry the cumin seeds until they pop, add the onions, ginger and garlic, fry until the onions are golden brown (6-7 minutes).

2. Add the turmeric, cinnamon, nutmeg, mixed spice, coriander and chili powder, stir and fry on low heat for 2-3 minutes.

3. Add the meat, stir and fry until the meat is brown and all the liquid evaporates.

4. Add the tomatoes and cook for 2-3 minutes stirring frequently.

5. Add the salt and water, bring to the boil, cover and cook on low heat for 15-20 minutes.

6. Beat the yogurt until it is smooth and add this to the meat along with the peas, bring to the boil again, cover and simmer for 5 minutes.

7. Stir in half the coriander leaves and remove from heat.

8. Melt the ghee or butter over medium heat in a non-stick or cast iron skillet and fry the potato sticks in a single layer until they are well browned and tender (5-6 minutes), reducing heat towards the end of the cooking time. You will need to do this in 2-3 batches. Drain the potato sticks on paper towels.

9. Season the potato sticks with the salt and chili powder.

10. Put the meat in the middle of a serving dish and arrange the potato sticks around it. Garnish with the remaining coriander leaves, if desired.

TIME Preparation takes 15 minutes, cooking takes 55 minutes.

SERVING IDEAS Serve with any Indian bread and Bhindi (Okra) Raita.

Classic Meat Dishes

MEAT MAHARAJA

A rich lamb curry cooked in the style favored by the great Maharajas of India.
Ground poppy seeds and almonds are used to thicken the sauce and also to add
a nutty flavor.

SERVES 4-6

4 tbsps ghee or unsalted butter

2 large onions, coarsely chopped

1-inch cube of root ginger, peeled and
    coarsely chopped

4-6 cloves garlic, peeled and coarsely
    chopped

1 fresh green chili pepper, seeded and
    chopped

1-2 dried red chili peppers, chopped

⅔ cup thick set plain yogurt

1 tsp cumin seeds or caraway seeds

Mix the following 4 ingredients in a small
bowl

3 tsps ground coriander

1 tsp garam masala

1 tsp ground turmeric

¼ tsp ground black pepper

2 tbsps white or black poppy seeds, ground
    in a coffee or spice grinder

2¼lbs leg of lamb, cut into 1-inch cubes

1¼ tsps salt or to taste

2 tbsps ground almonds

2 tbsps chopped coriander leaves

1 tbsp lemon juice

½ cup unsalted pistachio nuts, lightly
    crushed

1. Melt 2 tbsps ghee from the specified amount over medium heat and fry the onions, ginger, garlic, green and red chili peppers until the onions are just soft (3-4 minutes). Remove from heat and allow to cool slightly.

2. Put the yogurt into a blender or food processor, add the onion mixture and blend to a purée. Set aside.

3. Heat the remaining ghee or butter over low heat (do not overheat ghee) and add the cumin or caraway seeds followed by the spice mixture and the ground poppy seeds. Stir and fry for 1 minute.

4. Add the meat, adjust heat to medium-high, stir and fry until meat changes colour (4-5 minutes). Cover the pan and let the meat cook in its own juice for 15 minutes. Stir occasionally during this time.

5. Add the blended ingredients and mix thoroughly. Rinse out blender container with ¾ cup warm water and add this to the meat. Stir in the salt and bring the liquid to the boil, cover the pan and simmer until the meat is tender. Stir occasionally during the first half of cooking time, but more frequently towards the end to ensure that the thickened sauce does not stick to the bottom of the pan.

6. Stir in the ground almonds and half the coriander leaves, cook, uncovered for 2-3 minutes.

7. Remove the pan from heat and add the lemon juice, mix well. Garnish with the remaining coriander leaves and sprinkle the crushed pistachio nuts on top.

Classic Meat Dishes

MEAT DILRUBA

*This delicious meat curry is in a class of its own. It is cooked in two stages,
making it easier to get much of the preparation and cooking out of the
way in advance.*

SERVES 4-6

2¼lbs boned leg of lamb

1¼ tsps salt or to taste

½-inch cube of root ginger, peeled and
    finely chopped

3-4 cloves garlic, peeled and finely
    chopped

1 tsp ground turmeric

⅔ cup thick set plain yogurt

1 large onion, finely sliced

3-4 dried red chili peppers, coarsely
    chopped

⅔ cup water

Grind together in a coffee grinder

1 tbsp poppy seeds

1 tsp fenugreek seeds

¾cup flaked coconut ground in a food
    processor until very fine

2 tbsps ghee or unsalted butter

2 tbsps ground coriander

⅔ cup milk

½ cup finely chopped coriander leaves

1 fresh green chili pepper, remove seeds if
    preferred and chop finely

1. Trim off excess fat from the meat, wash
and pat dry, and cut into 1-inch cubes.

2. Put the ginger, garlic and salt in a pestle
and mortar and crush them to a pulp.

Alternatively, use a food processor, scraping
down the bowl frequently.

3. Mix together the ginger/garlic pulp,
turmeric and the yogurt and beat until the
yogurt is smooth. Add this to the meat, mix
thoroughly, cover the container and leave to
marinate for 4-6 hours or overnight in the
refrigerator.

4. Put the marinated meat into a heavy-
based saucepan, add the onions, red chili
peppers and the water. Bring to a slow
simmer over gentle heat. Cover the pan and
simmer for 50-60 minutes or until the meat
is tender. Remove from the heat.

5. Melt the ghee over medium heat and add
the ground coriander, stir and fry for 30
seconds. Add the ground poppy and
fenugreek seeds and fry until the mixture is
lightly browned, stirring constantly (1-2
minutes).

6. Lift the meat with a slotted spoon and
add to the poppy/fenugreek mixture. Stir
and fry over medium-high heat until all the
moisture evaporates (6-7 minutes). Add the
ground coconut, stir and fry for 2 minutes.
Now add the milk and the liquid in which
the meat was cooked. Stir and mix
thoroughly. Cook, uncovered, over low heat
for 4-5 minutes, stirring frequently.

7. Stir in the coriander leaves and the green
chili peppers and remove from the heat.

TIME Preparation takes 25-30 minutes plus time needed for marinating,
cooking takes 1 hour 15 minutes.

Classic Meat Dishes

NAWABI KHEEMA PILAU

A rich rice dish in which ground lamb is transformed into a wonderfully fragrant pilau by the addition of saffron, rose water and fried nuts.

SERVES 4-6

1½ cups basmati rice

4 tbsps ghee or unsalted butter

1 tbsp extra ghee or unsalted butter

1 tbsp raisins

¼ cup raw cashews, split into halves

2 tbsps milk

1 tsp saffron strands

6 cardamoms, split open on the top

4 whole cloves

1 tsp cumin seeds

2 bay leaves, crumpled

1-inch cube of root ginger, peeled and grated

2-3 cloves garlic, peeled and crushed

1-2 fresh green chili peppers, finely chopped and seeded if a milder flavor is preferred

1 tsp ground nutmeg

1 tsp ground cinnamon

1 tsp ground cumin

1 tbsp ground coriander

1lb lean ground lamb

2½ cups water

1½ tsps salt or to taste

⅔ cup single cream

2 tbsps rosewater (optional)

2 hard-boiled eggs, chopped

1. Wash and soak basmati rice in cold water for ½ hour, then drain.

2. Melt the 1 tbsp ghee or butter over low heat and fry the raisins until they swell up, then remove with a slotted spoon and set aside.

3. In the same fat, fry the cashews until they are lightly browned, remove with a slotted spoon and set aside.

4. Boil the milk, add the saffron strands and set aside. Alternatively, put the milk and the saffron strands in the microwave and boil on full power or about 45 seconds. Set aside.

5. Melt the remaining ghee or butter gently over low heat and fry the cardamoms, cloves, cumin seeds and the bay leaves for 1 minute.

6. Add the ginger, garlic and green chili peppers and stir fry for 30 seconds.

7. Add all the nutmeg, ground cinnamon, cumin and coriander and fry for 1 minute.

8. Add the lamb and adjust heat to medium. Stir and fry the lamb until all liquid dries up and it is lightly browned. This will take about 5 minutes.

9. Add the rice, stir and fry for about 5 minutes.

10. Add the water, salt, cream and the steeped saffron. Stir and mix well. Bring the liquid to the boil, cover the pan and simmer for 12-15 minutes without lifting the lid. Remove the pan from the heat and keep it undisturbed for a further 10-15 minutes.

11. Add half the nuts and raisins to the rice, then sprinkle the rosewater evenly on top, if using. Stir and mix the ingredients gently with a fork.

12. Put the pilau in a serving dish and garnish with the remaining nuts and raisins and the chopped hard-boiled eggs.

TIME Preparation takes 20-25 minutes, cooking takes 40-45 minutes.

Classic Meat Dishes

KOFTA BHOONA

Kofta Bhoona consists of tiny meatballs the size of marbles which are coated with a delicious spice paste.

SERVES 4-6

1lb fine lean ground lamb or beef

1 large clove of garlic, peeled and crushed

1 tsp garam masala

1-2 fresh green chili peppers, seeded and minced

2 tbsps fresh coriander leaves, minced

1½ tsps salt or to taste

3 tbsps cooking oil

1 large onion, finely chopped

¼-inch cube of root ginger, peeled and grated

2 tsps ground coriander

1 tsp ground cumin

Make a paste of the following 5 ingredients

½-1 tsp chilli powder

2 cloves garlic, peeled and crushed

½ tsp ground turmeric

2 tbsps tomato paste

½ cup cold water

1 cup warm water

⅓ cup frozen peas

¼ tsp garam masala

2 tbsps chopped coriander leaves

1. Put the meat in a large bowl and add the garlic, garam masala, green chili peppers, 1 tsp salt and the coriander leaves. Mix the ingredients thoroughly and knead until smooth.

2. Divide the mixture into about 28-30 marble-sized balls (koftas). Make the koftas by rolling the balls between the palms in a circular motion until they are smooth and round.

3. Heat the oil over medium heat, preferably in a nonstick or cast iron skillet, and fry the koftas in 2-3 batches. Turn the koftas as they brown and when they are brown all over, remove with a slotted spoon and drain on paper towels.

4. In the same oil, fry the onions and ginger until the onions are golden brown (6-8 minutes), stirring frequently.

5. Adjust heat to low and add the ground coriander, stir and fry for 30 seconds. Now add the ground cumin and fry for 30 seconds.

6. Adjust heat to medium and add 2 tbsps of the tomato paste mixture. Stir and fry until it dries up. Repeat the process until all the tomato paste mixture is used up.

7. Add the warm water and the remaining salt and bring to the boil.

8. Add the koftas, cover the pan and simmer for 10 minutes.

9. Now adjust heat to medium, bring the liquid to the boil, stir and cook for 4-5 minutes.

10. Add the peas and the ½ tsp garam masala. Continue to cook, uncovered, until the sauce is fairly thick, stirring frequently.

11. Stir in the coriander leaves and remove from heat.

TIME Preparation takes 25-30 minutes, cooking takes 50-55 minutes.

SERVING IDEAS Serve with Mushroom Pilau or Parathas and a Raita or salad.

Classic Meat Dishes

MEAT VINDALOO

Vindaloo is made by marinating the meat in vinegar and spices. It is traditionally a hot curry, but the quantity of chili peppers can be adjusted to suit individual taste.

SERVES 4-6

Grind the following 5 ingredients in a coffee grinder

2 tbsps coriander seeds

1 tbsp cumin seeds

6-8 dried red chili peppers

1 tbsps mustard seeds

½ tsp fenugreek seeds

3-4 tbsps cider or white wine vinegar

1 tsp ground turmeric

1-inch cube of root ginger, peeled and finely grated

3-4 cloves garlic, peeled and crushed

2¼lbs shoulder of lamb or chuck steak

4 tbsps cooking oil

1 large onion, finely chopped

1-2 tsps chili powder

1 tsp paprika

1¼ tsps salt or to taste

Scant 2 cups warm water

2-3 medium-sized potatoes

1 tbsp chopped coriander leaves, (optional)

1. In a large bowl, make a thick paste out of the ground spices, by adding the vinegar.

2. Add the turmeric, ginger and garlic. Mix thoroughly.

3. Trim off excess fat from the meat and cut into 1-inch cubes.

4. Add the meat and mix it well so that all the pieces are fully coated with the paste. Cover the bowl and leave to marinate for 4-6 hours or overnight in the refrigerator.

5. Put the meat in a pan and place this over medium heat. Allow the meat to heat through, stirring occasionally; this will take about 5 minutes. Cover the pan, and cook the meat in its own juice for 15-20 minutes or until the liquid is reduced to a thick paste. Stir occasionally during this time to ensure that the meat does not stick to the bottom of the pan. Remove from heat and set aside.

6. Heat the oil over medium heat and fry the onions until they are soft (about 5 minutes).

7. Add the meat and fry for 6-8 minutes stirring frequently.

8. Add the chili powder, paprika and salt. Stir and fry for a further 2-3 minutes.

9. Add the water, bring to the boil, cover and simmer for 40-45 minutes or until the meat is nearly tender (beef will take longer to cook, check water level and add more water if necessary).

10. Meanwhile, peel and wash the potatoes. Cut them into approximately 1½-inch cubes. Add this to the meat and bring to the boil again. Cover the pan and simmer until the potatoes are cooked (15-20 minutes).

11. Transfer the vindaloo to a serving dish and sprinkle the coriander leaves on top.

TIME Preparation takes 10-15 minutes plus time needed for marinating, cooking takes 1 hour 15 minutes.

Classic Meat Dishes

MARINATED LAMB CHOPS

This is an excellent way to cook lamb chops though a little unusual. The chops are tender and juicy and the sauce, made with chopped spinach, is delicious.

SERVES 4-6

2¼lbs lamb shoulder chops

⅔ cup thick set plain yogurt

1-inch cube of root ginger, peeled and coarsely chopped

2-3 cloves garlic, peeled and coarsely chopped

1-2 fresh green chili peppers, seeded and coarsely chopped

2 tbsps cooking oil

6 cardamoms, split open on the top

Combine the following 5 ingredients in a bowl

1 tbsp ground coriander

1 tsp ground cinnamon

1 tsp ground turmeric

¼ tsp chilli powder

1 tsp paprika

¾ cup warm water

1¼ tsps salt or to taste

1. Trim off excess fat from the chops, wash and pat them dry. Flatten the chops slightly by beating them with a meat mallet. This will help tenderize and absorb the spices better.

2. Put the yogurt, ginger, garlic and green chill peppers in a food processor and blend until smooth.

3. Pour the yogurt marinade over the chops and mix thoroughly. Cover the container and allow the chops to marinate in a cool place for 4-6 hours or overnight in the refrigerator.

4. Heat the oil over medium heat, when the oil is hot, remove the pan from heat and add the cardamoms and the combined spices. Stir the ingredients once and place the pan back on heat.

5. Add the chops, adjust heat to high and stir and fry the chops for 4-5 minutes.

6. Add the water and salt, bring to the boil, cover the pan and simmer until the chops are nearly tender (35-40 minutes).

7. Meanwhile, prepare the spinach

2 tbsps cooking oil

1 tsp cumin seeds

2-3 cloves garlic, peeled and finely chopped

1 tsp ground cumin

1 large onion, finely sliced

1lb leaf spinach; or 8oz frozen (defrosted and drained) chopped

1. Heat the oil over medium heat and fry the cumin seeds until they start popping.

2. Add the garlic and ground cumin and immediately follow with the onions. Fry until the onions are lightly browned (8-10 minutes), stirring frequently.

3. Add the spinach and stir fry over medium-high heat for 1-2 minutes, then stir it into the chops.

4. Cover the pan and simmer for 20-25 minutes. Remove from heat.

Classic Meat Dishes

ALOO GOSHT

*A well-known north-Indian lamb curry with a distinctive flavor from the ghee
which is used to brown the potatoes before they are added to the curry.*

SERVES 4-6

2¼lbs leg or shoulder of lamb

1¼ tsps salt or to taste

1-inch cube of root ginger, peeled and
    coarsely chopped

3-4 cloves garlic, peeled and coarsely
    chopped

2 tbsps ghee or unsalted butter

3 medium-sized potatoes, peeled and cut
    into 1½-inch cubes

3 tbsps cooking oil

1 large onion, finely chopped

3-4 dried red chili peppers

2 cinnamon sticks, 2-inch long each,
    broken up

*Make a paste of the following 5 spices by
adding 3 tbsps water*

1 tbsp ground coriander

1 tsp ground allspice

1 tsp paprika

1 tsp ground turmeric

¼-½ tsp chili powder

1 tbsp tomato paste

2 cardamoms, split open on the top

4-6 whole cloves

Scant 2 cups warm water

1 tbsp lemon juice

2 tbsps chopped coriander leaves

1. Trim off excess fat from the meat and cut it into 1½-inch cubes.

2. Add the salt to the ginger and garlic and crush to a pulp.

3. Melt the ghee or butter over medium heat in a non-stick or cast iron skillet and fry the potatoes until they are well-browned on all sides (about 10 minutes). Remove the potatoes with a slotted spoon and keep aside.

4. Add the oil to any remaining ghee in the pan and when hot, fry the onions, red chili peppers and cinnamon sticks until the onions are soft (about 5 minutes).

5. Add the ginger and garlic pulp, and fry for a further 2-3 minutes stirring frequently.

6. Adjust heat to low and add the spice paste, stir and fry for 3-4 minutes.

7. Add the meat, adjust heat to medium-high, stir and fry until the meat changes colour (5-6 minutes), then stir in the tomato paste.

8. Now add the cardamoms, cloves and the water. Bring to the boil, cover and simmer for 45-50 minutes or 20 minutes in the pressure cooker with the 15lbs weight on.

9. Add the potatoes, bring to the boil again, cover and simmer for 15-20 minutes or until the potatoes are tender; if using pressure cooker, bring pressure down first, remove lid and add the potatoes. Cover and cook the potatoes without the weight.

10. Remove from heat and add the lemon juice and coriander leaves.

TIME Preparation takes 20-25 minutes, cooking takes 1 hour 30 minutes.

Classic Meat Dishes

SHAHI KORMA

*The word 'Shahi' means royal, meaning that this particular korma was created
in the royal kitchens of the great Maharajas of India. The dish is rich and
creamy and is a perfect choice for a special occasion.*

SERVES 4-6

2¼lbs boned leg of lamb, fat trimmed and
   cut into 1½-inch cubes

⅔ cup thick set plain yogurt

½-inch cube of root ginger, peeled and
   grated

3-4 cloves of garlic, peeled and crushed

4 tbsps ghee or unsalted butter

2 medium-sized onions, finely chopped

*Grind the following ingredients in a coffee
grinder*

2 tbsps coriander seeds

8 green cardamoms with the skin on

10 whole black peppercorns

3-4 dried red chili peppers

*Mix the following 2 spices with the above
ground ingredients*

1 tsp ground cinnamon

1 tsp ground mace

3-4 tbsps chopped fresh mint or 1½ tsps
   dried mint

½ cup ground almonds

1¼ cups warm water

½ tsp saffron strands, crushed

1½ tsp salt or to taste

½ cup raw split cashews

⅔ cup cream

1 tbsp rosewater (optional)

1. Put the meat into a bowl and add the
yogurt, ginger and garlic. Mix thoroughly,
cover the bowl and leave to marinate for
2-4 hours or overnight in the refrigerator.

2. Put the marinated meat, along with any
remaining marinade in the container, in a
heavy-based saucepan and place it over
medium-low heat. Bring to a slow simmer,
cover and cook the meat in its own juice for
45-50 minutes stirring occasionally. Remove
the pan from the heat and remove the meat
with a slotted spoon. Transfer the meat to
another container and keep hot.

3. Melt the ghee over medium heat and fry
the onions until they are lightly browned
(8-9 minutes).

4. Adjust heat to low and add the ground
spices and the mint; stir and fry for 2-3
minutes. Add the half of the liquid in which
the meat was cooked, stir and cook for 1-2
minutes. Add the ground almonds and mix
thoroughly; add the remaining meat stock,
stir and cook for a further 1-2 minutes.

5. Adjust heat to medium and add the meat,
stir and fry the meat for 5-6 minutes.

6. Add the water, saffron strands, salt and
cashews, bring the liquid to a slow boil,
cover and simmer for 20 minutes.

7. Add the cream, stir and mix well, simmer
uncovered for 6-8 minutes.

8. Stir in the rosewater, if using, and remove
from the heat.

TIME Preparation takes 20-25 minutes, cooking takes 1 hour 30 minutes.

SERVING IDEAS Serve with Naan or Plain Fried Rice and Green Beans in
Garlic Butter.

143

Classic Meat Dishes

KHEEMA MATTAR

A popular dish all over India, especially in the north. Lean ground meat is combined with peas and ground almonds and garnished with sliced hard-boiled eggs to make an attractive and delicious dish.

SERVES 4

6 tbsps cooking oil
1 tsp cumin seeds
2 dried red chili peppers
1lb lean ground lamb or beef
1 large onion, finely chopped
1-inch cube of root ginger, peeled and
    finely grated
4 cloves garlic, peeled and crushed
½ tsp ground turmeric
2 tsps ground coriander
1½ tsps ground cumin
½ tsp chili powder
1 small can of tomatoes or 3-4 fresh
    tomatoes, skinned and chopped
1 tsp salt or to taste
1 tbsp plain yogurt
¾ cup warm water
⅔ cup fresh or frozen peas; shelled weight
1 tbsp ground almonds
½ tsp garam masala
2 hard-boiled eggs, sliced
Coriander leaves

1. Heat 1 tbsp oil over medium heat and add the cumin seeds, as soon as they pop add the red chili peppers and then the meat. Stir and cook until the meat is evenly browned.

2. Meanwhile, heat the remaining oil over medium heat and add the onions. Stir and fry until the onions are soft, add the ginger and garlic and stir and fry for a further 2-3 minutes.

3. Stir in the turmeric and then the coriander, cumin and chili powder.

4. Add the tomatoes along with all the juice, stir and cook for 3-4 minutes.

5. Add the meat and cook for 6-8 minutes, stirring frequently.

6. Add the salt and water and stir in the yogurt.

7. Cover the pan and simmer for 20 minutes.

8. Add the frozen peas and simmer for a further 10 minutes. If using fresh peas, boil until tender before adding to the meat.

9. Stir in the ground almonds and simmer for 2-3 minutes.

10. Remove from heat and stir in the garam masala.

11. Transfer onto a serving dish and arrange the sliced eggs on top. Garnish with the coriander leaves.

TIME Preparation takes 15 minutes, cooking takes 50 minutes.

SERVING IDEAS Serve with Chapattis, Parathas and/or Fried Brown Rice
and Potato Raita
Suitable for freezing if fresh peas are used.

Classic Meat Dishes

LAMB WITH BUTTER BEANS

Adding beans or pulses to meat not only makes a more interesting and wholesome dish, but also makes it go further. The lamb and the buttery taste of the beans make an excellent combination.

SERVES 6-8

---

1 cup butter beans, washed and soaked overnight in plenty of cold water

2¼ cups cold water

1¼ tsps salt or to taste

1-inch cube of root ginger, peeled and coarsely chopped

2-4 cloves garlic, peeled and coarsely chopped

5 tbsps cooking oil

2 medium-sized onions, finely chopped

2-3 dried red chili peppers

2 cinnamon sticks, each 2-inches long, broken up

Make a paste of the following 4 spices by adding 3 tbsps water

1½ tsps ground coriander

2½ tsps ground cumin

1 tsp ground turmeric

¼ tsp chili powder (optional)

2¼ lbs leg or shoulder of lamb, fat trimmed and cut into 1½-inch cubes

2 tbsps tomato paste

2-3 cardamoms, split open on the top

6 whole cloves

¾ cup warm water

Juice of half a lemon

2 tbsps chopped coriander leaves

1. Put the cold water and the butter beans in a saucepan and bring the liquid to the boil.

2. Partially cover the pan and cook over low heat for 15 minutes.

3. Now cover the pan tightly and simmer the beans for about 20 minutes. Remove the pan from heat and keep aside.

4. Add the salt to the ginger and garlic and crush to a pulp.

5. Heat the oil over medium heat and add the onions, red chili peppers and cinnamon sticks. Stir and fry until the onions are soft (about 5 minutes).

6. Add the ginger and garlic pulp and stir and fry for 2-3 minutes. Add the spice paste, adjust heat to low, stir and fry for a further 3-4 minutes.

7. Add the meat, turn heat up to medium-high and fry for 5-6 minutes, stirring frequently.

8. Stir in the tomato paste, then add the cardamoms, cloves and warm water. Bring to the boil, cover and simmer until the meat is tender, about 55-60 minutes.

9. Add the butter beans and the liquid in which they were cooked. Bring the liquid to the boil, cover the pan and simmer for 15 minutes.

10. Remove the pan from heat and add the lemon juice and coriander leaves.

TIME Preparation takes 20-25 minutes, cooking takes 1 hour 30 minutes.

SERVING IDEAS Serve with Plain Boiled Rice or Plain Fried Rice, or Naan. Suitable for freezing.

Classic Meat Dishes

MEAT MADRAS

This hot, but delicious curry is named after Madras, the major city in southern India, perhaps because in the humid south, people eat rather hot food. Strange though it may seem, the hotter the food, the cooler you'll feel.

SERVES 4-6

6 tbsps cooking oil

2 medium-sized onions, coarsely chopped

1-inch cube of root ginger, peeled and coarsely chopped

3-4 cloves garlic, peeled and coarsely chopped

4-6 dried red chili peppers

2 large cloves garlic, peeled and crushed

1-2 fresh green chili peppers, sliced lengthwise

1 small can of tomatoes

3 tsps ground cumin

1 tsp ground coriander

½-1 tsp chilli powder

1 tsp ground turmeric

2¼lbs leg or shoulder of lamb, fat removed and cut into 1½-inch cubes

¾ cup warm water

1¼ tsps salt or to taste

1 tsp garam masala

1. Heat 3 tbsps oil from the specified amount over medium heat and fry the onions, coarsely chopped ginger, garlic and red chili peppers until the onions are soft (8-10 minutes), stirring frequently. Remove from heat and allow to cool.

2. Meanwhile, heat the remaining oil over medium heat and fry the crushed garlic and green chili peppers until the garlic is lightly browned.

3. Add half the tomatoes, along with the juice; stir and cook for 1-2 minutes.

4. Add the cumin, coriander, chili powder and turmeric, adjust heat to low and cook for 6-8 minutes, stirring frequently.

5. Add the meat and adjust heat to medium-high. Stir and fry until meat changes color (5-6 minutes).

6. Add the water, bring to the boil, cover and simmer for 30 minutes.

7. Place the fried onion mixture in a blender or food processor and add the remaining tomatoes. Blend until smooth and add this to the meat – bring to the boil, add salt and mix well. Cover the pan and simmer for a further 35-40 minutes or until the meat is tender.

8. Stir in the garam masala and remove from heat.

TIME Preparation takes 25-30 minutes, cooking takes 1 hour 20 minutes.

SERVING IDEAS Serve with Plain Boiled Rice or any Indian bread accompanied by Saag Bhaji and/or a Raita.
Suitable for freezing.

WATCHPOINT Meat Madras is meant to be hot, to make it less so, omit the chili powder and seed the green chili peppers.

Classic Meat Dishes

KHEEMA SHAHZADA

Kheema, or ground meat, is not at all an under-rated item in Indian cooking and in fact, the recipe below elevates it to gourmet status. Make sure that the meat is lean and coarsely ground.

SERVES 4

4 heaped tbsps ghee or unsalted butter

1 large onion, coarsely chopped

1-inch cube of root ginger, peeled and coarsely chopped

2-4 cloves garlic, peeled and coarsely chopped

Grind the following ingredients in a coffee or spice grinder

1 cinnamon stick, 2-inches long; broken up

4 cardamoms

4 whole cloves

4-6 dried red chili peppers

1 tbsp coriander seeds

Grind the following 2 ingredients separately

1 tbsp poppy seeds

1 tbsp sesame seeds

1lb lean coarse ground meat

½ tsp ground turmeric

½ cup raw cashews, split into halves

1 tsp salt or to taste

1¼ cups warm water

⅔ cup milk

2 hard-boiled eggs, quartered lengthwise

A few sprigs of fresh coriander

1. Melt 2 tbsps ghee or butter from the specified amount, over medium heat and fry the onions, ginger and garlic until the onions are soft (about 5 minutes). Squeeze out excess fat by pressing the fried ingredients onto the side of the pan and then transfer them to a plate. Allow to cool.

2. Add the remaining ghee or butter to the pan and fry the ground ingredients, including the poppy and sesame seeds, for 1 minute, stirring constantly.

3. Add the meat and fry until all the liquid evaporates (about 10 minutes), stirring frequently.

4. Add the turmeric, stir and fry for 30 seconds.

5. Add the salt, cashews and the water, bring to the boil, cover the pan and cook over low heat for 15 minutes, stirring occasionally.

6. Meanwhile, put the milk into a food processor followed by the fried onions, garlic and ginger. Blend until the ingredients are smooth and stir into the mince. Bring to the boil again, cover the pan and simmer for 10-15 minutes or until thickened.

7. Put the meat into a serving dish and garnish with the hard-boiled eggs and the coriander leaves.

TIME Preparation takes 25-30 minutes, cooking takes 40-45 minutes.

SERVING IDEAS Serve with Naan or Plain Pilau and Tomato & Cucumber Salad.
Suitable for freezing.

Classic Meat Dishes

LAMB WITH MUNG BEANS

Mung beans are available from specialist grocers and health food stores. Prepare this dish a day in advance because the flavor develops when it is left to stand.

SERVES 6-8

---

1 cup whole mung beans

1¼ tsp salt or to taste

1-inch cube of root ginger, peeled and coarsely chopped

2-4 cloves garlic, peeled and coarsely chopped

1½lbs leg or shoulder of lamb, cut into 1-inch cubes

Scant 2 cups water

1 large onion, finely chopped

Grind the 6 following ingredients in a coffee grinder

2 dried red chili peppers

1½ tsps cumin seeds

2 tsps coriander seeds

4 whole cloves

1 cinnamon stick, 2-inches long; broken up

4 black peppercorns

1 tsp ground turmeric

1 small can of tomatoes or 4 ripe tomatoes, skinned and chopped

2 tbsps chopped coriander leaves

1. Soak the mung beans overnight in plenty of cold water and drain well. Pulses sometimes contain a certain amount of small stones; make sure you pick over the beans and wash them several times before soaking.

2. Add the salt to the ginger and garlic and crush them to a smooth pulp.

3. Place the meat and water in a large pan and bring the liquid to the boil. Cover the pan and simmer for 45 minutes.

4. Add the mung beans along with the onions. Bring back to the boil, cover the pan and cook on low heat for 25 minutes.

5. Add the ginger/garlic pulp, the ground spices, turmeric and the tomatoes. Simmer for 10 minutes, uncovered.

6. Remove from heat and stand aside for several hours before serving. The longer you let it stand, the better.

7. Reheat the curry and stir in the coriander leaves and simmer for 5 minutes before serving.

TIME Preparation takes 15-20 minutes plus time needed to soak the beans, cooking takes 1 hour 20 minutes.

SERVING IDEAS Serve with Plain Boiled Rice and Tomato and Cucumber Salad.
Suitable for freezing.

VARIATION Add a small eggplant, cut into chunky pieces, along with the mung beans.

Classic Meat Dishes

BHOONA GOSHT

*The word "Bhoon" means to fry and "Gosht" means meat; Bhoona Gosht,
therefore, means fried meat. This dish needs particular care and attention
during frying. It is important to follow carefully the different levels of temperature
during the different stages of frying.*

SERVES 4-6

2¼lbs leg or shoulder of lamb

5 tbsps cooking oil

3 large onions, finely chopped

1-inch cube of root ginger, peeled and
    grated or finely chopped

3-4 cloves garlic, peeled and crushed

1 tsp ground turmeric

2 tsps ground cumin

1 tbsp ground coriander

½-1 tsp chili powder

Scant 1 cup warm water

1¼ tsps salt or to taste

2 medium-sized ripe tomatoes, skinned and
    chopped; canned tomatoes can be used

4-5 whole fresh green chili peppers

1 tsp garam masala

1 tbsps chopped coriander leaves

2 small ripe tomatoes, sliced

---

1. Trim off excess fat from the meat, wash
and cut into 1-inch cubes. Drain on paper
towels.

2. Heat the oil over medium heat and add
the onions, ginger and garlic. Fry until the
onions are just soft (about 5 minutes).

3. Lower heat and add the turmeric, cumin,
coriander and chili powder. Stir and fry for
2-3 minutes.

4. Add the meat, turn heat to medium and
fry for 5 minutes stirring frequently. Cover
the pan and cook on medium heat until all
the liquid dries out (15-20 minutes). Stir
frequently.

5. Turn heat to high and fry the meat for 2-3
minutes stirring continuously. Reduce heat
to medium and fry for a further 7-8 minutes
stirring frequently. The meat should now
look fairly dry and the fat should be floating
on the surface. Some of the fat can be
drained off at this stage, but be careful not
to drain off any of the spices.

6. Add the water and salt, bring to the boil,
cover and simmer for 50-60 minutes or until
the meat is tender. Add more water if
necessary. At the end of the cooking time,
the thick spice paste should be clinging to
the pieces of meat.

7. Add the chopped tomatoes and the
whole green chili peppers. Stir and fry for
3-4 minutes.

8. Stir in the garam masala and half the
coriander leaves and remove from heat.

9. Put the bhoona gosht into a serving dish
and arrange the sliced tomatoes round the
meat. Sprinkle the remaining coriander
leaves on top.

TIME Preparation takes 25-30 minutes, cooking takes 1 hour 45 minutes.

Classic Meat Dishes

MEAT DILPASAND

A delectable lamb dish with a slightly creamy texture and a wonderfully nutty flavor derived from roasted and ground poppy seeds.

SERVES 4-6

2¼lbs leg of lamb

⅔ cup thick set plain yogurt

1 tsp ground turmeric

2 tbsps white or black poppy seeds

1-inch cube of root ginger, peeled and coarsely chopped

4-5 cloves garlic, peeled and coarsely chopped

1-2 fresh green chili peppers, seed them if a milder flavor is preferred

2 onions

3 tbsps ghee or unsalted butter

½ tsp chili powder

1 tsp paprika

1 tbsp ground cumin

1 tsp garam masala

1 tbsp tomato paste

1¼ tsps salt or to taste

¾ cup warm water

2 tbsps flaked coconut

2 tbsps chopped coriander leaves

---

1. Trim off any fat from the meat, wash and dry on paper towels and cut into 1½-inch cubes.

2. Add yogurt and turmeric, mix thoroughly, cover the container and leave to marinate for 4-6 hours or overnight in the refrigerator.

3. Roast the poppy seeds without fat over gentle heat until they are a shade darker – allow to cool.

4. Place the ginger, garlic and green chili peppers in a blender or food processor. Chop one onion, from the specified amount, and add to the ginger and garlic

mixture. Blend until fairly smooth.

5. Chop the remaining onions finely.

6. Melt the ghee or butter over medium heat and fry onions until golden brown. This will take 10 to 12 minutes.

7. Adjust heat to low and add chili powder, paprika, cumin and ½ tsp garam masala from the specified amount. Stir and fry for 2-3 minutes.

8. Now add the blended ingredients and fry for 10 to 12 minutes, stirring frequently. If during this time the spices tend to stick to the bottom of the pan, sprinkle with about 1 tbsp of water at a time as and when necessary.

9. Add the meat and adjust heat to medium-high. Fry for 4-5 minutes stirring constantly.

10. Add the tomato paste, salt and water, stir and mix, bring to the boil, cover and simmer for 45 minutes or until the meat is tender. Stir occasionally during the first half of cooking, but more frequently towards the end to ensure that the thickened sauce does not stick to the bottom of the pan.

11. Grind coconut in a spice grinder or a food processor until very fine.

12. Grind the poppy seeds in a spice grinder along with the coconut and stir both into the meat. Cover and simmer for 15 minutes.

13. Stir in the coriander leaves and the remaining garam masala. Remove from heat.

Classic Meat Dishes

PASANDA BADAM CURRY

Pasanda is a classic north Indian dish where the meat is cut into thin slices and cooked in a rich sauce containing saffron, yogurt and cream.

SERVES 4-6

2lbs boned leg of lamb

1-inch cube of root ginger, peeled and coarsely chopped

4-6 cloves garlic, peeled and coarsely chopped

2 fresh green chili peppers, seeded and coarsely chopped

4 tbsps plain yogurt

4 tbsps ghee or unsalted butter

3 medium-sized onions, finely sliced

½ tsp ground turmeric

1 tsp ground cumin

2 tsps ground coriander

½ tsp ground nutmeg

¼-½ tsp chili powder

1 cup warm water

1¼ tsps salt or to taste

⅔ cup cream

¼ cup ground almonds

1 tsp garam masala or ground mixed spice

2 tbsps rosewater (optional)

½ tsp paprika

1. Beat the meat with a meat mallet to flatten it to ¼-inch thickness, then cut into thin slices (about 1½-inch long and ½-inch wide).

2. Put the ginger, garlic, green chili peppers and yogurt into a blender or food processor and blend until smooth.

3. Melt the ghee or butter over medium heat and fry the onions until they are lightly browned (6-8 minutes).

4. Add the turmeric, cumin, coriander, nutmeg and chili powder; adjust heat to low, stir and fry for 2-3 minutes.

5. Add the meat and fry it over high heat for 3-4 minutes or until it changes color.

6. Add about 2 tbsps of the blended ingredients and cook for 1-2 minutes, stirring frequently. Repeat this process until all the yogurt mixture is used up.

7. Now fry the meat over medium heat for 4-5 minutes stirring frequently. When the fat begins to seep through the thick spice paste and floats on the surface, add the water, bring to the boil, cover the pan and simmer until the meat is tender (about 60 minutes), stirring occasionally.

8. Add the salt, cream and ground almonds and let it simmer without the lid for 5-6 minutes.

9. Stir in the garam masala and rosewater, if using, and remove from heat.

10. Put the pasanda into a serving dish and sprinkle the paprika on top, if desired.

TIME Preparation takes 30 minutes, cooking takes 1 hour 20 minutes.

SERVING IDEAS Serve with Mattar Pilau and Cabbage and Mint Salad.

VARIATION Use chuck steak.

Classic Meat Dishes

MEAT DURBARI

The word 'Durbar' means forum or formal gathering. This wonderful lamb dish originated in the royal kitchens and was served at special gatherings held by the great Mughal Emperors.

SERVES 4

2¼lbs leg of lamb

Grind the following 9 ingredients in a spice or coffee grinder and make a paste by adding the vinegar

1 tbsp mustard seeds

1 tbsp sesame seeds

2 tbsps poppy seeds

10 black peppercorns

2-4 dried red chili peppers

1 bay leaf

2-inch piece of cinnamon stick, broken up

4 whole cloves

The inner seeds of 2 black cardamoms

3 tbsps white wine vinegar

1¼ tsp salt or to taste

3-4 cloves garlic, peeled and coarsely chopped

3 tbsps ghee or unsalted butter

1 large onion, finely chopped

1-inch cube of root ginger, peeled and finely grated

¾ cup warm water

1 tbsp tomato paste

2 fresh green chili peppers, slit lengthwise into halves, seeded for a milder flavor

2 tbsps chopped coriander leaves

1. Trim off excess fat from the meat and cut into 2-inch cubes.

2. Rub the spice paste well into the meat and leave to marinate for 4-6 hours, or overnight in the refrigerator.

3. Add the salt to the garlic and crush to a smooth pulp.

4. Melt the ghee or butter gently over low heat, add the onions and ginger, adjust heat to medium and fry them until the onions are soft (3-4 minutes).

5. Add the garlic paste and fry for a further 2-3 minutes stirring frequently.

6. Add the meat and cook in the onion mixture until all sides of meat are sealed and brown.

7. Add the water, bring to the boil, cover and simmer until the meat is tender.

8. Add the tomato paste, green chili peppers and coriander leaves – adjust heat to medium and cook for 3-4 minutes stirring continuously. Remove the pan from the heat.

TIME Preparation takes 20-25 minutes plus time needed to marinate, cooking takes 1 hour 10 minutes.

SERVING IDEAS Serve with Mushroom Pillau and Saagwalla Dhal; with Parathas or Rotis and Cauliflower with Lentil Flour. Serve any chutney or relish for a traditional touch.
Suitable for freezing.

Classic Meat Dishes

KHEEMA-PALAK (GROUND MEAT WITH SPINACH)

In India, ground meat is rarely cooked on its own. Various combinations are used to make it more interesting. Meat and spinach is one of the most popular.

SERVES 4-6

4 tbsps cooking oil

½ tsp mustard seeds

1 tsp cumin seeds

1 fresh green chili pepper, finely chopped and seeded if a milder flavor is preferred

1-inch cube of root ginger, peeled and finely grated

6 cloves garlic, peeled and crushed

1lb lean ground lamb or beef

1 large onion, finely sliced

2 cinnamon sticks, 2-inches long each, broken up

½ tsp ground turmeric

1 tbsp ground cumin

½ tsp ground black pepper

1lb fresh spinach leaves, chopped or 8oz frozen spinach, defrosted and drained

1 tsp salt or to taste

1 small can of tomatoes, drained and chopped or 3-4 medium sized ripe tomatoes, skinned and chopped

1 tsp garam masala

1. Heat half the oil in a skillet over medium heat and fry the mustard seeds until they crackle. Add the cumin seeds and immediately follow with the chili pepper, ginger and half the garlic. Stir and fry for 30 seconds.

2. Add the meat, stir and fry until all the liquid evaporates – this will take 8-10 minutes. Remove the pan from the heat and set aside.

3. In a separate pan, heat the remaining oil over medium heat and stir in the rest of the garlic. Add the onions and cinnamon sticks and fry until the onions are lightly browned (6-8 minutes), stirring frequently.

4. Adjust heat to low and add the turmeric, cumin and black pepper. Stir and fry for 1 minute. Add the spinach and mix thoroughly.

5. Add the meat and stir until the spinach and the other ingredients are thoroughly mixed. Cover the pan and simmer for 15 minutes.

6. Adjust heat to medium, add salt and the tomatoes, stir and cook for 2-3 minutes.

7. Add the garam masala, stir and cook for a further 2-3 minutes. Remove the pan from heat.

TIME Preparation takes 15-20 minutes, cooking takes 40 minutes.

SERVING IDEAS Serve with Loochis or Rotis and Sour-hot Potatoes. With Plain Boiled Rice, Spicy Channa Dhal and Cucumber and Onion Raita.

TO FREEZE Suitable for freezing if fresh spinach is used.

Classic Meat Dishes

SAVORY MEAT & EGGS

A very attractive and unusual way to present ground meat which also makes an economical and filling family meal.

SERVES 4-6

4 tbsps cooking oil

1 large onion, coarsely chopped

1-inch cube of root ginger, peeled and coarsely chopped

4-6 cloves garlic, peeled and coarsely chopped

⅔ cup thick set plain yogurt

1 tsp cumin seeds

1 tsp ground turmeric

1 tsp ground coriander

1lb lean coarse ground meat, lamb or beef

1 tsp paprika

1¼ cups warm water

1 tsp salt or to taste

1 tbsp tomato paste

½ tsp garam masala

2 tbsps chopped coriander leaves

4-6 small eggs (1 per person)

1. Heat 2 tbsps of oil from the specified amount over medium heat and fry onion, ginger and garlic for 3-4 minutes stirring frequently. Remove from heat and allow to cool slightly.

2. Put the yogurt and fried onion mixture into a blender or food processor and blend until smooth. Set aside.

3. Heat the remaining oil and fry the cumin seeds until they pop.

4. To prevent the spices from burning, remove the pan from the heat and add the turmeric and coriander, stir and mix thoroughly.

5. Place the pan back on the heat and add the meat. Fry over medium heat until lightly browned.

6. Add the paprika, water and salt, bring to the boil, cover and simmer for 15 minutes. Stir occasionally.

7. Add the blended ingredients and tomato paste, bring to the boil again, cover and simmer for a further 15 minutes. Stir occasionally.

8. Stir in the garam masala and the coriander leaves. Remove from heat.

9. Preheat oven to 375°F.

10. Put the meat into an ovenproof dish. Make 4-6 hollows, according to the number of eggs used, about 1-inch apart. Break an egg into each hollow; do not worry about the egg white spilling over the hollow. Bake in the center of the oven for 30 minutes or until the eggs are set. Bake for a few minutes longer if you like the yolks hard.

11. Garnish with the remaining coriander leaves.

TIME Preparation takes 10-15 minutes, cooking takes 55 minutes.

SERVING IDEAS Serve with Parathas or Rotis. Aloo ki Bhaji makes a good accompaniment. It is also excellent with garlic bread.

TO FREEZE Freeze before adding the eggs.

VARIATION Add ½ cup frozen peas in stage 7.

microwave

SPICED ALMONDS

These toasted, lightly spiced almonds are a real treat for a cocktail party or pre-dinner drinks. Be sure to stir and reposition the almonds during cooking, from the outside of the dish to the center, to ensure even distribution of energy.

SERVES 6-8

3½ cups whole almonds
½ tsp salt or to taste
1 tbsp water
1 tbsp cooking oil
½ tsp chili powder
½ tsp ground coriander

1. Place the almonds in a bowl. Dissolve the salt in the water and add to the almonds. Mix thoroughly and let stand for 15 minutes.

2. Stir the almonds again and spread them into a 12-inch diameter plate or large dish.

3. Cook on 100% power (High) for 7 minutes. Stir and reposition the almonds every 2 minutes.

4. Remove and sprinkle the oil evenly on them. Stir and mix well.

5. Sprinkle the chili powder and coriander and mix until the spices coat the almonds.

6. Place the almonds back in the microwave and cook on 100% power (High) for a further 3 minutes. Stir and reposition halfway through.

7. Allow the almonds to cool completely. It is best to wait several hours before serving them, as the longer they are allowed to stand, the crunchier they taste.

TIME Preparation takes 15 minutes, cooking takes 10 minutes.

SHRIMP IN GARLIC AND TAMARIND

A quick and tasty dish using frozen shrimp and boiled, diced potatoes. The potatoes help to thicken the sauce and add an extra dimension to the dish.

SERVES 4

2 medium-sized potatoes
2 tsps ground coriander
1 tsp chili powder or to taste
1 tsp paprika
3 tbsps cooking oil
4-5 cloves garlic, peeled and crushed
1 onion, finely chopped
⅓ cup hot water
1 level tsp tamarind concentrate or 1½ tbsps
    lemon juice
1 tsp salt or to taste
1lb frozen shrimp, defrosted and drained
1 tbsp besan (chick pea flour), sieved

1. Put the potatoes in a 2-3 pint dish and add 4 tbsps hot water. Cover and cook on 100% power (High) for 2½ minutes. Turn the potatoes over, re-cover and cook on 100% power (High) for a further 2 minutes.

2. Leave the potatoes to stand for 8 minutes then immerse them in cold water until they are completely cold. Peel and dice them evenly.

3. Put the coriander, chili powder and paprika in small glass bowl and heat on 100% power (High) for 1½ minutes. Stir and stand aside.

4. Mix 2 tbsps oil from the specified amount, half the garlic and all the onion in a 3-pint casserole, cover and cook on 100% power (High) for 5 minutes, stirring every 1½ minutes.

5. Add the spice mixture and cook, uncovered, on 100% power (High) for 2 minutes, stirring halfway through.

6. Add the water, tamarind, salt and the shrimp. Stir and mix well. Cover and cook on High for 4 minutes, stirring every 2 minutes.

7. Add the potatoes, re-cover and cook on High for 2 minutes.

8. Preheat a browning dish on 100% power (High) for 4-5 minutes, add the remaining oil and cook on High for 1 minute. Add the garlic and cook on 100% power (High) for 30 seconds to 1 minute until golden brown. Stir the garlic oil into the shrimp.

9. Sprinkle the besan evenly on the shrimp, stir and mix thoroughly. Cook, uncovered, on 100% power (High) for 2 minutes, stirring halfway through.

10. If you are using lemon juice instead of tamarind, simply add this with the besan and mix well, then cook for specified time.

TIME Preparation takes 15-20 minutes, cooking takes 20 minutes.

SERVING IDEAS Serve with Plain Boiled Rice or Cinnamon Rice and Cauliflower Upkari.

VARIATION Substitute corn starch for the besan if you can't find the latter.

EGGPLANT CURRY

The tangy, slightly hot taste of this dish enhances the natural flavor of eggplant. Sliced eggplant absorbs the coconut sauce beautifully and every bite tastes delicious.

SERVES 4-6

1-12oz eggplant
1½ tsp ground cumin
½ tsp garam masala
¼-½ tsp chili powder
14oz can of tomatoes
4 fresh green chili peppers, sliced
    lengthwise and seeded for a milder
    flavor
10-12 curry leaves (or 1 tbsp curry powder)
1¼ tsps salt or to taste
⅓ cup hot water
⅓ cup finely grated fresh coconut

1. Quarter the eggplant lengthwise and cut each quarter into ¼-inch thick slices. Soak in salted cold water for 15 minutes and drain. Rinse well.

2. Mix the cumin, garam masala and chili powder in a small glass bowl and heat on 100% power (High) for 2 minutes. Stir and stand aside.

3. Put the tomatoes, along with all the juice, and the green chili peppers in a 4-pint casserole or bowl. Cover with a lid or pierced plastic wrap and cook on 100% power (High) for 3 minutes.

4. Stir the tomatoes and add the eggplant, curry leaves or powder, salt and water. Re-cover and cook on 100% power (High) for 6 minutes, stirring every 2 minutes.

5. Stir in the heated spices and mix thoroughly. Cover and cook on 100% power (High) for 5 minutes, stirring as before.

6. Add the coconut, cover and cook on 100% power (High) for 5 minutes, stirring and re-positioning the eggplant halfway through cooking time.

7. Leave the dish to stand for 10 minutes before serving.

TIME Preparation takes 22 minutes including soaking the eggplant, cooking takes 21 minutes.

SERVING IDEAS Serve with Plain Boiled Rice and Seekh Kababs.

MUSTARD FISH

A traditional dish from Assam and Bengal, the two eastern states of India. Mustard powder and flaked coconut have been used in this recipe to make preparation quick and easy.

SERVES 4

1½lbs skinned fillets of firm white fish
3 tbsps flaked coconut
1½ tbsps mustard powder
4 fresh green chili peppers
½ cup water
1 tsp salt or to taste
1 tomato, cut into 8 pieces
2 tbsps finely chopped coriander leaves

1. Wash the fish gently in cold water and pat dry.

2. Cut each fillet into ½-inch thick and 2-inch long pieces.

3. Grind the coconut in a spice grinder or a food processor until it is fine.

4. Slice two chili peppers lengthwise and leave the other two whole. Seed them if a milder flavor is preferred.

5. Put the coconut in a bowl and add the rest of the ingredients except chili peppers, tomatoes and coriander. Stir and mix until a thick batter-like mixture is formed.

6. Pour this mixture over the fish and mix thoroughly, but gently with a metal spoon.

7. Place the whole chili peppers at the bottom of a 3-pint casserole and arrange half the fish on top.

8. Place the sliced chili peppers and half the coriander leaves on the layer of fish and cover with the remaining fish. Arrange the tomatoes on top.

9. Cover the dish with a lid or pierced plastic wrap and cook on 50% power (Medium) for 5 minutes, then stir and cook as before for a further 5 minutes.

10. Allow to stand for 8 minutes and garnish with the remaining coriander leaves.

TIME Preparation takes 15-20 minutes, cooking takes 10 minutes.

SERVING IDEAS Serve with Plain Boiled Rice and Mixed Vegetable Bhaji. Suitable for freezing.

CHICKEN KORMA

In addition to being quick, the microwave oven method retains all the delicious and distinctive flavor of Chicken Korma.

SERVES 4

1½lbs chicken breasts, skinned and boned
⅔ cup thick set plain yogurt
2 cloves garlic, peeled and crushed
¼-inch cube of root ginger, peeled and crushed or grated

Mix together the following 5 ingredients
2 tsps ground coriander
½ tsp freshly ground black pepper
½ tsp ground cinnamon
½ tsp ground cardamom
¼ tsp ground turmeric

1 tbsp ghee or unsalted butter
1 medium-sized onion, finely sliced
Scant ⅓ cup cream
¾ tsp salt or to taste
½ cup ground almonds
1 tbsp sliced almonds, toasted

1. Cut the chicken breast into 1-inch cubes.

2. Mix the yogurt, garlic and ginger together, add the chicken and mix until the chicken pieces are fully coated. Cover the container and leave to marinate in a cool place for 2 hours.

3. Put the bowl containing the ground spices in the microwave and heat on 100% power (High) for 2 minutes. Stir and set aside.

4. Put the ghee in a 3-pint casserole and melt on 100% power (High) for 45 seconds.

5. Stir in the onion, cover and cook on 100% power (High) for 4 minutes, stirring halfway through.

6. Stir in the heated spices and cook, uncovered, on 100% power (High) for 1½ minutes.

7. Stir the spices, then add the chicken. Stir and mix well. Cover and cook on 100% power (High) for 4 minutes, stirring after 2 minutes, then on 50% power (Medium) for 4 minutes.

8. Add the cream, cover and cook on for 4 minutes.

9. Stir in the salt and ground almonds; mix thoroughly. Cook, uncovered, on 50% power (Medium) for 3 minutes. Stir halfway through.

10. Stand for 6 minutes and garnish with the toasted almonds.

TIME Preparation takes 20-25 minutes plus marinating time, cooking takes 15½ minutes.

SERVING IDEAS Serve with Pilau Rice or Cinnamon Rice.
Suitable for freezing.

MARINATED TROUT

*A delicately flavored dish with a slightly hot and tangy taste. The flavor improves
if you cook the fish in advance and allow it to stand. It reheats perfectly.*

SERVES 4

2 trout (total weight about 1½lbs)
2-3 cloves garlic, peeled and coarsely
   chopped
1 tsp salt or to taste
½ tsp chili powder
½ tsp tamarind concentrate or 1 tbsp lemon
   juice
1 tbsp water
1 tbsp olive oil

1. Remove the heads of the fish and slit
along the belly right down to the tail. Gut
and wash inside and out gently in cold
water. Filleted trout are also available.

2. Put the fish on a board, on its stomach
and gently but firmly run your fingers along
the center bone. This will loosen the bone,
turn the fish over and gently pull out the
bone. If it does not come away in one
piece, simply pull away the remaining
pieces in exactly the same way.

3. Now cut the fish lengthwise into half. Cut
each half into 3 pieces.

4. Crush the garlic and salt together to a
smooth pulp. Add the rest of the ingredients
and mix thoroughly.

5. Put 1 tsp of the marinade over each piece
of fish and spread it so that it coats the
entire surface. Place any remaining
marinade on the fish and place the fish in a
covered container. Leave to marinate in the
refrigerator for 3-4 hours. Remove from the
refrigerator 30 minutes before cooking.

6. Arrange the fish, skin side down, in a
shallow dish, with the thin end towards the
center of the dish. Cover with pierced
plastic wrap. Cook on 50% power
(Medium) for 4 minutes.

7. Turn the fish over (skin side up), and
cook, covered as before, for a further 2
minutes.

8. Allow to stand for several hours, then
reheat on 50% power (Medium) setting and
serve.

TIME Preparation takes 20-25 minutes plus time for marinating, cooking
takes 6 minutes.

SERVING IDEAS Serve with Tarka Dhal and Plain Boiled Rice.
Suitable for freezing.

MACKEREL WITH COCONUT SAUCE

A popular Saraswat recipe converted for the microwave.
It is traditionally known as 'Amshi-Tikshi' meaning sour-hot. The quantity of
chili powder, however, can be adjusted to suit individual taste.

SERVES 4

1½lbs mackerel
3-4 cloves garlic, peeled and coarsely
    chopped
1¼ tsps salt or to taste

Mix together the following 4 ingredients
1½ tsps ground coriander
¼ tsp ground turmeric
1 tsp paprika
1-1½ tsps chili powder

1 cup warm water
1 cup flaked coconut
1 level tsp tamarind concentrate or 2 tbsps
    lemon juice

1. Remove the head from the fish, and cut the fish into about 2-inch wide pieces; do not cut along the belly.

2. Wash each piece of fish gently in cold water inside and out.

3. Add the salt to the garlic and crush it to a pulp.

4. Heat the spice mixture on 100% power (High) for 1½ minutes, stir and set aside.

5. Put the water, coconut and tamarind into a 3-pint casserole, cover and cook on 100% power (High) for 6 minutes, stirring halfway through.

6. Add the spice mixture and the garlic to the coconut mixture, stir and mix thoroughly.

7. Arrange the pieces of fish in the coconut mixture in a single layer and spoon some of it over the fish. Cover as before and cook on 50% power (Medium) for 6 minutes, reposition pieces in dish after every 2 minutes. Add lemon juice during this time and mix gently.

8. Set dish aside for 5 minutes before serving.

TIME Preparation takes 10-15 minutes, cooking takes 13 minutes.

SERVING IDEAS Serve with Plain Boiled Rice and Cauliflower Upkari.
Suitable for freezing.

CHICKEN WITH CASHEWS

This Mughlai-style recipe has a rich and creamy sauce made by blending raw cashews with milk. Diced, par-boiled potatoes are added towards the end, which also helps to thicken the sauce.

SERVES 4

2 small potatoes

Mix together the following 7 ingredients in a glass bowl

½ tsp ground cinnamon

½ tsp ground cardamom

½ tsp ground allspice

1 tsp ground coriander

½ tsp freshly ground black pepper

1 tsp paprika

¼ tsp ground turmeric

½ cup raw cashews

½ cup milk

1 fresh green chili pepper, chopped

1 medium-sized onion, finely chopped

½-inch cube of root ginger, peeled and grated

2 tbsps oil

2 cloves garlic, peeled and crushed

¾ cup hot water

1½lbs boned chicken breasts, skinned and cut into 1-inch cubes

1 tsp salt or to taste

1. Put the potatoes in a 2-3 pint casserole and add 4 tbsps hot water. Cover and cook on 100% power (High) for 3 minutes. Turn the potatoes over, re-cover and cook on for 2 minutes.

2. Stand the potatoes for 6-8 minutes, then immerse them in cold water until they are completely cold. Peel and dice the potatoes evenly.

3. Heat the spice mixture on 100% power (High) for 2 minutes. Stir and stand aside.

4. Put the cashews, milk and chili pepper in a food processor and blend until smooth.

5. In a 4-pint casserole, mix the oil, onions, ginger and garlic. Cover with a lid or pierced plastic wrap and cook on 100% power (High) for 4½ minutes, stirring halfway through.

6. Add the spice mixture, stir and mix thoroughly. Cook, uncovered, on 100% power (High) for 2 minutes and stir.

7. Now add the water and chicken, stir and mix well. Cover and cook on 100% power (High) for 4 minutes, stirring after 2 minutes. Cook for a further 4-6 minutes on 50% power (Medium), stirring after every two minutes.

8. Add the salt and the cashew paste, cover and cook on 100% power (High) for 2 minutes.

9. Add the potatoes, stir and mix well. Cook, uncovered, on 100% power (High) for 3 minutes, stirring halfway through.

TIME Preparation takes 10-15 minutes, cooking takes 20 minutes.

SERVING IDEAS Serve with Cinnamon Rice and Green Beans in Garlic Butter.

TO FREEZE Suitable for freezing, but freeze before adding the potatoes.

SHRIMP CURRY

A north-Indian style shrimp curry adapted for the microwave with amazingly delicious result! Use fresh or frozen shrimp but make sure that frozen ones are defrosted and drained first.

SERVES 4

Mix together the following 5 ingredients in a small glass bowl

2 tsps ground coriander
½ tsp garam masala
½-1 tsp chili powder
1 tsp paprika
¼ tsp ground turmeric

1 cup water
2 cloves garlic, peeled and crushed
1 tsp salt or to taste
⅓ cup flaked coconut, finely ground
1lb peeled shrimp
3 tbsps cooking oil
1 medium-sized onion, finely chopped
2 fresh green chili peppers, seeded and
    sliced lengthwise
Juice of half a lemon
2 tbsps chopped coriander leaves

1. Put the bowl of spice mixture in the microwave and heat, uncovered, on 100% power (High) for 2 minutes. Stir and set aside.

2. Put the water, garlic, salt, coconut and spice mixture in a 3-pint casserole and mix thoroughly.

3. Add the shrimp and mix. Cover with a lid or pierced plastic wrap and cook on 50% power (Medium) for 6-8 minutes. Stir halfway through.

4. Preheat the browning dish on 100% power (High) for 4-5 minutes. Add the oil and heat as before for 1 minute. Add the onion to the hot oil and fry on 100% power (High) for 4-5 minutes until they are lightly browned, stirring frequently. Stir the onion into the shrimp along with the chili peppers and half the coriander leaves. Cover and cook on 100% power (High) for 1½ minutes.

5. Remove from the oven, stir in the lemon juice and stand for 5 minutes.

6. Garnish with the coriander leaves.

TIME Preparation takes 10 minutes, cooking takes 14 minutes.

SERVING IDEAS Serve with plain boiled rice and Caulilower Upkari. Suitable for freezing, if fresh shrimp are used.

COOK'S TIP If you do not have a browning dish heat the oil over a medium heat and fry the onions until they are lightly browned. Stir the onion into the shrimp along with the chili peppers and half the coriander leaves. Cover and cook on 100% power (High) for 1½ minutes.

CHICKEN AND MUSHROOM CURRY

The combination of chicken and mushroom is delicious. Here, the traditional garam masala is replaced with allspice, which has the flavor of cloves, cinnamon and nutmeg.

SERVES 4

1 tsp ground coriander
½ tsp ground cumin
½ tsp ground turmeric
½ tsp chili powder
½ tsp ground allspice
2 tbsps cooking oil
1 medium-sized onion, finely chopped
½-inch cube of root ginger, peeled and finely chopped or grated
1-2 cloves garlic, peeled and crushed
1½lbs chicken thighs, skinned and boned
1½ tbsps tomato paste
⅓ cup hot water
3 cups mushrooms, thickly sliced
1 tsp salt or to taste
¼ cup flaked almonds
2 tbsps chopped coriander leaves

1. Put the ground coriander, cumin, turmeric, chili powder and allspice in a small glass bowl and heat, uncovered, on high for 2 minutes. Stir and stand aside.

2. Put the oil, onion, ginger and garlic in a 3-pint casserole or bowl, cover with a lid or pierced plastic wrap and cook on 100% power (High) for 2½ minutes.

3. Stir in the spice mixture and cook, uncovered, for 2 minutes.

4. Add the chicken, tomato paste and water, and stir and mix thoroughly. Cover as before and cook on 100% power (High) for 4 minutes. Stir every 2 minutes. Reduce temperature setting to 50% power (Medium) and cook for 6 minutes. Stir after 3 minutes.

5. Add the mushrooms and salt, stir and mix well. Cover again and cook on 50% power (Medium) for 4 minutes, stir after 2 minutes.

6. Stir in the flaked almonds and cook, uncovered, on 25% power (Low) for 3 minutes. Stir halfway through.

7. Remove and stir in half the coriander leaves. Use the remaining coriander leaves to garnish the curry.

8. Allow the dish to stand for 6 minutes before serving.

TIME Preparation takes 15 minutes, cooking takes 23 minutes.

SERVING IDEAS Serve with Cardamom Rice or Plain Boiled Rice.
Suitable for freezing.

SHRIMP WITH COCONUT MILK

Adapted for the microwave, this is a specialty from the coastal region of India where large shrimp are found. The sauce is fragrant with coconut and ginger, and spicy with fresh chili pepper.

SERVES 4

1 cup flaked coconut, finely ground

1 fresh green chili pepper, chopped and
    seeded if a milder flavor is liked

½-inch cube of root ginger, peeled and
    finely grated

1 tsp salt or to taste

⅔ cup hot water

1lb peeled frozen shrimp, defrosted and
    drained

⅔ cup frozen peas

2 tsps ground coriander

½-1 tsp chili powder

2 tbsps cooking oil

1 medium-sized onion, finely chopped

1½ tbsps lemon juice

1. Put the coconut, chili pepper, ginger, salt and water into a 2-pint casserole or bowl, cover with a lid or plastic wrap. Pierce the plastic wrap and cook on 100% power (High) for 2 minutes.

2. Stir and mix the ingredients thoroughly, re-cover and cook on 100% power (High) for a further 2 minutes or until the coconut is fully softened.

3. Add the shrimp and mix well, cover and cook on 100% power (High) for 2 minutes.

4. Add the peas, cover as before and cook on 100% power (High) for 1½ minutes. Stir the contents and stand for 5 minutes.

5. Put the coriander and chili powder in a small glass bowl and heat on 100% power (High) for 1½ minutes, when the spices will release their aroma. Let the mixture stand for 45 seconds then stir into the shrimp.

6. Preheat a microwave browning dish on high for 4-5 minutes. Add the oil and heat on 100% power (High) for 1 minute. Add the onion and 'fry' in the oil on High for 5-6 minutes until lightly browned, stirring frequently. Stir the onions into the shrimp.

7. Add the lemon juice and mix thoroughly.

TIME Preparation takes 10 minutes, cooking takes 9 minutes plus 5 minutes
45 seconds standing time.

SERVING IDEAS Serve with Plain Boiled Rice and Cauliflower Upkari.

COOK'S TIP If you do not have a microwave browning dish, heat the oil in
a skillet over a medium heat and fry the onions until they are lightly
browned, stirring frequently. Stir the onions into the shrimp.

SAFFRON RICE

A wonderfully fragrant rice cooked in a full-flavored stock prepared with a few whole spices and saffron strands. A pinch of powdered saffron can be used instead of the strands, though the strands have more flavor and color.

SERVES 4

1 cup basmati rice

2 cups water

1 cinnamon stick, 2-inches long, broken up
    into 2-3 pieces

3 green cardamoms, bruised

3 whole cloves

2 bay leaves, crumbled

⅛ tsp saffron strands

1 tsp salt or to taste

1 tsp butter

1. Wash the rice and soak it in cold water for 30 minutes. Drain well.

2. Put the water, cinnamon, cardamom, cloves, bay leaves and saffron in a 2-pint bowl and cover with plastic wrap. Puncture the wrap and cook on 100% power (High) for 5 minutes. Stand aside for 5 minutes.

3. Put the rice, salt and butter in a 4-5 pint bowl (be sure to use the correct size to avoid boiling over).

4. Strain the spiced liquid over the rice, stir and mix well. Cook on 100% power (High) for 8 minutes, then cook on 50% power (Medium) for 2 minutes.

5. Stand for 5 minutes. Fork through the rice before serving.

TIME Preparation takes 30 minutes to soak the rice, cooking takes 15 minutes plus 10 minutes standing time.

SERVING IDEAS Serve with Chicken Tikka Masala or Tandoori Chicken Masala.
Suitable for freezing.

PLAIN BOILED RICE

Cooking rice in the microwave is so simple as it does not need the slightest attention. The best result is achieved by using two levels of power control rather than cooking the rice on 100% power (High) throughout.

SERVES 4-6

1¼ cups basmati rice, washed and soaked
    in cold water for 30 minutes
2½ cups hot water
1 tsp butter
1 tsp salt

1. Drain the rice thoroughly.

2. Put all the ingredients in a 5-pint casserole or other dish, cover with a lid or pierced plastic wrap and cook on 100% power (High) for 6 minutes, then on 50% power (Medium) for 4 minutes.

3. Stand for 6-8 minutes. Fork through the rice before serving.

TIME Preparation takes 30 minutes to soak the rice, cooking takes 10 minutes.

SERVING IDEAS Plain Boiled Rice can be served with almost any curry, but it tastes particularly good with dishes like Bhoona Gosht, Chicken Kohlapuri and Mustard Fish.
Suitable for freezing.

CINNAMON RICE

A delicious boiled rice, flavored with cinnamon and bay leaves. Frozen peas are added for color.

SERVES 4

1 cup basmati rice, washed and soaked in
    cold water for 30 minutes

⅔ cup frozen peas or pre-cooked fresh
    peas

2 cups hot water

2 cinnamon sticks, 2-inches long each,
    broken up

2 bay leaves, crumbled

1 tsp butter

½ tsp salt

1. Drain the rice thoroughly.

2. Put all the ingredients together in a 5-pint casserole or bowl and mix well. Cover with a lid or pierced plastic wrap and cook on 100% power (High) for 8 minutes, then on 50% power (Medium) for 4 minutes.

3. Set aside for 10 minutes. Fork through the rice before serving. Remove cinnamon and bay leaves if liked.

TIME Preparation takes 30 minutes to soak the rice, cooking takes 12 minutes.

SERVING IDEAS Serve with Chicken Korma or Chicken with Cashews. Suitable for freezing if fresh peas are used.

TOMATO RICE

*In this delicious recipe basmati rice is cooked with cinnamon, bay leaves and
canned tomatoes to give it a soft red color, and a fragrant spicy taste.*

SERVES 4

1 cup basmati rice
Small can of tomatoes
1 cinnamon stick, 2-inches long; broken up
    into 2-3 pieces
1 bay leaf, crumbled
1-2 fresh green chili peppers, seeded and
    sliced lengthwise
1 tsp salt or to taste
1 tsp butter
A few sprigs of fresh coriander leaves

1. Wash the rice, soak in cold water for 30
minutes and drain well.

2. Sieve the tomatoes and mix the pulp
with enough hot water to make up to
2¼ cups.

3. Put the tomato-flavored water into a bowl
and add the cinnamon and bay leaf. Cover
and cook on 100% power (High) for 3½
minutes. Stir and leave to stand, covered,
for 15-20 minutes.

4. Put the rice in a 5-pint casserole or bowl
and add the spiced liquid, chili peppers,
salt and butter. Cover with pierced plastic
wrap; cook on 100% power (High) for 12
minutes.

5. Stand for 5-6 minutes.

6. Fork through the rice, remove cinnamon,
bay leaf and chili peppers and garnish with
the sprigs of fresh coriander.

TIME Preparation takes 30 minutes to soak the rice, cooking takes 15
minutes.

SERVING IDEAS Serve with Bhoona Gosht, Fish Bhoona or Tarka Dhal,
Saagwalla Dhal and Kababs.
Suitable for freezing.

TARKA DHAL

This delicious tarka dhal recipe requires less than half the time used for the conventional method of cooking.

SERVES 4

1 cup masoor dhal (red split lentils), cleaned and washed

2¼ cups hot water

½-inch cube of root ginger, peeled and finely chopped or grated

¼ tsp ground turmeric

2 ripe tomatoes, skinned and chopped

4 fresh green chili peppers, whole

¾ tsp salt or to taste

2 tbsps oil or ghee

1 tsp mustard seeds

10-12 curry leaves (or 1 tbsp mild curry powder)

10-12 fenugreek seeds

3-4 dried red chili peppers, whole

1 tbsp chopped coriander leaves

1. Put the dhal, water, ginger and turmeric in 4-5 pint casserole or bowl, cover with a lid or pierced plastic wrap, and cook on 100% power (High) for 5 minutes.

2. Stir the dhal, re-cover and cook on 50% power (Medium) for 10 minutes, stirring every 3 minutes.

3. Add the tomatoes, green chili peppers and salt; stir and mix well. Cover and cook on 100% power (High) for 2½ minutes.

4. Preheat a browning dish on 100% power (High) for 4-5 minutes, add the oil and heat for 1 minute on 100% power (High). Add the mustard seeds, cook on High for 30 seconds-1 minute until they pop. Now add the curry leaves or powder, fenugreek and red chili peppers.

5. Stir the hot oil seasoning into the dhal and garnish with the coriander leaves.

TIME Preparation takes 10 minutes, cooking takes 18 minutes.

SERVING IDEAS Serve with Cinnamon Rice and Marinated Trout. Suitable for freezing.

VARIATION If you do not have a browning dish, heat the oil in a frying pan, add the mustard seeds and fry over high heat. As soon as the seeds begin to pop, add the curry leaves or powder, fenugreek and red chili peppers. Remove from heat and stir the hot oil seasoning into the dhal.

CAULIFLOWER UPKARI

The microwave has transformed the taste of this traditional recipe. The pieces of cauliflower stay firm yet tender and succulent and the flavor of the whole spices comes through beautifully.

SERVES 4-6

1 large cauliflower
1 tbsp cooking oil
½ tsp mustard seeds
8-10 curry leaves (or 2 tsps curry powder)
2-4 dried red chili peppers, whole
¾ tsp salt or to taste

1. Cut the cauliflower into ½-inch flowerettes and soak in plenty of lightly salted water for 30 minutes. Drain and rinse well.

2. Pour oil into a 4-5 pint casserole or bowl and add the mustard seeds, curry leaves or powder and chili peppers.

3. Arrange the cauliflower evenly over the spices, cover with a lid or plastic wrap. Pierce plastic and cook on 100% power (High) for 5 minutes without stirring.

4. Sprinkle the salt evenly over the cauliflower, then stir and mix well. Cover again and cook on 100% power (High) for 7 minutes, stirring every 2 minutes.

5. Stand for 5-7 minutes.

TIME Preparation takes 10 minutes, cooking takes 12 minutes.

SERVING IDEAS Serve with Shrimp or Mackerel with Coconut and Plain Boiled Rice.

ALOO MATTAR

You would need twice the amount of spices if you cooked this dish conventionally. The microwave oven brings out the flavors of everything you cook in it.

SERVES 4-6

3 large potatoes
1 cup hot water
½ tsp garam masala
1 tsp ground cumin
¼ tsp ground turmeric
½ tsp chili powder
2 tbsps cooking oil
1 small onion, finely chopped
8-10 curry leaves (or 2 tsps curry powder)
⅔ cup frozen peas
¾ tsp salt or to taste
1 tbsp tomato paste

1. Put the water and the potatoes in a casserole or bowl, cover and cook on 100% power (High) for 4½ minutes.

2. Turn the potatoes over, cover again and cook on 100% power (High) for 4 minutes. Stand for 6-8 minutes. Allow the potatoes to cool thoroughly.

3. Peel and dice the potatoes evenly.

4. Put the garam masala, cumin, turmeric and chilli powder in a small glass bowl and heat on 100% power (High) for 1 minute. Stir and set aside for 5 minutes.

5. Put the oil, onion and curry leaves or powder in a 3-pint casserole and mix well. Cover with a lid or pierced plastic wrap and cook on 100% power (High) for 3½ minutes. Stir halfway through cooking time.

6. Add the heated spice mixture and mix thoroughly. Cook, uncovered, on 100% power (High) for 3 minutes, stir after 1 minute.

7. Add the peas, potatoes, salt, tomato paste and the remaining water and mix thoroughly. Cover and cook on 100% power (High) for 2½ minutes. Stir the contents, re-cover and cook on 50% power (Medium) for 3½ minutes.

8. Stir the curry, cover and stand for 6-8 minutes.

TIME Preparation takes 15 minutes, cooking takes 20 minutes.

SERVING IDEAS Serve with Loochis or Puris accompanied by Kababs or Tandoori Chicken.

MIXED VEGETABLES WITH CINNAMON

A colorful and attractive combination of vegetables which is delicious served with roast lamb or beef.

SERVES 4-6

2 tbsps cooking oil

1-2 fresh green chili peppers, seeded and sliced lengthwise

2 cinnamon sticks, 2-inches long each, broken up into 2-3 pieces

1 tsp cumin seeds

1 small onion finely sliced

1 head green cabbage, finely shredded

¾ cup carrots, scraped and coarsely grated

1¼ tsp salt or to taste

¼ tsp chili powder (optional)

1. In a large bowl or casserole put the oil, green chili peppers, cinnamon sticks and cumin seeds. Cover the ingredients with the sliced onions.

2. Cover the dish with a lid or pierced plastic wrap, and cook on 100% power (High) for 2½ minutes, stirring after 1 minute.

3. Add the vegetables and sprinkle with the salt and chili powder (if used). Stir and mix well then cover the dish as before and cook on 100% power (High) for 8 minutes, stirring every two minutes.

4. Uncover the dish and cook on 50% power (Medium) for 2 minutes. Stir and let it stand for 5 minutes.

TIME Preparation takes 15 minutes, cooking takes 12 minutes.

SERVING IDEAS Serve as an accompaniment with rice or chapattis and Aloo Gosht or Bhoona Gosht.

POTATO GUSHI

A delicious potato curry adapted for the microwave from the fascinating range of Saraswat cookery. Their cooking methods are simple and health-conscious. The art of mixing only two or three spices in different combinations and creating a numerous range of delicious flavors is unique to this style of cooking.

SERVES 4-6

3 medium-sized potatoes
4 tbsps hot water
1 cup warm water

Grind the following 2 ingredients in a spice or coffee grinder
4 tbsps flaked coconut
3-4 dried red chili peppers

¾ tsp salt or to taste
2 tbsps cooking oil
2-3 cloves garlic, peeled and crushed
1 tsp ground coriander
1 tbsp lemon juice

1. Put the potatoes in a 3-pint dish and add the hot water. Cover and cook on 100% power (High) for 4 minutes.

2. Turn the potatoes over, re-cover and cook on 100% power (High) for a further 4 minutes. Stand for 10 minutes, then keep them immersed in cold water until they are completely cold.

3. Peel and dice the potatoes evenly.

4. Put the potatoes in a 2-pint casserole and pour over the warm water. Add the ground coconut mixture and salt. Stir and mix thoroughly. Cover and cook on 100% power (High) for 2 minutes.

5. Stir the potatoes, cover again and cook on 50% power (Medium) for 4 minutes.

6. Preheat a browning dish for 4 minutes. Add the oil and heat for 1 minute, remove and add the garlic. Cook for 30 seconds to 1 minute on 100% power (High) until golden brown. Stir in the ground coriander.

7. Stir the hot oil seasoning into the potatoes and mix thoroughly.

8. Add the lemon juice and mix well.

TIME Preparation takes 15 minutes plus cooling time for the potatoes, cooking takes 15 minutes.

SERVING IDEAS Serve with Mackerel in Coconut Sauce and Plain Boiled Rice or with Puris/Loochis and Kababs or Masala Machchi.

COOK'S TIP If you do not have a browning dish, heat the oil in a skillet, add the garlic and fry slightly brown. Stir in the ground coriander and remove from heat.

MIXED VEGETABLE BHAJI

A combination of fresh and frozen vegetables is used to make this delicious side dish. The flavor of the dish will blend well with almost any meat, fish or chicken curry.

SERVES 4

---

3 small potatoes

2 tbsps cooking oil

½ tsp black or white mustard seeds

3-4 dried red chili peppers, whole

1 fresh green chili pepper, seeded and coarsely chopped

10-12 curry leaves (or 1 tbsp curry powder)

1 medium-sized onion, finely sliced

¾ cup fresh carrots, scraped or peeled and cut into matchstick strips

⅔ cup frozen sliced green beans, defrosted and drained

¾ tsp salt or to taste

---

1. Put the potatoes in a 1-pint dish or bowl and add 4 tbsps hot water. Cover and cook on 100% power (High) for 3 minutes. Turn them over, re-cover and cook for a further 2 minutes. Leave to stand for 8 minutes, then keep them immersed in cold water until they are completely cold.

2. Peel and dice the potatoes evenly.

3. Put the oil, mustard seeds, red and green chili peppers and curry leaves or powder in a 4-pint casserole. Spread the onion on top, cover and cook on high for 5 minutes without stirring.

4. Spread the carrots over the onion and add 1 tbsp hot water. Cover and cook on 100% power (High) for 3 minutes, stirring halfway through.

5. Add the beans, cover and cook on high for 4 minutes, stirring halfway through.

6. Add the potatoes and salt, stir and mix well. Cook, uncovered on 100% power (High), for 1½ minutes.

7. Stir and leave to stand for 5 minutes before serving.

TIME Preparation takes 10-15 minutes, cooking takes 18 minutes.

SERVING IDEAS Serve as an accompaniment with any meat, fish or chicken curry and Chapattis, Rotis, Parathas or rice.

CABBAGE BHAJI

*A simple, tasty way to cook cabbage. The coconut absorbs all the cabbage juices
as the dish cooks and gives this ordinary vegetable a lift.*

SERVES 4-6

---

2 tbsps cooking oil

½ tsp black or white mustard seeds

8-10 fenugreek seeds (optional)

10-12 curry leaves (or 1 tbsp curry powder)

2-4 dried red chili peppers

2 fresh green chili peppers, seeded and
    sliced lengthwise

1 head green or white cabbage, finely
    shredded

1 tsp salt or to taste

⅓ cup flaked coconut, finely ground

1 ripe tomato, sliced

1 tbsp finely grated coconut

1. Put the oil, mustard, fenugreek, (if used) curry leaves or powder and chili peppers in a 4-pint casserole and cover with the cabbage.

2. Cover the casserole with a lid or pierced plastic wrap and cook on 100% power (High) for 6 minutes, stirring halfway through cooking time.

3. Add the salt and the ground coconut; stir and mix well. Re-cover and cook on 100% power (High) for a further 6 minutes, stirring every 2 minutes.

4. Arrange the sliced tomato on the cabbage and sprinkle with the extra 1 tbsp of coconut. Cover and cook on 100% power (High) for 1½ minutes. Stand for 5 minutes before serving.

TIME Preparation takes 10 minutes, cooking takes 13 minutes.

SERVING IDEAS Serve accompanied by Prawns in Garlic, and Tamarind
and Plain Boiled Rice.

SOUR-HOT POTATOES

The tangy taste in this dish comes from tamarind. Ready-to-use tamarind concentrate is available from specialist grocers. If you can't find it, use lemon juice.

SERVES 4

---

3 medium-sized potatoes

¾ tsp tamarind concentrate or 1½ tbsps lemon juice

⅔ cup hot water

2 cloves garlic, peeled and crushed

1 tsp salt or to taste

½ tsp chili powder

1 tsp paprika

4 tbsps cooking oil

1 tsp black or white mustard seeds

1 large onion, finely chopped

1½ tsps ground coriander

---

1. Put the potatoes in a 2-pint bowl or casserole and add 4-5 tbsps hot water. Cover with a lid or pierced plastic wrap and cook on High for 3 minutes.

2. Turn the potatoes over, re-cover and cook on 100% power (High) for a further 3½ minutes. Stand for 5 minutes.

3. Immerse the potatoes in cold water and allow them to cool completely; or cook the potatoes in advance and leave them in the refrigerator.

4. Peel and cut the potatoes into 1-inch cubes.

5. Put the tamarind or lemon juice and the water into a 2-pint bowl or casserole and cook, uncovered, on 100% power (High) for 50 seconds.

6. Stir and mix thoroughly then add the garlic, salt, chili powder and paprika. Cover and cook on High for 45 seconds.

7. Add the potatoes and cook, uncovered, on 100% power (High) for 3 minutes, stirring halfway through.

8. Preheat a microwave browning dish for 4-5 minutes on 100% power (High). Add the oil and heat on High for 1 minute.

9. Add the mustard seeds. Cook until they start popping – 30 seconds-1 minute. Add the onion.

10. Cook on 100% power (High) for 4-6 minutes until golden brown, stirring after each minute. Add the coriander, stir and cook for an additional 30 seconds. Stir this mixture into the potatoes.

TIME Preparation takes 10-15 minutes plus cooling time for the potatoes, cooking takes 15 minutes.

SERVING IDEAS Serve with Puris or Loochis or as a side dish with rice, Tarka Dhal and Kababs.

COOK'S TIP If you do not have a microwave browning dish, use a skillet to fry the mustard seeds over high heat until they crackle. Add the onions and fry until golden brown, stirring frequently. Add the ground coriander, stir and fry for 1 minute. Stir this mixture into the potatoes.

CAULIFLOWER WITH CASHEWS

*An interesting combination of textures and flavors and a speedy preparation
and cooking method make this dish the perfect choice for entertaining.*

SERVES 4

1 tsp ground coriander
½ tsp garam masala
¼ tsp ground turmeric
½-1 tsp chili powder or cayenne pepper
⅔ cup milk
¾ cup raw cashews, split into halves
1 large cauliflower cut into ½-inch
   flowerettes
¾ tsp salt or to taste
¼ cup ground almonds
1 tbsp chopped coriander leaves

1. Put the coriander, garam masala, turmeric and chili powder or cayenne in small glass bowl and heat on 100% power (High) for 1½ minutes. Stir and stand aside for 5 minutes.

2. Put the milk, cashews and the heated spices into a 3-pint casserole, cover with a lid or pierced plastic wrap and cook on 100% power (High) for 3 minutes, stirring halfway through cooking time.

3. Add the cauliflower and salt, re-cover and cook on 100% power (High) for 6 minutes, stirring every 2 minutes.

4. Stir in the ground almonds and cook, uncovered, on 100% power (High) for 3 minutes, stirring every minute.

5. Garnish with the fresh coriander leaves.

TIME Preparation takes 10 minutes, cooking takes 13 minutes.

SERVING IDEAS Serve with Chicken Korma, Meat Durbari, Shahi Korma
and rice or bread.

ZUCCHINI WITH COCONUT & GREEN CHILI PEPPERS

An unusual way to cook zucchini that goes well with broiled fish and poultry.
Coconut gives the vegetables extra crunch and offsets the hot chili peppers.

SERVES 2-4

1 tbsp cooking oil

4-6 fresh green chili peppers, seeded and
   sliced lengthwise

1 clove garlic, peeled and crushed

2 ripe tomatoes, skinned and chopped

3 zucchini, cut into ¼-inch thick slices

½ tsp salt or to taste

4 tbsps chopped coriander leaves

2 tbsps flaked coconut

1. Put the oil, green chili peppers, garlic and tomatoes into a 2-pint casserole. Cover with pierced plastic wrap and cook on 100% power (High) for 3 minutes, stirring halfway through cooking time.

2. Add the zucchini, salt and coriander leaves. Stir and mix well. Re-cover and cook as before for 3 minutes, stirring halfway through cooking time.

3. Stir in the coconut, cover as before and cook for 3 minutes, stirring as before.

4. Allow the dish to stand for 4 minutes before serving.

TIME Preparation takes 5-10 minutes, cooking takes 9 minutes.

SERVING IDEAS Serve with Chicken & Mushroom Curry and Plain Boiled
Rice.

217

LETTUCE AND COCONUT CHUTNEY

Here is a very tasty way to use up lettuce leaves which are not crisp enough to use in a salad.

SERVES 8-10

¾ cup flaked coconut

1¼ cups hot water

About ½ a lettuce head, washed and coarsely chopped

1-2 fresh green chili peppers, seeded and chopped

1 level tsp tamarind concentrate or 1½ tbsps lemon juice

½ tsp salt or to taste

½ tsp ground cumin

1. Put half the water and all the coconut in a 4-pint bowl or casserole. Cover and cook on 100% power (High) for 2 minutes.

2. Stir the coconut and add the remaining water. Spread the lettuce leaves on top evenly, re-cover and cook on 100% power (High) for 2 minutes.

3. Stir the contents, cover and let it stand for 5 minutes, then uncover and allow it to cool for 15-20 minutes.

4. Put the coconut and lettuce mixture, chili peppers and tamarind or lemon juice in a food processor and chop coarsely.

5. Add the salt and cumin and blend for a few seconds longer.

TIME Preparation takes 10-15 minutes, cooking takes 4 minutes.

SERVING IDEAS Serve with Kababs and Pakoras or as a relish with a main meal.
Suitable for freezing.

TOMATO CHUTNEY

The prominent flavors in this chutney are green chili peppers and cinnamon.
Together they create an unusual and mouth-watering accompaniment to any
Indian dish. Fresh tomatoes were used for this recipe, but canned tomatoes can
be used if well drained.

SERVES 8-10

1lb tomatoes, coarsely chopped
1 large onion, peeled and finely chopped
½-inch cube of root ginger, peeled and
    finely sliced
2-3 cloves garlic, peeled and crushed
1-2 fresh green chili peppers, seeded and
    chopped
1 cinnamon stick; 2-inches long, broken up
2 tsps caster sugar
1 tsp salt or to taste

1. Put all the ingredients, except sugar and salt, in a bowl, cover and cook on 100% power (High) for 4 minutes, stirring the contents halfway through. Uncover, add sugar and salt and cook for a further 4 minutes.

2. Allow to cool, then put into a blender or food processor and blend until smooth.

3. Strain to remove seeds. Push as much pulp as possible through the strainer.

4. Store in an airtight container in the refrigerator for up to 10 days.

TIME Preparation takes 5-10 minutes, cooking takes 8 minutes.
SERVING IDEAS Serve with Onion Bhajiyas and Pakoras, or Kababs.

ZUCCHINI CHUTNEY

A rich tasting chutney, made by cooking the zucchini briefly and blending with coconut, root ginger and fresh green chili peppers.

SERVES 8-10

¾ cup flaked coconut

3 zucchini, washed and coarsely chopped

1 cup water

¾ tsp salt or to taste

1 level tsp tamarind concentrate or 1 tbsp lemon juice

1-2 fresh green chili peppers, seeded and coarsely chopped

½-inch cube of root ginger, peeled and coarsely chopped

2-3 tbsps finely chopped onions

1. Put the coconut, zucchini and water in a 3-pint bowl or casserole, cover and cook on 100% power (High) for 10 minutes. Stir every 2-3 minutes.

2. Let the ingredients stand for 5 minutes, then stir in the salt and the tamarind. Allow the mixture to cool.

3. Put the zucchini and coconut mixture in a food processor and add the chili peppers and ginger, blending until the ingredients are finely chopped.

4. If using lemon juice, add this to the rest of the ingredients in the processor.

5. Stir in the onions before serving.

TIME Preparation takes 5 minutes, cooking takes 10 minutes.

SERVING IDEAS Serve with any snacks or as a side dish with rice and Lamb with Mung Beans or Chicken Kohlapuri.
Suitable for freezing.

VARIATION Use tender summer squash.

SAVORY RICE CAKE

A healthy snack that's full of fiber. Brown lentils give the cake a rich color. Don't substitute brown rice, though.

SERVES 6-8

1 cup white rice
½ cup brown lentils
1¼ cups water
1 tsp salt or to taste
1 tsp ground cumin
1 tsp freshly milled black pepper
Oil or ghee for shallow frying

1. Wash and soak the rice and lentils separately overnight in cold water. Drain thoroughly.

2. Put the rice into a food processor and add ¼ cup water from the specified amount. Switch on for a few seconds or until coarsely chopped, but sticky.

3. Transfer the rice to a bowl or pan which has been rinsed in hot water.

4. Now put the lentils in the food processor and add ⅔ cup water from the specified amount. Purée this to a smooth paste. Stir the contents once or twice to ensure even blending.

5. Add the lentils to the rice and stir in the remaining water, mix thoroughly, cover the container and leave to ferment in a warm place.

6. When fermented, the mixture will look light and frothy. It can take between 6 and 8 hours to ferment.

7. Add the salt, cumin and pepper, mix thoroughly.

8. Line a 6-8 inch souffle dish or similar container with wax paper. Spoon the mixture into the dish and put the dish on an inverted glass plate or pie dish.

9. Cook on 100% power (High) for 8 minutes, then on 50% power (Medium) for 2½ minutes.

10. When cool, turn out the cake on a board, cut into about ¼-inch thick slices, then cut each slice into 2-3 pieces.

11. Preheat the browning dish for 4-5 minutes on 100% power (High). Add the oil or ghee and heat for 1 minute, then add the rice cake slices and cook on 100% power (High) for 5-6 minutes, turning frequently, until golden brown. They may have to be fried in batches.

TIME Preparation takes 6-8 hours or overnight for soaking, 6-8 hours for fermenting, cooking takes 10½ minutes, frying takes 8-10 minutes.

SERVING IDEAS Serve as a snack with Lettuce and Coconut Chutney or any other Chutney.
Suitable for freezing. Freeze before frying.

COOK'S TIP If you do not have a microwave browning dish – shallow fry slices in ghee or oil in a skillet until golden brown on both sides. They will need to be fried in 2-3 batches.

bread
and rice

NAAN

Naan is traditionally cooked in the Tandoor, although you will get good results in a very hot oven. The only thing that will be missing is the distinctive taste of clay cooking.

MAKES 8 Naan

4 cups plain flour

1 tsp salt

1 tsp Kalonji-onion seeds, (optional)

1 tsp sugar

1½ packages fast action yeast

⅓ cup milk

⅔ cup plain yogurt

1 medium-sized egg, beaten

4 tbsps ghee or butter

2 tbsps sesame seeds

1. Put the flour, salt, kalonji, sugar and yeast into a large bowl and mix well.

2. Warm the milk until it is lukewarm, reserve 1 tbsp yogurt and add the rest to the milk and blend thoroughly.

3. Beat the egg and keep aside.

4. Melt the butter or ghee.

5. Add the milk and yogurt mixture, egg and ghee or butter to the flour, knead with your hands or in the food processor or mixer until a soft and springy dough is formed.

6. Place the dough in a large plastic bag and tie the top so that the dough has enough room to expand.

7 Rinse a bowl (preferably stainless steel, which retains heat better) with hot water and put the bag of dough in it. Put the bowl in a warm place, until risen to double in volume, about 30 minutes to 1 hour)

8. Divide the dough into 8 balls, cover them and set aside for 10-15 minutes.

9. Preheat oven to 450°F and put an ungreased baking sheet into the oven to preheat for about 10 minutes. Remove baking sheet from the oven and line with non-stick or baking paper.

10. Take one of the balls and stretch it gently with both hands to make a teardrop shape. Lay this on the baking sheet and press it gently to stretch it to about 6-7-inches in length, maintaining the teardrop shape at all times. Make 2-3 similar shapes at a time and brush with the reserved yogurt, then sprinkle with the sesame seeds. Bake on the top shelf of the oven for 10-12 minutes, or until puffed and browned.

TIME Preparation takes 10-15 minutes plus time needed to prove the dough, cooking takes 20-25 minutes.

SERVING IDEAS Serve with any meat, chicken or vegetable curry. Suitable for freezing.

VARIATION Use 1 tsp caraway or cumin seeds instead of the onion seeds while making the dough.

TANDOORI ROTI

Tandoori Rotis, like Naan, are cooked in the Tandoor – a barrel-shaped clay oven which distributes an even and fierce heat. Tandoori rotis can be cooked in a very hot conventional oven, too. They are equally delicious though the flavor is different.

MAKES 8 Rotis

⅔ cup plain yogurt

4 cups plain flour

1 tsp sugar

1 tsp baking powder

½ tsp salt

1½ packages fast action yeast

1 level tbsp ghee or unsalted butter

1 medium egg, beaten

⅔ cup warm milk

---

1. Beat the yogurt until smooth, and set aside.

2. In a large bowl, sift the flour with the sugar, baking powder, salt and yeast. Add ghee and mix thoroughly. Add yogurt and egg and knead well, using a mixer with a dough hook, or food processor, if preferred.

3. Gradually add the warm milk and keep kneading to form a smooth and springy dough.

4. Place the dough in a large plastic food bag and tie the top part of the bag so that the dough has enough room to expand.

5. Rinse a large bowl with hot water and put the bag of dough in it. Use a stainless steel, metal or enamel bowl to retain heat better, or use a saucepan if you do not have a suitable bowl. Place the bowl in a warm place for ½-¾ hour when it will be almost double in volume.

6. Preheat oven to 450°F.

7. Line a baking sheet with non-stick baking paper.

8. Divide the dough into 8 equal-sized balls. Place a ball between your palms and flatten by pressing it down.

9. Dust the ball lightly in a little flour and roll it out gently to a 4-inch disc. Place in the prepared baking sheet. Make the rest of the rotis the same way.

10. Bake on the top rung of the oven for 10-12 minutes. Turn the rotis over and bake for a further 2 minutes.

TIME Preparation takes 10-15 minutes, cooking takes 25 minutes.

SERVING IDEAS Serve with any meat, chicken or vegetable curry. Suitable for freezing.

VARIATION Use wholemeal flour.

CHAPATTIS

*A Chapatti is a dry roasted unleavened bread best eaten as soon as it is cooked.
Not as filling as Rotis or Parathas, 2-3 chapattis per person
is the usual serving.*

MAKES 14 Chapattis

3 cups fine wholewheat flour or Atta/
    Chapatti flour (if available)
½ tsp salt
1 tbsp butter or ghee
¾-1¼ cups warm water
    (quantity depends on the texture of the
    flour)
1 tbsp extra flour

1. Mixer Method: Place flour, salt and fat together in the bowl and mix thoroughly at the medium-to-low speed until well incorporated. Turn speed down to minimum and gradually add the water. When the dough is formed, knead it until it is soft and pliable. Cover the dough with a well-moistened cloth and set aside for ½-1 hour.

2. Hand Method: Put the flour and salt in a large bowl and rub in the fat. Gradually add the water and keep mixing and kneading until a soft and pliable dough is formed. Cover the dough as above and keep aside.

3. Divide the dough into 14 walnut-sized portions. Roll each portion in a circular motion between the palms to make a smooth round ball, then flatten the ball to make a round cake. Place 1 tbsp flour on a plate. Dip each cake into the flour and roll the chapatti into a circle of about 6-inch diameter.

4. A cast iron griddle is normally used for cooking chapattis, but if you do not have one, then make sure you use a heavy-based frying pan as the chapattis need even distribution of heat during cooking. Overheating of the pan will cause the chapattis to stick and burn.

5. Heat the griddle or frying pan over medium heat and place a chapatti on it, cook for 30 seconds and turn the chapatti over. Cook until brown spots appear on both sides, turning it over frequently.

6. To keep the chapattis warm, line a piece of aluminum foil with paper towels and place the chapattis on one end, cover with the other end and seal the edges.

TIME Preparation takes 20-25 minutes, cooking takes 35-40 minutes.

SERVING IDEAS Serve with any meat, chicken or vegetable curry.
Suitable for freezing.

PURIS

This deep-fried unleavened bread is one of those items which needs last minute preparation. The dough can be made in advance, but rolling out and frying should be done simultaneously and once fried, they should be served immediately.

MAKES 14-15 Puris

2½ cups fine wholewheat flour or atta or chapatti flour (if available)

½ tsp salt

¼ tsp sugar

1 tbsp margarine or oil

⅔ cup-1¼ cups warm water (quantity will depend on the texture of the flour – fine textured flour will absorb less water than the coarser variety)

Oil for deep frying

1. In a bowl, mix flour, salt and sugar. Rub in the margarine or oil. Now add the water very slowly and keep mixing and kneading until a stiff dough has formed. Alternatively, put the flour, salt, sugar and fat in a food processor or mixer with a dough hook and switch on. When the fat is well incorporated into the flour, gradually add the water. Once the dough has been formed and kneaded for a few seconds, switch off the machine.

2. Divide the dough into 14-15 equal portions, each about 1½-inch diameter. Make the balls by rolling a portion of the dough between your palms in a circular motion. Have a little dry flour ready in a bowl or a plate. Dust each ball lightly in this and flatten the ball into a round cake. Treat all the balls the same way and cover them with a damp cloth.

3. Roll out the puris to about 3½-inch diameter circles. Roll out evenly to ensure tight edges which help the puris to puff up when they are dropped in hot oil. A flat perforated spoon is ideal for frying puris.

4. It is easier to roll and fry one puri at a time. If you wish to roll out all of them spread them out on a large work surface as they should not be piled together.

5. Careful handling is needed while rolling and frying the puris – if they are damaged or pierced, they will not puff up.

6. Heat the oil to 300°F in a deep fryer. Place one puri at a time in the oil and gently press it down – as soon as the puri puffs up turn it over and cook for about 30 seconds. Drain on paper towels. Fry the remaining puris in the same way.

7. Do not stack the puris as they are finished. Place them on a tray in one layer, so they don't flatten.

TIME Preparation takes 5-10 minutes, cooking takes 15-20 minutes.

SERVING IDEAS Serve with Aloo Gosht or Murghi Jhal Frezi and Aloo ki Bhaji.

LOOCHIS

Loochis are similar to puris – the main difference is that they are made with all-purpose white flour instead of wholewheat or chapatti flour (atta) and with certain dishes they do taste better than puris.

MAKES 14-15 Loochis

1½ cups all purpose flour plus 1 tbsp extra
    flour for dusting
½ tsp salt
¼ tsp sugar
1 tsp kalonji (onion seeds); optional
1 tbsp butter, margarine or ghee
⅔-¾ cup warm water (this will depend on
    the texture of the flour)
Oil for deep frying

1. In a large bowl, mix the flour, salt, sugar and kalonji. Rub in the fat and gradually add the water. Either knead with your hands or in the food processor until a stiff dough is formed.

2. Divide the dough into 14-15 walnut-sized balls. Take each ball between your palms and roll it in a circular motion. Press it down gently to make a flat, about ½-inch thick round cake. When you have made all the round cakes, cover them with a damp cloth.

3. Dust each flattened cake lightly with the extra flour and roll out to about 3½-inch circles. It is easier to roll out and fry one loochi at a time unless you have someone to help you. If you roll out all of them first, they need to be kept in a single layer – piling on each other may cause them to stick together.

4. Loochis puff up like balloons during frying. To ensure that the loochis are beautifully puffed, roll them out carefully and evenly without damaging or piercing them. Use a flat perforated spoon for frying.

5. Heat the oil to 300°F in a deep fryer. Place one loochi at a time in the hot oil – it will soon float to the surface and start puffing up. It helps to cook the loochis evenly if you press them down gently by touching the spoon only to the edge. As soon as each loochi puffs up, turn it over gently and cook for about 30 seconds or until lightly browned. Drain on paper towels. Fry the rest of the loochis the same way.

6. Keep the fried loochis in a single layer, i.e. do not pile one on top of the other as this will flatten them.

TIME Preparation takes 10-15 minutes, cooking takes 15-20 minutes.

SERVING IDEAS Serve with Bhoona Gosht accompanied by Aloo Mattar as an optional side dish. For entertaining, add a pilau or biriani with Raita and Popadoms.

TO RE-HEAT To enjoy them at their best, serve as soon as they are fried. They can be reheated, however, in a hot oven for 5-6 minutes; put them in a large tray in a single layer.

BATURA

Batura is a yeast bread, made from all purpose flour and yogurt. Then it's deep-fried, so it's soft and light with a velvet-like texture.

SERVES 6

3 cups all purpose flour
1 tsp salt
2 tsps fast action yeast
1 egg, beaten
⅔ cup plain yogurt
2-3 tbsps warm water
Oil for deep frying

1. Put the flour, salt and yeast in a bowl and mix well.

2. Add the egg, yogurt and water and knead until a soft and pliable dough is formed. Alternatively, put all the ingredients into the bowl of a food processor, mix the dough and knead it.

3. Put the dough in a large plastic bag and tie the top part of the bag, leaving room for the dough to expand.

4. Put the bag in a stainless steel or metal bowl which has been rinsed out in hot water. Leave the dough in a warm place for 3-4 hours for it to rise.

5. Remove the dough from the bag and divide it into 6 equal portions.

6. Roll each portion gently between your palms in a circular motion and flatten it to a round cake.

7. Dust the cake lightly in a little flour and roll it out gently to a large dish, about 6-inch diameter.

8. Heat the oil to 350°F. Make sure it doesn't overheat. Place a batura in the hot oil and fry it for 1 minute; turn it over and fry the other side for a further minute or until it is a rich creamy colour. Drain on paper towels.

9. Make and fry all the baturas the same way. It is easier to roll out and fry one batura at a time rather than rolling them all out first.

TIME Preparation takes 5-10 minutes plus 35-40 minutes for proving the dough, cooking takes 12-15 minutes.

SERVING IDEAS Serve with Marinated Lamb Chops, Kheema Mattar or Chicken Liver Masala.

VARIATION Use equal quantity of plain and wholewheat flour.

ROTIS

Rotis are a type of unleavened wholewheat bread. The dough is enriched with ghee or butter as for Parathas, but is much easier to make. If you cannot get chapatti flour, use equal quantities of wholewheat flour and all purpose flour.

MAKES 8 Rotis

½ tsp salt

4 tbsps butter, or ghee

3 cups chapatti flour or 1 ½ cups each of wholewheat and all purpose flour

¾-1¼ cups warm water
(quantity depends on the texture of the flour)

2 tbsps ghee or unsalted butter for frying

1. Hand Method: Rub the salt and fat into the flour until you reach a coarse breadcrumb consistency. Gradually add the water and knead until a soft and pliable dough is formed.

2. Mixer Method: Put the salt, fat and flour into the bowl and switch on to minimum speed. When the fat has completely broken up and incorporated well into the flour, gradually add the water and knead until the dough is soft and pliable.

3. Divide the dough into 8 balls. Hold each ball between your palms and roll it until it is smooth and round. Flatten the ball into a round cake and dust it very lightly in a little flour. Roll it out to about 6-inch diameter; cover the rest of the balls with a damp cloth while you are working on one.

4. Heat a heavy-based frying pan or griddle over medium heat. A heavy-based pan is important as the rotis need even distribution of heat.

5. When the pan is hot, place a roti on it and flip it over after about 30 seconds. Spread 1 tsp ghee or butter over it and turn the roti over. Repeat the process for the other side. Brown both sides evenly and remove from heat.

6. Line a piece of aluminum foil with paper towels and put the cooked rotis on one end, cover with the other end and seal the edges. This will keep the rotis warm for 30-40 minutes.

TIME Preparation takes 15-30 minutes, cooking takes 25-30 minutes.

SERVING IDEAS Serve with any meat, chicken or vegetable curry.
Suitable for freezing.

PARATHAS

A Paratha is a crisp, rich unleavened bread. The dough is made with a fair amount of fat and each paratha is rolled out, spread with a little ghee or butter, folded and rolled out again to its final shape. It is like making puff pastry, but a lot simpler!

MAKES 4 Parathas

3 cups wholewheat flour or chapatti flour
   plus 1 tbsp extra flour for dusting
½ tsp salt
⅔ cup ghee or unsalted butter
½-⅔ cup warm water

1. Sift the flour and the salt together. Rub 4 tbsps fat from the specified amount into the flour until thoroughly mixed.

2. Gradually pour in the water and knead the mixture until you get a soft and pliable dough.

3. Divide the dough into 4 equal sized balls and flatten them between your palms, pressing gently.

4. Dust each flattened portion of dough with the flour and roll out to 8-inch diameter. Spread evenly with 1 tsp fat.

5. With your hands, roll up the dough from the edge until you have a tube about an inch wide and 8 inches long. Gently stretch the dough lengthways and then curl each end inwards to resemble a backwards 'S'.

6. Now fold the upper half over the lower half and flatten. Lightly dust all over with flour and roll out again until the dough is an 8-inch circle about one-eighth-of-an-inch thick.

7. Melt remaining fat and set aside; heat the frying pan (preferably a cast iron one) over medium heat and place the paratha on it. Flip it over in about 30 seconds.

8. Spread 1 tbsp of the melted fat on the paratha. Flip it over again. Lower heat. Spread 1 tbsp of the melted fat on this side as well.

9. With a metal or a wooden spatula press the paratha gently into the frying pan, especially at the edges. Flip it over after one minute and press again. Cook the second side for one minute.

10. Continue turning to cook both sides evenly until the paratha is uniformly light brown.

TIME Preparation takes 30 minutes, cooking takes 20 minutes.

SERVING IDEAS Serve with Chicken Do-Piaza, Kheema Mattar or Saagwalla Dhal. If there is rice on the menu, the parathas can be cut into halves or quarters.
Suitable for freezing.

VARIATION Use equal quantity of plain flour and wholewheat flour.

PLAIN FRIED RICE

Plain fried rice is very versatile as the mild taste blends in happily with other flavors. The recipe below is perfect when you want to cook something quick, but a little more special than boiled rice.

SERVES 4-6

1¼ cups basmati or other long grain rice, washed and soaked in cold water for ½-1 hour
2 tbsps ghee or 3 tbsps cooking oil
1 tsp fennel seeds
1 tsp salt or to taste
2¼ cups water for basmati rice or 2½ cups for other long grain rice.

1. Drain the rice and set aside.

2. Heat the oil or ghee over medium heat and fry the fennel seeds until they are brown. Add the rice and salt, stir and fry for 4-5 minutes then lower heat for the last 2-3 minutes of cooking.

3. Add the water and bring to the boil. Cover the pan and simmer for 12 minutes for basmati rice and 15-18 minutes for other long grain rice without lifting the lid.

TIME Preparation takes a few minutes plus time needed to soak the rice, cooking takes 20-25 minutes.

SERVING IDEAS Serve with Meat Madras, Meat Vindaloo, Bengal Fish Curry or Fish Bhoona. A complementary vegetable dish, such as Cabbage with Lentil Flour or Green Bean & Potato Bhaji is an excellent accompaniment. Suitable for freezing.

WATCHPOINT There is no need to lift the lid to check the rice during cooking. This will only result in the loss of vital steam which helps to cook the rice leaving each grain separate.

PLAIN BOILED RICE

A few simple rules will produce perfect results every time. Do not lift the lid while the rice is cooking. Do not stir the rice at any time during cooking or immediately after it has been removed from the heat. This ensures fluffy and separate grains every time.

SERVES 4-6

1¼ cups basmati or other long grain rice, washed and soaked in cold water for 30 minutes
1 tsp butter or ghee
½ tsp salt
2¼ cups water

1. Drain the rice thoroughly and put into a saucepan with the water.

2. Bring to the boil, stir in the salt and the butter.

3. Place the lid on the saucepan and simmer: 12 minutes for basmati rice, 15 minutes for other long grain rice.

4. Remove from heat and keep the pot covered for a further 10-12 minutes.

5. Fork through the rice gently before serving. Use a metal serving spoon as wooden ones tend to squash the grains.

TIME Preparation takes 30 minutes, cooking takes 12-15 minutes.

SERVING IDEAS Plain Boiled Rice can be served with any curry. The rice can be garnished with fried onion rings or fresh coriander leaves.
Suitable for freezing.

FRIED BROWN RICE

This is the traditional rice dish which accompanies chicken or meat dhansak. It can also be served with a host of other dishes.

SERVES 4-6

1¼ cups basmati or other long grain rice

4 tbsps cooking oil

4 tsps sugar

1 tsp cumin seeds

2 cinnamon sticks, 2-inches long each, broken up

6 whole cloves

6 black peppercorns

2 bay leaves, crumpled

2½ cups water

1 tsp salt

1. Wash the rice and soak in cold water for 30 minutes. Drain well.

2. In a heavy-based saucepan, heat the oil over medium heat and add the sugar.

3. The sugar will gradually begin to change color to a golden brown. As soon as it does, add the cumin seeds, cinnamon, cloves, black peppercorns and bay leaves. Fry for 30 seconds.

4. Add the rice and fry for about 5 minutes, stirring frequently and lowering heat towards the last minute or two.

5. Add the water and salt. Bring to the boil, cover and simmer without lifting the lid: 12-15 minutes for basmati rice, 15-18 minutes for other long grain rice.

6. Remove the pan from heat and keep it undisturbed for a further 10-15 minutes before serving.

TIME Preparation takes a few minutes plus time needed to soak the rice, cooking takes 20-25 minutes.

SERVING IDEAS Serve with Chicken Dhansak, Meat Dilpasand or Kheema Mattar.
Suitable for freezing.

WATCHPOINT If the lid is lifted and the rice is stirred during cooking, the loss of steam will cause the rice to stick and turn soggy. Do not stir the rice immediately after it has been cooked, to ensure dry and separate grains.

PILAU RICE

Pilau is usually a beautifully fragrant rice or a combination of rice and meat, poultry, fish or vegetables. It is always cooked in pure butterfat ghee, but unsalted butter is a good substitute.

SERVES 4-6

1¼ cups basmati rice

4 tbsps ghee or unsalted butter

1 large onion, finely sliced

2-4 cloves garlic, peeled and finely chopped

8 whole cloves

8 green cardamoms, split open on the top

2 cinnamon sticks, 2-inches long each, broken up

8 whole peppercorns

1 tsp ground turmeric

2½ cups water

1¼ tsps salt or to taste

1 heaped tsp butter

2 tbsps seedless raisins

¼ cup sliced almonds

1. Wash the rice and soak in cold water for 30 minutes. Drain well.

2. In a heavy-based pan melt the ghee or butter over medium heat and fry onions until they are soft but not brown (about 5 minutes).

3. Add the garlic, cloves, cardamoms, cinnamon sticks and peppercorns. Stir and fry until the onions are golden brown (3-4 minutes).

4. Add the rice and turmeric, stir and fry for 1-2 minutes. Adjust heat to low, stir and fry the rice for a further 2-3 minutes.

5. Add the water and the salt, bring to the boil, cover and simmer for 15 minutes without lifting the lid.

6. Remove the pan from heat and keep it undisturbed for a further 10-12 minutes.

7. Melt the 1 tsp butter over gentle heat and fry raisins until they change color and swell up (1 minute). Transfer the raisins to a plate and in the same fat fry the almonds until they are lightly browned. Remove and keep separate.

8. Put the pilau rice into a serving dish and, using a fork, gently mix in the fried sultanas and almonds.

TIME Preparation takes 10 minutes plus time needed to soak the rice, cooking takes 25-30 minutes.

SERVING IDEAS Serve with Chicken Korma, Tandoori Chicken Masala, or Meat Maharaja.
Suitable for freezing.

VARIATION Omit the almonds and use a hard-boiled sliced egg to garnish.

CARDAMOM RICE

*When time may be short to cook a Pilau Rice or when you may feel like having
a milder flavored rice, Cardamom Rice is the answer as it can be served
with a whole host of dishes.*

SERVES 4-6

1½ cups basmati or other long grain rice
4 tbsps ghee or unsalted butter
6 green cardamoms; split open on the top
1 tsp black cumin seeds or caraway seeds
1 tsp salt or to taste
2¼ cups water for basmati rice or
    2½ cups for other long grain rice

1. Wash the rice, soak in cold water for ½-1 hour and drain thoroughly.

2. Melt the ghee or butter over low heat and fry cardamom and caraway seeds for 1 minute.

3. Add the rice, stir and fry over medium heat for 2-3 minutes, adjust heat to low, stir and fry for a further 2-3 minutes.

4. Add salt and water and mix well. Bring to the boil, cover the pan and simmer for 12 minutes for basmati rice and 15-18 minutes for other long grain rice without lifting the lid.

5. Remove from heat and keep the pot undisturbed for 6-8 minutes.

TIME Preparation takes 5-10 minutes plus time needed to soak the rice,
cooking takes 20-25 minutes.

SERVING IDEAS This rice can be served with almost any Indian dish.
Suitable for freezing.

WATCHPOINT Do not lift the lid or stir the rice during cooking. Do not stir
immediately after the rice has been cooked.

CARROT PILAU

An imaginative way to turn plain boiled rice, left over or freshly cooked, into a colorful and flavorful pilau which can be served with meat, fish or chicken curry.

SERVES 4-6

1¼ cups basmati rice, washed and soaked in cold water for ½ hour

2¼ cups water

1 tsp salt or to taste

1 tsp butter or ghee

2 tbsps ghee or unsalted butter

1 tsp cumin or caraway seeds

1 medium-sized onion, finely sliced

2 cinnamon sticks, each 2-inches long, broken up

4 green cardamoms, split open on the top

1 tsp garam masala or ground mixed spice

¾ cup coarsely grated carrots

⅔ cup frozen peas

½ tsp salt or to taste

---

1. Drain the rice thoroughly and put into a saucepan with the water.

2. Bring to the boil, stir in the salt and the butter.

3. Allow to boil steadily for 1 minute.

4. Place the lid on the saucepan and simmer for 12-15 minutes. Do not lift the lid during cooking.

5. Remove the pan from heat and keep it covered for a further 10 minutes.

6. Meanwhile, prepare the rest of the ingredients.

7. Melt the ghee or butter over medium heat and fry cumin or caraway seeds until they crackle.

8. Add the onions, cinnamon and cardamom. Fry until the onions are lightly browned (4-5 minutes), stirring frequently.

9. Add the garam masala or ground mixed spice, stir and cook for 30 seconds.

10. Add the carrots, peas and the salt, stir and cook for 1-2 minutes.

11. Now add the rice, stir and mix gently using a metal spoon or a fork as wooden spoon or spatula will squash the grains. Remove the pan from heat.

TIME Preparation takes 10-15 minutes plus time needed to soak the rice, cooking takes 25-30 minutes.

SERVING IDEAS Serve with Fish Bhoona, Chicken Kohlapuri or Bhoona Gosht. Mint and Onion Raita makes and excellent accompaniment. Suitable for freezing.

MIXED VEGETABLE PILAU

Vegetable lovers will adore this pilau; the rice and the vegetables are cooked together with a selection of spices and their individual flavors blend beautifully.

SERVES 6-8

4 tbsp ghee or unsalted butter

1 large onion, finely sliced

3-4 cloves garlic, peeled and finely chopped

Grind the following 7 ingredients in a spice or coffee grinder

1 tsp cumin seeds or caraway seeds

1 tsp coriander seeds

6 black peppercorns

1 bay leaf

2 dried red chili peppers

1 cinnamon stick, 2-inches long; broken up

6 cardamoms

½ tsp ground turmeric

½ head cauliflower, cut into ½-inch flowerettes

1 small green pepper, white pith removed and cut into 1-inch strips

½ cup carrots, scraped and thinly sliced

1¼ cups basmati rice, washed and soaked in cold water for 30 minutes and drained

⅓ cup frozen peas or fresh peas boiled until nearly tender

⅓ cup frozen corn

1½ tsp salt or to taste

2½ cups water

1. Melt the ghee or butter over medium heat and fry the onions and garlic until the onions are golden brown (6-8 minutes).

2. Add the ground spices and the turmeric and fry for 2 minutes over low heat, stirring frequently.

3. Add the cauliflower, green pepper and carrots, stir and fry for 2-3 minutes.

4. Add the rice and fry for a further 2-3 minutes stirring constantly.

5. Add the peas, corn and salt, and mix well. Now add the water, bring to the boil, cover the pan and simmer until the rice has absorbed all the water (12-15 minutes). Allow about 18 minutes for other types of long grain rice. Do not lift the lid or stir the rice during cooking.

6. Remove the pan from the heat, uncover and allow steam to escape for 2 minutes. Do not stir the rice immediately after cooking. Cover the pan and keep it undisturbed for 10 minutes before serving.

TIME Preparation takes 30 minutes, cooking takes 25-30 minutes.

SERVING IDEAS Serve with Barrah Kababs, Tandoori Chicken, Nargisi Kababs and a Raita or Chutney.

VARIATION Omit the cauliflower and use 2 cups mushrooms, halved or quartered.

MATTAR PILAU

An easy to prepare pilau rice, great when time to cook is short. Seed the chili peppers if you like things less hot.

SERVES 4-6

1¼ cup basmati rice

⅓ cup ghee or unsalted butter

2 tsp fennel seeds

2-3 dried red chili peppers

6 whole cloves

2 cinnamon sticks, 2-inches long each, broken up

6 cardamoms, split open on the top

2 bay leaves, crumbled

1 large onion, finely sliced

⅔ cup frozen peas

1 tsp ground turmeric

1¼ tsps salt or to taste

2½ cups water

1. Wash the rice and soak it in cold water for half an hour. Drain thoroughly.

2. Melt the butter over medium heat and fry the fennel seeds until they are brown.

3. Add the chili peppers, cloves, cinnamon, cardamom and bay leaves. Stir once and add the onions. Fry until the onions are lightly browned, stirring frequently.

4. Add the rice, peas, turmeric and salt. Stir and fry until the rice is fairly dry (4-5 minutes), lowering heat towards the last 1-2 minutes.

5. Add the water and bring to the boil. Cover the pan and simmer for 12-15 minutes without lifting the lid. Remove the pan from heat and leave it undisturbed for a further 10-15 minutes.

TIME Preparation takes 10 minutes plus time needed to soak the rice, cooking takes 25-30 minutes.

SERVING IDEAS Serve with Pasanda Badam Curry, Meat Maharaja or Murgh Dilkush.

VARIATION Use ⅓ cup frozen corn and ⅓ cup peas.

MUSHROOM PILAU

Delicate mushrooms blend happily with the distinctive flavor and aroma of basmati rice and the whole spices used in this pilau. Other long grain rice can be used, but the pilau will not be as fragrant and delicious as with basmati rice.

SERVES 4-6

1¼ cups basmati rice

2 tbsps ghee or unsalted butter

1 tsp caraway seeds

1 large onion, finely sliced

2 cinnamon sticks, each 2-inches long;
  broken up

2 cups button mushrooms, thickly sliced

½ tsp ground turmeric

1¼ tsps salt or to taste

2¼ cups water

6 green cardamoms, split open on the top

6 whole cloves

2 bay leaves, crumbled

1. Wash and soak the rice in cold water for 30 minutes. Drain and set aside.

2. Melt the ghee or butter over medium heat and fry the caraway seeds for 30 seconds.

3. Add the onions and cinnamon sticks, stir and fry until the onions are golden brown (6-8 minutes).

4. Add the rice and fry, stirring constantly, for 3-4 minutes. Add the mushrooms, turmeric and salt, stir and fry for a further 2-3 minutes over low heat.

5. Add the water, cardamoms, cloves and bay leaves; bring to the boil, cover the pan and simmer for 12-15 minutes. Do not lift the lid or stir the rice during cooking.

6. Remove from the heat, uncover and allow steam to escape for 1-2 minutes. Cover the pan and keep aside for 10-15 minutes before serving.

TIME Preparation takes 20-25 minutes plus time needed to soak the rice, cooking takes 25-30 minutes.

SERVING IDEAS Serve with Chicken Korma, Murghi Badami or Meat Maharaja.
Suitable for freezing.

side dishes

GREEN BEANS IN GARLIC BUTTER

Tender green beans, cooked in their own juice, make a mouth-watering accompaniment to any rich meat, fish or poultry dish.

SERVES 4-6

2 tbsps unsalted butter
½ tsp cumin seeds
3-4 cloves garlic, peeled and crushed or finely chopped
¼-½ tsp chili powder
3 cups whole green beans
½ tsp salt or to taste

1. Melt the butter over low heat and fry the cumin seeds for 30 seconds.

2. Add the garlic and fry for 1 minute.

3. Add the chili powder and immediately follow with the beans. Stir and fry for 1-2 minutes.

4. Add the salt and mix thoroughly. Cover the pan and simmer the beans in their own juice until they are tender (10-12 minutes), stirring occasionally.

5. Remove from the heat.

TIME Preparation takes 5-10 minutes, cooking takes 15 minutes.

SERVING IDEAS Serve with Chicken Korma, Fish Shahjahani, or Murghi Badami.

VARIATION Use cauliflower cut into tiny pieces.

POTATOES WITH POPPY SEEDS

This quick and easy, but thoroughly delicious, potato dish comes from Assam.
Serve it as a side dish or as a snack with Puris – simply gorgeous!

SERVES 4-6

5 tbsps cooking oil

½ tsp Kalonji (onion seeds), optional

1 tsp cumin seeds

4-6 cloves garlic, peeled and crushed

1 tsp freshly ground black pepper

½ tsp ground turmeric

4 potatoes, peeled and diced

1 fresh green chili pepper, finely chopped

6 tbsps white or black poppy seeds

1 tsp salt or to taste

1. Heat the oil in a non-stick or cast iron skillet until smoking. Remove the pan from heat and add the kalonji (if used) and cumin seeds.

2. As soon as the seeds start crackling, add the garlic and place the pan over medium heat.

3. Add the ground black pepper and turmeric, stir briskly and add the potatoes and the chili pepper. Fry the potatoes for 2-3 minutes stirring constantly.

4. Reduce heat to low, cover the pan and cook until the potatoes are tender (12-15 minutes), stirring occasionally.

5. Meanwhile, grind the poppy seeds in a coffee or spice grinder into a coarse mixture. Add this to the potatoes, adjust heat to medium and fry the potato and poppy seed mixture for 5-6 minutes, stirring frequently.

6. Stir in the salt and remove the pan from heat.

TIME Preparation takes 10 minutes, cooking takes 20 minutes.

SERVING IDEAS Serve with Puris or Loochis as a snack or make a meal by adding Seekh Kababs and Date Sauce to the menu.

WATCHPOINT Make sure the potatoes are cut into small cubes, if cut into chunky pieces it will be difficult to cook them thoroughly in the specified time.
Use a non-stick or cast iron skillet, otherwise the potatoes will stick.

CAULIFLOWER MASALA

This dish, with potatoes and peas, is flavored with a few basic ingredients and the finished dish is semi-dry, making it an ideal accompaniment to rice and curry or Indian bread.

SERVES 4-6

1 medium-sized cauliflower

2 medium-sized potatoes

4 tbsps cooking oil

1 tsp cumin seeds

1 large onion

½ tsp ground turmeric

1 tsp ground coriander

1 tsp ground cumin

¼-½ tsp chili powder

2 ripe tomatoes, skinned and chopped

¾ cup warm water

½ cup shelled peas, fresh or frozen (cook fresh peas until they are tender before using)

1-2 fresh green chili peppers, seeded and slit lengthwise into halves

1 tsp salt or to taste

½ tsp garam masala

1 tbsp chopped coriander leaves

1. Cut the cauliflower into ½-inch diameter flowerettes – wash and drain.

2. Peel and cut the potatoes lengthwise into thick strips about ½-inch.

3. Heat the oil over medium heat and add the cumin seeds. As soon as they start popping, add the onions and fry until they are soft (about 5 minutes).

4. Turn heat down to low and add the turmeric, coriander, cumin and chili powder. Stir and fry for 2-3 minutes and add the chopped tomatoes. Fry for a further 2-3 minutes stirring continuously.

5. Add the potatoes and the water. Bring to the boil, cover the pan and simmer until the potatoes are half-cooked.

6. Add the cauliflower, cover the pan again and simmer until the potatoes are tender (about 10 minutes).

7. Stir in the peas, chili peppers, salt and garam masala. Cover and cook for 5 minutes.

8. Remove from heat and stir in the coriander leaves.

TIME Preparation takes about 25 minutes, cooking takes 30-35 minutes.

SERVING IDEAS Serve with Kofta Pilau or Plain Boiled Rice accompanied by Meat Madras or Meat Bhoona. Also excellent with Puris or Loochis. Not suitable for freezing as the potatoes will turn mushy when defrosted and cauliflower does not freeze well once cooked.

VARIATION Cook in 3 tbsps ghee instead of oil for a richer flavour.

269

KHUMBI AUR BESAN KI BHAJI

The use of mushrooms is somewhat limited in Indian cooking. However, in the West the abundant supply of mushrooms throughout the year makes it possible to create mouthwatering dishes at any time.

SERVES 4

2½ cups mushrooms

2 tbsps cooking oil

2-3 cloves garlic, peeled and crushed

½ tsp salt or to taste

½ tsp chili powder

2 tbsps finely chopped coriander leaves

1 tbsp lemon juice

2 tbsps besan (lentil flour or chick pea flour), sieved

1. Wash the mushrooms and cut them into quarters.

2. Heat the oil over medium heat and add the garlic. Allow garlic to turn slightly brown and add the mushrooms, stir and cook for 2 minutes.

3. Add salt, chili powder and coriander leaves, stir and cook for 1 minute.

4. Add the lemon juice and mix well.

5. Sprinkle the besan over the mushroom mixture, stir and mix immediately. Remove from heat.

TIME Preparation takes 15 minutes, cooking takes 6-8 minutes.

SERVING IDEAS Serve as a side dish.
Suitable for freezing.

VARIATION Omit besan, if unavailable. Cook a minute or two longer to reduce any liquid from the mushrooms.

GOBI ALOO

Gobi Aloo, or cauliflower with potatoes, is a classic north Indian dish. The potatoes are first boiled and the cauliflower is blanched. The two are then braised together gently with a few spices to give it a subtle but distinctive flavor.

SERVES 4-6

3 medium-sized potatoes

1 medium-sized cauliflower

5 tbsps cooking oil

½ tsp mustard seeds

½ tsp cumin seeds

12-15 fenugreek seeds

1-2 dried red chili peppers, coarsely
    chopped

1 medium-sized onion, coarsely chopped

1 fresh green chili pepper, coarsely
    chopped

½ tsp ground turmeric

½ tsp ground cumin

1 tsp ground coriander

1¼ tsp salt or to taste

1 tbsp chopped coriander leaves (optional)

1. Boil the potatoes in their skins and allow to cool thoroughly. The potatoes can be boiled and left in the refrigerator for 2-3 days.

2. Peel the potatoes and cut them into 2-inch squares.

3. Blanch the cauliflower in boiling water for 2 minutes, do not over-boil; it should remain firm after cooking. Allow the cauliflower to cool and cut it into ½-inch diameter flowerettes.

4. Heat the oil over medium heat in a large skillet pan, preferably non-stick or cast iron.

5. Add the mustard seeds, and as soon as they begin to pop, add the cumin and fenugreek seeds and then the red chili peppers.

6. Add the onions and the green chili pepper, stir and fry until the onions are golden brown (8-10 minutes).

7. Add the cauliflower, reduce heat to low, cover the pan and cook for 6-8 minutes.

8. Add the potatoes, turmeric, cumin, coriander and salt. Stir gently until all the ingredients are mixed thoroughly. Cover the pan and cook until the potatoes are heated through (6-8 minutes).

9. Stir in the coriander leaves (if used) and remove from the heat.

TIME Preparation takes 25-30 minutes, cooking takes 15-20 minutes.

SERVING IDEAS Serve as an accompaniment to any meat or chicken curry or Chapattis and Rotis. Excellent with Puris or Loochis.

TO FREEZE Freeze before adding the potatoes. Add the potatoes during reheating.

VARIATION Add ½ cup frozen peas with the cauliflower.

CAULIFLOWER CUTLETS

This unusual recipe makes an excellent vegetarian dish or an unusual accompaniment to any meat dish.

MAKES 10-12 Cutlets

1 small cauliflower

2 medium-sized potatoes

2 tbsps cooking oil plus oil for shallow frying

¼ tsp mustard seeds

½ tsp cumin seeds

1 large onion, finely chopped

1 fresh green chili pepper, seeded and finely chopped

1 tsp ground fennel

1 tsp ground coriander

¼-½ tsp chili powder or cayenne

½ tsp salt or to taste

½ cup plain flour

2 tbsps chopped coriander leaves

1. Cook the whole cauliflower in boiling water for 6-8 minutes, drain and cool.

2. Boil the potatoes in their skins and peel them.

3. Chop the cauliflower coarsely and mash it with the potatoes.

4. Heat the 2 tbsps oil over medium heat and fry mustard seeds until they crackle, then add the cumin seeds.

5. Add the onions and chili peppers, stir and fry until the onions are soft (4-5 minutes).

6. Adjust heat to low, add the ground fennel, ground coriander, chili powder or cayenne and salt, stir and cook for 2-3 minutes.

7. Remove the pan from heat and add the potatoes, cauliflower, flour and coriander leaves. Stir and mix thoroughly.

8. Allow the mixture to cool completely, then divide it into 10-12 portions.

9. Form each portion into a cutlet shape and flatten to about one eighth of an inch thickness.

10. Heat the oil over medium heat in a heavy-based frying pan, preferably cast iron or non-stick, and fry the cutlets in a single layer until they are golden brown on both sides.

11. Drain on paper towels.

TIME Preparation takes 30-35 minutes, cooking takes 15-20 minutes.

SERVING IDEAS Serving ideas: Serve with a pilau rice such as Nawabi Kheema Pilau, Kofta Pilau and Raita or a vegetable curry.

MIXED VEGETABLE BHAJI

In this delicious dish all the vegetables are cooked in a tightly covered dish in their own juice until tender, but firm. The dish has no sauce and is a perfect partner for most curries.

SERVES 4

3 tbsps cooking oil

½ tsp mustard seeds

½ tsp cumin seeds

2-4 dried red chili peppers, whole

3-4 cloves garlic, peeled and crushed

¼-½ tsp chili powder

¾ cup carrots, scraped and cut into match stick strips

¾ cup green beans, cut to the same length as the carrots

1 large potato, peeled and cut into matchstick strips

1 small onion, finely shredded

¾ tsp salt or to taste

¼ cup fresh coriander leaves, including the tender stalks, finely chopped

1. Heat the oil in a large skillet over medium heat.

2. Add the mustard seeds and as soon as they begin to pop, add the cumin seeds and the red chili peppers.

3. Add the garlic and chilli powder and immediately follow with all the vegetables and the onions.

4. Add the salt, stir and cook for 2-3 minutes. Cover the pan tightly and reduce heat to minimum setting. Let the vegetables sweat for 20-25 minutes, stirring occasionally.

5. Add the coriander leaves and stir-fry the vegetables over medium heat for 1-2 minutes and remove from the heat.

TIME Preparation takes 25 minutes, cooking takes 30 minutes.

SERVING IDEAS Serve with any meat/chicken/fish curry.

TO FREEZE Suitable for freezing, but as cooked potatoes do not freeze well, they should be omitted. Alternatively, add pre-boiled potatoes during re-heating.

GOBI MATTAR (CABBAGE WITH PEAS)

A quick and easy side dish to prepare which not only tastes good, but also looks colorful and attractive.

SERVES 4-6

1 small head green cabbage
3 tbsps cooking oil
¼ tsp mustard seeds
½ tsp cumin seeds
10-12 fenugreek seeds (optional)
2-4 dried red chili peppers, whole
1 small onion, finely sliced
½ tsp ground turmeric
⅔ cup frozen peas
¾ tsp salt or to taste
1 tsp ground coriander
¼-½ tsp chili powder
2 small ripe tomatoes, skinned and
   chopped
1 tbsp chopped coriander leaves (optional)

1. Shred or chop the cabbage finely.

2. Heat the oil over medium heat and fry the mustard seeds until they pop.

3. Add the cumin seeds followed by the fenugreek (if used), chili peppers and the onions. Stir and fry until the onions are soft (about 5 minutes).

4. Stir in the turmeric and add the cabbage. Stir and mix thoroughly.

5. Add the peas and salt, stir and cover the pan. Lower heat to minimum and cook for 5 minutes.

6. Add the ground coriander, the chili powder and the chopped tomatoes. Stir until it is completely dry.

7. Remove from heat and stir in half the coriander leaves.

8. Put the cabbage into a serving dish and sprinkle the remaining coriander leaves on top (if used).

TIME Preparation takes 15 minutes, cooking takes 10-15 minutes.

SERVING IDEAS Serve as an accompaniment with Meat Madras, Murghi Jhal Frezi or Lamb with Butter Beans.

TO FREEZE Suitable for freezing if pre-boiled fresh peas are used.

ALOO CHOLE

Chick peas are delicious cooked with spices and diced potatoes. They need long slow cooking before they are tender. If you have one, a pressure cooker will speed up the process.

SERVES 4-6

1 cup chick peas, picked over and washed

3¾ cups water

½-inch cube of root ginger, peeled and grated

1 large potato, peeled and cut into 1½-inch cubes

1 tsp ground cumin

½ tsp ground turmeric

¼-½ tsp chili powder, optional

1-2 fresh green chili peppers, slit lengthwise into halves; seeded for a milder flavor

2 tbsps ghee or unsalted butter

1 large onion, finely chopped

1¼ tsp salt or to taste

½ tsp garam masala

1 tbsp lemon juice

1 tbsp chopped fresh mint or 1 tsp dried mint

1. Soak the chick peas overnight in plenty of cold water. Rinse several times and drain well.

2. Put the chick peas, water and ginger into a saucepan and place over a high heat, bring to the boil, cover the pan and simmer for 1¼-1½ hours or until the peas are tender. Alternatively, put the peas and the ginger in a pressure cooker and add a scant 2 cups water. Bring to the boil, then following the usual method for pressure cooking, cook under 15lbs pressure for 20 minutes. Let pressure reduce before opening the lid.

3. Add the potatoes, cumin, turmeric, chili powder and the chili peppers, and the mint, if dried. Bring to the boil again, cover the pan and simmer for a further 15-20 minutes or until the potatoes are tender.

4. Melt the ghee over medium heat and fry the onions until they are lightly browned (6-8 minutes). Stir this into the chick peas along with the salt and garam masala.

5. Remove the pan from heat and stir in the lemon juice and fresh mint.

TIME Preparation takes 10-15 minutes plus time needed to soak the peas, cooking takes 1½-1¾ hours.

SERVING IDEAS Serve with Puris or Loochis or as a side dish with meat/fish/chicken curry. Avoid serving with Mughlai dishes (rich and creamy curries).

TO FREEZE Suitable for freezing, but freeze before adding the potatoes.

SAAG BHAJI

Spinach simmered in spices and combined with diced, fried potatoes.

SERVES 4-6

6 tbsps cooking oil

½ tsp mustard seeds

1 tsp cumin seeds

8-10 fenugreek seeds (optional)

1 tbsp curry leaves (or 1 tsp curry powder)

2-3 cloves garlic, peeled and finely chopped

2-4 dried red chili peppers, coarsely chopped

1lb fresh leaf spinach or 8oz frozen leaf spinach, finely chopped

1 tbsp ghee or unsalted butter

1 large potato, peeled and diced

1 large onion, finely sliced

½ tsp ground turmeric

1 tsp ground cumin

½ tsp garam masala

¼-½ tsp chili powder

2-3 ripe tomatoes, skinned and chopped

1 tsp salt or to taste

1. Heat 2 tbsps oil from the specified amount over medium heat and fry mustard seeds until they pop.

2. Add the cumin seeds, fenugreek (if used) and curry leaves or powder and immediately follow with the garlic and chili peppers. Allow garlic to turn slightly brown.

3. Add the spinach, stir and mix thoroughly. Cover and simmer for 15 minutes stirring occasionally.

4. Melt the ghee or butter over medium heat and brown the diced potatoes. Remove from heat and keep aside.

5. Heat the remaining oil over medium heat and fry onions until well browned (about 10 minutes), be sure not to burn the onions or they will taste bitter.

6. Adjust heat to minimum and add turmeric, cumin, garam masala and chili powder, stir and fry for 2-3 minutes.

7. Add the spinach, potatoes, tomatoes and salt, cover and simmer for 10 minutes or until the potatoes are tender, stirring occasionally. Remove from heat.

TIME Preparation takes 25-30 minutes, cooking takes 50 minutes.

SERVING IDEAS Serve with Dahl Gosht and Plain Boiled Rice or Murghi Jhal Frezi and Parathas/Rotis/Chapattis.

TO FREEZE Freeze before adding the potatoes.

283

ALOO KI BHAJI

Boiled potatoes, diced and braised with a few whole spices and onions make a quick and easy side dish.

SERVES 4-6

4 large potatoes
5-6 tbsps cooking oil
½ tsp mustard seeds
2-3 dried red chili peppers
⅛ tsp fenugreek seeds
1 large onion, finely sliced
1-2 fresh green chili peppers, sliced
   lengthwise and seeded if a milder flavor
   is preferred
1 tsp ground turmeric
1 tsp salt or to taste
¼ cup chopped coriander leaves

1. Boil the potatoes in their skins and allow to cool thoroughly. Boiled potatoes can be left for a day or two in the refrigerator.

2. Peel the potatoes and dice them evenly.

3. Heat the oil over medium heat in a large skillet and fry the mustard seeds until they pop.

4. Add the red chili peppers and the fenugreek seeds; immediately follow with the onions and green chili peppers.

5. Fry the onions until they are golden brown (8-10 minutes).

6. Add the turmeric, potatoes and salt. Stir and fry gently until the potatoes are heated through (8-10 minutes).

7. Remove from heat and stir in the coriander leaves.

TIME Preparation takes 15-20 minutes plus time needed to boil and cool the potatoes, cooking takes 20 minutes.

SERVING IDEAS Serve with Puris or Loochis to make a substantial snack or as a side dish with rice, chicken or meat curry.

CABBAGE WITH CINNAMON

The taste of cinnamon fried with onions is unusual and delicious. The dish is not particularly spicy, but this flavor combination gives it a special touch.

SERVES 4-6

4 tbsps cooking oil

1 large onion, finely sliced

2 fresh green chili peppers, sliced lengthwise, seeds removed

3 cinnamon sticks, each 2-inches long; broken up into 2-3 pieces

1 large potato, peeled and cut into 1-inch cubes

½ tsp ground turmeric

¼ tsp chili powder

½ cup warm water

1 small white cabbage, finely shredded

1 tsp salt or to taste

1 tbsp chopped coriander leaves

1. Heat the oil over medium heat and fry the onions, chili peppers and cinnamon sticks until the onions are soft (about 5 minutes).

2. Add the potatoes, stir and fry on low heat for 6-8 minutes.

3. Stir in the turmeric and chili powder.

4. Add the water and bring it to the boil, cover the pan and simmer until the potatoes are half cooked (6-8 minutes).

5. Add the cabbage and salt, stir and mix well. Lower the heat to minimum setting, cover the pan and cook until the vegetables are tender (the cabbage should not be mushy). The finished dish should be fairly moist but not runny. If there is too much liquid left in the pan, take the lid off and cook rapidly so the liquid evaporates.

6. Stir in the coriander leaves and remove the pan from heat.

TIME Preparation takes 25 minutes, cooking takes 25 minutes.

SERVING IDEAS Serve with any Indian bread or rice and Rogan Josh, Bhoona Gosht or Murgh Dilkush.

TO FREEZE If you wish to freeze it, cook the cabbage only and add pre-boiled diced potatoes during reheating.

VARIATION For more color, add frozen peas.

POTATOES WITH GARLIC AND CHILI PEPPERS

These are rather like spicy French fries, but are not deep fried. They are a perfect alternative when you want a touch of spice with plain meat, fish or chicken.

SERVES 4-6

3-4 potatoes, peeled and washed
3 tbsps cooking oil
½ tsp mustard seeds
½ tsp cumin seeds
4 cloves garlic, peeled and crushed
¼-½ tsp chili powder
½ tsp ground turmeric
1 tsp salt or to taste

1. Cut the potatoes to the thickness of French fries, but half their length.

2. In a large non-stick or cast iron skillet, heat the oil over medium heat.

3. Add the mustard seeds and then the cumin. When the seeds start popping, add the garlic and allow it to turn lightly brown.

4. Remove the pan from the heat and add the chili powder and turmeric.

5. Add the potatoes and place the pan back on heat. Stir and turn heat up to medium.

6. Add the salt, stir and mix, cover the pan and cook for 3-4 minutes and stir again. Continue to do this until the potatoes are cooked and lightly browned. Remove from the heat.

TIME Preparation takes 15-20 minutes, cooking takes 15 minutes.

SERVING IDEAS Serve with any curry and rice or Chapattis/Rotis.

VARIATION Use cauliflower flowerettes, cut into small pieces.

GREEN BEAN & POTATO BHAJI

Sliced green beans and potatoes are braised together with a mixture of whole and powdered spices to make this quick side dish. A saucepan or frying pan with a tight-fitting lid lets the vegetables cook in their own juice, for a wonderful flavor.

SERVES 4-6

4-5 tbsps cooking oil

½ tsp mustard seeds

½ tsp cumin seeds

1 large onion, finely sliced

3-4 dried red chili peppers, coarsely chopped

10-12 fenugreek seeds

¼ cup coriander leaves, finely chopped

½ tsp ground turmeric

1 large potato, peeled and cut into matchstick strips

2 cups beans, sliced

1 tsp salt or to taste

1 tsp ground cumin

1. Heat the oil over medium heat and add the mustard seeds. As soon as the seeds pop, add the cumin seeds, then the onions, red chillies and fenugreek. Fry the ingredients for 3-4 minutes, stirring frequently.

2. Add the coriander leaves and turmeric, stir and fry for 1 minute.

3. Add the potatoes, beans and salt. Stir until the ingredients are mixed thoroughly. Cover the pan and cook on lowest setting until the vegetables are tender (about 25 minutes), stirring occasionally.

4. Add the ground cumin, stir and cook for 2-3 minutes and remove from the heat.

TIME Preparation takes 15 minutes, cooking takes 30 minutes.

SERVING IDEAS Serve with Chicken Do-Piaza, Meat Vindaloo or Fish Bhoona.

KASHMIRI DUM ALOO

This is a lovely way to serve new potatoes. The potatoes are boiled, then fried until they are golden brown, and finally simmered gently in plain yogurt and spices.

SERVES 4

8 small new potatoes
2 tbsps ghee or unsalted butter
1 tsp fennel seeds

Mix the following 5 ingredients in a small bowl
½ tsp ground cumin
1 tsp ground coriander
¼ tsp freshly ground black pepper
½ tsp ground turmeric
½ tsp ground ginger

⅔ cup thick set plain yogurt
1 tsp salt or to taste
¼ tsp garam masala
1 tbsp chopped coriander leaves
1 fresh green chili pepper, seeded and finely chopped

1. Boil the potatoes in their skins, cool and peel them. Prick the potatoes all over with a tooth pick to help the spices to penetrate deep inside.

2. Melt the ghee over medium heat in a non-stick or cast iron skillet (stainless steel or enamel pans will cause the potatoes to stick and break up).

3. When the ghee is hot, fry the potatoes in a single layer until they are well browned (8-10 minutes), turning them over frequently. Remove them with a slotted spoon and set aside.

4. Remove the pan from the heat and stir in the fennel seeds followed by the spice mixture. Adjust heat to low and place the pan back on the heat, stir the spices and fry for 1 minute.

5. Add the yogurt and salt, and mix well. Add the potatoes, cover the pan and simmer for 10-12 minutes. Add the garam masala and remove the pan from the heat.

6. Stir in the coriander leaves and the green chilli.

TIME Preparation takes 30-35 minutes including boiling the potatoes, cooking takes 20-25 minutes.

SERVING IDEAS Serve as a side dish with Chicken Korma, Meat Maharaja or Murghi Badami.

SPICED GREEN BEANS

Sliced green beans are braised with a few spices, then tossed in roasted, ground sesame seeds to create the unique flavor of this dish.

SERVES 4-6

2 tbsps sesame seeds

3 tbsps cooking oil

¼ tsp mustard seeds

4-6 cloves garlic, peeled and finely chopped

1-2 dried red chili peppers, coarsely chopped

½ tsp ground turmeric

1 tsp ground coriander

1lb frozen sliced green beans, defrosted and drained

¾ tsp salt or to taste

1 tbsp flaked coconut

1. Heat a cast iron griddle or other heavy-based skillet over medium heat and dry-roast the sesame seeds until they are lightly browned, stirring constantly. Transfer them to a plate and allow to cool.

2. Heat the oil over medium heat and add the mustard seeds. When they begin to pop, add the garlic and allow it to turn slightly brown.

3. Add the red chili peppers, turmeric and coriander, stir briskly and add the beans and salt. Mix thoroughly, lower heat to minimum setting, cover the pan tightly and cook until the beans are tender (15-20 minutes), stirring occasionally.

4. Grind the sesame seeds and the coconut in a spice grinder and stir into the beans. Remove the pan from the heat.

TIME Preparation takes 10-15 minutes, cooking takes 25-30 minutes

SERVING IDEAS Serve with Chicken Tikka Masala, Murgh Musallam or Shahi Korma.

BHINDI (OKRA) WITH COCONUT

A quick and delicious way to cook okra. Roasted and ground poppy and sesame seeds with coconut make a special recipe.

SERVES 4

½lb bhindi (okra)

2 tbsps sesame seeds

1 tbsp white poppy seeds

1-2 dried red chili peppers

2 tbsps flaked coconut

1 fresh green chili pepper, coarsely chopped

3 tbsps cooking oil

½ tsp mustard seeds

¼ tsp fenugreek seeds

2 cloves garlic, peeled and finely chopped or crushed

½ tsp salt or to taste

1. Wash the bhindi, trim off head and cut each bhindi into two or three pieces.

2. Heat an iron griddle or other heavy-based skillet over medium heat and dry-roast the sesame and poppy seeds until they are lightly browned. Transfer the seeds to a plate and allow them to cool.

3. Reheat the griddle and dry-roast the coconut until the coconut is lightly browned, stirring constantly. Transfer the coconut to a plate and allow it to cool.

4. Put the sesame and poppy seeds and the dried red chili peppers in a coffee grinder or food processor and switch on; when half done, add the coconut and the green chili pepper and grind until smooth.

5. Heat the oil over medium heat and add the mustard seeds, as soon as the seeds pop add the fenugreek followed by the garlic. Allow garlic to turn slightly brown and add the bhindi and salt; stir and mix thoroughly. Lower heat to the minimum setting, cover the pan and cook for about 10 minutes, stirring occasionally.

6. Stir in the ground ingredients and mix well. Remove from the heat.

TIME Preparation takes 15-20 minutes, cooking takes 12-15 minutes.

SERVING IDEAS Serve with Shahi Korma or Murghi Badami.

ALOO MATTAR

In India, unlike in the west, potatoes are not eaten instead of rice, but as well as rice. The recipe below is a semi-moist dish which goes well with meat, chicken or fish curries.

SERVES 4-6

4 tbsps cooking oil

1 medium-sized onion, finely chopped

2 cinnamon sticks, each 2-inches long, broken up

½-inch cube of root ginger, peeled and finely chopped

½ tsp ground turmeric

2 tsps ground cumin

¼ tsp chili powder

¼ tsp freshly ground black pepper

3-4 potatoes, peeled and cut into 1-inch cubes

1-2 whole fresh green chili peppers

1 tbsp tomato paste

1 tsp salt or to taste

1 cup warm water

½ cup frozen peas

1 tbsp chopped coriander leaves (optional)

1. Heat the oil over medium heat and fry the onion, cinnamon and ginger for 4-5 minutes, stirring frequently.

2. Reduce heat to low and add the turmeric, cumin, chili powder and black pepper. Stir and fry for one minute.

3. Add the potatoes and the green chili peppers, stir and cook until the spices are blended thoroughly (2-3 minutes).

4. Stir in the tomato paste and salt.

5. Add the water, bring to the boil, cover the pan and cook over medium to low heat until the potatoes are half cooked (about 10 minutes).

6. Add the peas, cover the pan and cook until the potatoes are tender.

7. Remove the pan from the heat, stir in half the coriander leaves (if used) and sprinkle the remainder on top.

TIME Preparation takes 10-15 minutes, cooking takes 25-30 minutes.

SERVING IDEAS Serve with Puris or Loochis or with rice and any meat, fish or chicken curry.

CABBAGE WITH LENTIL FLOUR

A truly delicious and very quick dish to prepare which is a distinctive feature of the Saraswat style of cooking.

SERVES 4-6

4 tbsps cooking oil
½ tsp mustard seeds
½ tsp cumin seeds
8-10 fenugreek seeds
3-4 cloves garlic, peeled and crushed
Pinch of asaphoetida (optional)
1 medium-sized onion, finely shredded
¼ tsp ground turmeric
½ tsp chili powder
1 small head white cabbage, finely shredded
1 tsp salt or to taste
¼ cup water
2 heaped tbsps besan (lentil flour or chick pea flour), sieved

1. Heat the oil in a wide shallow pan over medium heat and fry mustard seeds until they pop.

2. Add the cumin seeds followed by the fenugreek.

3. Stir in the garlic and allow it to turn slightly brown.

4. Add the asaphoetida (if used) and immediately follow with the onions, turmeric and chili powder. Stir and fry for 1-2 minutes.

5. Add the cabbage and salt, stir and mix thoroughly. Reduce heat to low, cover the pan and cook for 8-10 minutes, stirring occasionally. The cabbage should be tender but firm.

6. Sprinkle the water evenly on the cabbage, then sprinkle the besan and cook for 1-2 minutes stirring continuously. Remove from heat.

TIME Preparation takes 10-15 minutes, cooking takes 15 minutes.

SERVING IDEAS Serve as an accompaniment to any meat, fish or chicken curry, but avoid serving with Mughlai dishes (rich and creamy curries).

VARIATION Omit the onion and use half green cabbage and half leek. Substitute a few crushed fennel seeds for the asaphoetida. Omit besan and cook until liquid evaporates.

BHINDI (OKRA) MASALA

*Okra is available from specialist grocers and many supermarkets.
For this recipe, choose the small tender ones, scrub each one gently and wash
thoroughly.*

SERVES 4

½lb bhindi (okra)
2 tbsps cooking oil
1 tsp ground coriander
¼ tsp ground cumin
¼ tsp ground turmeric
Small can of tomatoes
¼ tsp chili powder
½ tsp salt or to taste
1 tbsp chopped coriander leaves

1. Scrub each bhindi gently, wash them and slice off the tops.

2. Heat the oil over medium heat in wide shallow pan. When hot, remove the pan from the heat and add the ground coriander, cumin, garam masala and turmeric. The pan is removed from the heat so the spices don't burn.

3. Place the pan back on the heat and add the tomatoes and the chili powder. Stir and cook for 2-3 minutes.

4. Add the whole bhindis and the salt. Stir and cover the pan. Lower heat to the minimum setting and cook for about 10 minutes. Stir once or twice during this time. When cooked, the bhindi should be tender but firm.

5. Put the bhindi onto a serving dish and sprinkle the coriander leaves on top.

TIME Preparation takes 10 minutes, cooking takes 12-15 minutes.

SERVING IDEAS Serve with Bhoona Gosht, Fish Bhoona or Chicken Kohlapuri.

303

EGGPLANT BHARTA

*Bharta is a puréed or mashed vegetable which is flavored with spices.
This recipe is traditionally made by roasting the eggplant over charcoal or burnt-
down ashes of a wood fire. For the recipe below, however, it has been broiled.*

SERVES 4

1 large eggplant

4 tbsps cooking oil

½ tsp mustard seeds

½ tsp fennel seeds

1-inch cube of root ginger, peeled and
    grated

2-3 cloves garlic, peeled and crushed

1 fresh green chili pepper, finely chopped

1 large onion, finely chopped

½ tsp ground turmeric

¼-½ tsp chili powder (optional)

2 small ripe tomatoes, skinned and
    chopped

1 tsp salt or to taste

1 small tomato, sliced

¼ cup fresh coriander leaves, finely
    chopped

1. Wash the eggplant and make 2-3 small incisions on it. This will prevent it from bursting during cooking.

2. Preheat the broiler to medium and cook the eggplant for 12-15 minutes or until tender to the touch. Turn it frequently during cooking. Remove the eggplant and allow it to cool.

3. Cut lengthwise into two. Scrape the flesh off gently with a knife. Discard the skin.

4. Purée the flesh or mash it with a fork. Heat the oil over medium heat and add the mustard seeds; as soon as they begin to pop add the fennel seeds, then the ginger, garlic and chili pepper. Stir fry the ingredients for 1 minute then add the onions. Stir and fry the onions until they are just soft.

5. Stir in the turmeric and chili powder.

6. Add the tomatoes, stir and cook for 2 minutes.

7. Add the eggplant and salt, and stir and cook for 2-3 minutes.

8. Stir in half the coriander leaves and remove the pan from heat.

9. Put the eggplant in a serving dish and garnish with the sliced tomatoes. Sprinkle the remaining coriander leaves on top.

TIME Preparation takes 10-15 minutes, cooking takes 30-35 minutes.

SERVING IDEAS Serve with Chicken Pilau, Kofta Pilau or Chicken Do-
Piaza, Bhoona Gosht, and rice.
Suitable for freezing.

TARKA DHAL (SPICED LENTILS)

Dhal of some sort is always cooked as part of a meal in an Indian household.
As a vast majority of the Indian population is vegetarian, dhal provides a good
source of protein.

SERVES 4

¾ cup Masoor dhal (red split lentils)
2⅔ cups water
1 tsp ground turmeric
1 tsp ground cumin
1 tsp salt or to taste
2 tbsps ghee or unsalted butter
1 medium-sized onion, finely chopped
2 cloves garlic, peeled and finely chopped
2 dried red chili peppers, coarsely chopped

1. Put the dhal, water, turmeric, cumin and salt into a saucepan and bring the liquid to the boil.

2. Reduce heat to medium and cook uncovered for 8-10 minutes, stirring frequently.

3. Now cover the pan and simmer for 30 minutes, stirring occasionally.

4. Remove the dhal from the heat, allow to cool slightly and mash through a strainer.

5. Melt the ghee or butter over medium heat and fry the onion, garlic and red chili until the onions are well browned (8-10 minutes).

6. Stir in half the fried onion mixture to the dhal and put the dhal in a serving dish. Arrange the remaining fried onions on top.

TIME Preparation takes about 10 minutes, cooking takes about 50 minutes.

SERVING IDEAS Serve with Plain Boiled Rice and Murghi Jhal Frezi.

WATCHPOINT Pulses tend to froth and boil over. The initial cooking without the lid in stage 2 should help to eliminate this problem, so will partially covering the pan until the froth settles down, which should take only a few minutes.

SPICY CHANNA DHAL

This is a specialty of the north-eastern region of India. In Assam and Bengal this dhal is invariably served during weddings and other special gatherings. Channa dhal is available from some specialist grocers, but if it is difficult to get, yellow split peas can be used.

SERVES 4-6

1 cup channa dhal or yellow split peas

3 tbsps ghee or unsalted butter

1 large onion, finely sliced

2 cinnamon sticks, each 2-inch long, broken up into 2-3 pieces

6 cardamoms, split open on the top

2-4 dried red chili peppers, coarsely chopped

½ tsp ground turmeric

¼-½ tsp chili powder

1¼ tsps salt or to taste

2½ cups warm water

2 bay leaves, crumpled

¼ cup flaked coconut

2 ripe tomatoes, skinned and chopped

2 tbsps chopped coriander leaves (optional)

1. Clean and wash the channa dahl or the yellow split peas and soak them for at least 2 hours. Drain well.

2. Melt the ghee or butter over medium heat and fry the onions, cinnamon, cardamom and chili peppers until the onions are lightly browned (6-7 minutes).

3. Add the dhal, turmeric, chili powder and salt. Stir-fry the dhal for 2-3 minutes. Adjust heat to low and fry the dhal for a further 3-4 minutes, stirring frequently.

4. Add the water, bay leaves, coconut and tomatoes. Bring to the boil, cover the pan and simmer for 35-40 minutes.

5. Stir in the coriander leaves (if used) and remove from the heat.

TIME Preparation takes 5-10 minutes plus time needed to soak the dhal, cooking takes 50-55 minutes.

SERVING IDEAS Serve with rice or any Indian bread and Masala Machchi, Kababs or Chicken Chaat.
Suitable for freezing.

Saagwalla Dhal

*Spinach and skinless split moong dhal complement each other extremely well.
The dish is easy to make and full of essential nutrients. If you cannot get moong
dhal, use yellow split peas.*

SERVES 6-8

¾ cup skinless split moong dhal or yellow
  split peas

2 heaped tbsps ghee or unsalted butter

1 large onion, finely sliced

1 fresh green chili pepper, sliced
  lengthwise, seeded for a milder flavor

2 cinnamon sticks, 2-inch long each; broken
  up into 2-3 pieces

½ tsp ground turmeric

½ tsp garam masala

¼ tsp chili powder

1 tsp salt or to taste

1 tsp ground cumin

2 ripe tomatoes, skinned and chopped

2½ cups warm water

2 tbsps cooking oil

½ tsp mustard seeds

2-3 cloves garlic, peeled and finely
  chopped

1-2 dried red chili peppers, coarsely
  chopped

5oz frozen leaf spinach, defrosted and
  finely chopped or 10oz fresh spinach;
  stalks removed and finely chopped

1. Wash and soak the dhal for 1½-2 hours
and drain well.

2. Melt the ghee or butter over medium
heat in a non-stick or cast iron skillet and
fry the onions, chili pepper and cinnamon
until the onions are lightly browned (6-8
minutes).

3. Add the turmeric and garam masala, stir
and mix well.

4. Add the dhal, chili powder and salt, stir
and fry for 8-10 minutes over low heat.

5. Add the cumin and tomato, stir and cook
for 3-4 minutes.

6. Add the water, bring to the boil, cover
and simmer for 30-35 minutes, stirring
occasionally.

7. Meanwhile, heat the oil over medium
heat and fry the mustard seeds until they
pop.

8. Add the garlic and allow it to turn slightly
brown.

9. Add the dried red chili peppers and then
the spinach, stir and mix thoroughly. Cover
the pan and simmer for 5 minutes.

10. Add the spinach to the dhal, cover and
cook over low heat for 10 minutes, stirring
occasionally. Remove the pan from heat.

TIME Preparation takes 10-15 minutes plus time needed to soak the dhal,
cooking takes 1 hour 10 minutes.

SERVING IDEAS Serve with rice or Parathas/Rotis. Kababs, Tandoori
Chicken and Murghi Jhal Frezi are perfect to complement the meal.
Suitable for freezing.

VARIATION Use cauliflower flowerettes instead of the spinach.

CARROT & COCONUT SALAD

Grated carrots and coconut make a simple but appetizing salad.

SERVES 4-6

3-4 carrots
2 tbsps finely grated coconut
2 tbsps finely shredded onion
1 tbsp lemon juice
2 tbsps chopped coriander leaves
1 fresh green chili pepper, seeded and
   coarsely chopped (optional)
½ tsp salt or to taste

1. Peel and grate the carrots.

2. Combine all the ingredients in a bowl except salt.

3. Stir in the salt just before serving.

TIME Preparation takes 10 minutes.

SERVING IDEAS Serve with Kheema Mattar, Meat Vindaloo or Bhoona Gosht.

VARIATION Add 1 tbsp finely chopped fresh mint.

CABBAGE & MINT SALAD

An unusual touch is given to this salad by the mint jelly and plain yogurt used to coat the ingredients.

SERVES 4-6

1 small head white cabbage
1 small onion, finely chopped
1 fresh green chili pepper, finely chopped
    and seeded if a milder flavor is preferred
2-3 tbsps thick set plain yogurt
2 tsps mint jelly
½ tsp salt or to taste

1. Grate the cabbage (use the coarse side of a grater or coarse blade of a food processor) and put it into a large mixing bowl.

2. Add the rest of the ingredients and mix thoroughly.

3. Put the salad into a serving dish, cover and chill before serving.

TIME Preparation takes 10 minutes.

SERVING IDEAS Serve with Meat or Chicken Biriani, or rice and curry such as Kofta Curry, Chicken Kohlapuri or Chicken Do Piaza.

TOMATO & CUCUMBER SALAD

*The combination of cucumber, tomato and roasted peanuts makes a
mouthwatering side dish, just right with hot spicy food.*

SERVES 4-6

½ a cucumber

2 tomatoes

1 bunch green onions, coarsely chopped

1 tbsp lemon juice

1 tbsp olive oil

¼ tsp salt

¼ tsp freshly ground black pepper

1 tbsp chopped coriander leaves

¼ cup roasted salted peanuts, crushed

1. Peel the cucumber and chop finely.

2. Chop the tomatoes finely.

3. Put cucumber, tomatoes and green onions into a serving bowl.

4. Combine the lemon juice, olive oil, salt, pepper and coriander leaves and set aside.

5. Just before serving, stir in the peanuts and the dressing.

TIME Preparation takes 10 minutes.

SERVING IDEAS Serve with any meat, fish, chicken or vegetable curry.

VARIATION Omit the lemon juice and use 3 tbsps plain yogurt.

CARROT & MOOLI SALAD

This salad has a nutty flavor which is from the mustard seeds fried in hot oil.
Mooli or Daikon radishes are available in many supermarkets.

SERVES 4-6

1 tbsp cooking oil
½ tsp mustard seeds
½ tsp cumin seeds
¾ cup carrots, peeled and coarsely grated
1½ cups mooli, peeled and coarsely grated
½ tsp salt
2-3 tbsps finely chopped onion
1 tbsp lemon juice
1 tbsp finely chopped coriander leaves

1. Heat the oil over medium heat and fry the mustard seeds until they pop, add the cumin and remove from heat.

2. Add the grated carrots and mooli and allow to cool.

3. Stir in the salt, onion, lemon juice and coriander leaves before serving.

TIME Preparation takes 15 minutes, cooking takes 5 minutes.

SERVING IDEAS Serve as a side dish with any curry and rice. Avoid serving with rich and creamy curries.

POTATO RAITA

Raitas normally involve no cooking, but this is one of the few where the potatoes are first cooked in a hot oil and spice mixture, then cooled and mixed with plain yogurt.

SERVES 4-6

2 tbsps cooking oil
¼ tsp fennel seeds
1 clove garlic, peeled and finely chopped
2 large potatoes, peeled and diced
½ tsp ground cumin
½ tsp salt or to taste
⅔ cup plain yogurt
½ tsp sugar
¼ tsp chili powder or paprika

1. Heat the oil over medium heat and fry the fennel seeds until they are brown.

2. Add the garlic and cook until slightly brown.

3. Add the potatoes and stir well. Cover the pan and cook until the potatoes are tender and brown, stirring frequently.

4. Stir in the cumin and salt, mix thoroughly and remove from heat. Allow to cool completely.

5. Beat the yogurt and sugar until smooth. Add the spiced potatoes along with any oil/spice mixture that remains in the pan. Stir and mix well.

6. Put the raita in a serving dish and sprinkle the chili powder or paprika on top.

TIME Preparation takes 10-15 minutes, cooking takes 10-15 minutes.

SERVING IDEAS Can be served with all types of curry, either chilled or at room temperature.

CUCUMBER RAITA

This raita is very cooling with the taste of the roasted cumin seeds.

SERVES 4-6

1 small cucumber
1 tsp cumin seeds
⅔ cup thick set plain yogurt
¼ tsp salt
¼ tsp paprika

1. Peel the cucumber and cut lengthwise into two halves. Remove seeds, if necessary. Slice each half finely.

2. Heat a small pan over low heat and dry roast the cumin seeds until they turn a shade darker. Allow the seeds to cool, then crush them with a rolling pin or pestle and mortar.

3. Beat the yogurt until smooth. Stir in the cumin along with the salt.

4. Add the cucumber to the yogurt and mix thoroughly, coating cucumber well.

5. Put the raita into a serving dish and chill if not serving immediately.

6. Sprinkle the paprika evenly on the sliced cucumber.

TIME Preparation takes 15 minutes.

SERVING IDEAS Serve with Meat Vindaloo or Chicken Kohlapuri.

VARIATION Use half cucumber and half finely sliced radishes.

BHINDI (OKRA) RAITA

*Crisp fried okra coated with plain yogurt and flavored with
a hot oil seasoning.*

SERVES 6-8

Oil for deep frying
½lb bhindi (okra), cut into about one-
    eighth of an inch rounds
½ tsp salt or to taste
1 fresh green chili pepper, seeded and
    coarsely chopped
⅔ cup thick set plain yogurt
½ tsp dry mustard powder
1 tbsp cooking oil
½ tsp mustard seeds
1 tbsp curry leaves (or 1 tsp curry powder)

1. Deep fry the bhindi in an electric fryer until they are well browned and crisp. Drain on paper towels. Allow to cool completely.

2. Add the salt to the chili pepper and crush to a pulp.

3. Beat the yogurt with a fork until smooth, add the mustard and green chilli mixture, stir and mix well.

4. Gently stir in the fried bhindi.

5. Heat the 1 tbsp oil in a small pan and fry the mustard seeds until they crackle, then add the curry leaves or powder and fry for 15-20 seconds.

6. Remove the pan from heat and stir the seasoned oil into the bhindi raita along with all the seasonings.

TIME Preparation takes 15 minutes, cooking takes 5-6 minutes.

SERVING IDEAS Serve with Kheema Palak, Kofta Pilau or Meat Biriani.

NOTE The curry powder will give the raita a creamy yellow color.

Mint & Onion Raita

Raw onions are frequently served with an Indian meal – on their own or occasionally in a yogurt-based dressing.

SERVES 4-6

⅔ cup thick set plain yogurt
1 small onion, finely chopped
1 tbsp chopped fresh mint or 1 tsp mint jelly
1 fresh green chili pepper, seeded and
   chopped
¼ tsp paprika
½ tsp salt or to taste

1. Beat the yogurt until smooth.

2. Add the rest of the ingredients, except paprika, and beat again.

3. Put the raita into a serving dish and sprinkle the paprika on top.

TIME Preparation takes 10 minutes.

SERVING IDEAS Serve with Meat Biriani, Mixed Vegetable Pilau or Aubergine Pilau.

VARIATION Add a few finely sliced radishes.

CARROT & PEANUT RAITA

A very tasty and easy to prepare side dish that's nutritious, too.

SERVES 4-6

2 carrots
½ cup roasted salted peanuts
1 small clove of garlic, peeled and coarsely chopped
1 fresh green chili pepper, seeded and coarsely chopped
¼ tsp salt or to taste
⅔ cup thick set plain yogurt
½ tsp sugar
1 tbsp finely chopped coriander leaves (optional)

1. Peel and grate the carrots coarsely.

2. Crush peanuts with a wooden pestle or rolling pin.

3. Mix garlic, chili pepper and salt and crush to a pulp.

4. Beat the yogurt until smooth and stir in the garlic mixture.

5. Add the carrots, peanuts, sugar and coriander leaves (if using) and mix thoroughly.

TIME Preparation takes 10-15 minutes.

SERVING IDEAS This raita complements almost any meal and can be served as a relish with Kababs or Pakoras.

CUCUMBER AND ONION RAITA

Raitas and salads are an integral part of an Indian meal. This raita is particularly easy to make and the roasted cumin seeds add a special flavor.

SERVES 4-6

1 tsp cumin seeds
⅔ cup plain yogurt
3 tbsps finely chopped onions
½ a cucumber
½ tsp salt or to taste

1. Heat a cast iron or other heavy-based skillet and dry-roast the cumin seeds until they release their aroma. Allow to cool and crush them lightly.

2. Beat the yogurt with a fork until smooth, add the onions and the crushed cumin seeds. Mix thoroughly. Cut three thin slices of cucumber and chop the rest. Add to the yogurt.

3. Put the raita in a serving dish and arrange sliced cucumber on top.

TIME Preparation takes 10-15 minutes.

SERVING IDEAS Serve with any curry, especially suitable to serve with Meat Vindaloo and Meat Madras.

EGGPLANT RAITA

For this recipe, the eggplant is traditionally cooked over charcoal or burnt-down ashes of a wood fire. If you are having a barbecue, use the coals to cook the eggplant. Alternatively, broil it indoors.

SERVES 6-8

1 eggplant
½ tsp salt or to taste
½-inch cube of root ginger, peeled and
    coarsely chopped
1 fresh green chili pepper, coarsely
    chopped and seeded for a milder flavor
⅔ thick set plain yogurt
2-3 tbsps finely chopped onions
2 tbsps chopped coriander leaves

1. Make one or two small incisions in the eggplant to prevent it from bursting during cooking.

2. Preheat broiler to medium. Broil whole eggplant for 10 minutes, turning it over once. Allow to cool completely.

3. Add the salt to the ginger and chili pepper and crush them to a pulp.

4. Slit the eggplant lengthwise into two halves and scoop out the flesh. Chop the flesh finely or mash it.

5. Beat the yogurt until smooth. Add ginger mixture. Stir and mix well. Add the eggplant and mix thoroughly.

6. Stir in the onions and half the coriander leaves just before serving. Garnish with the remaining coriander leaves.

TIME Preparation takes 10 minutes, cooking takes 10 minutes.

SERVING IDEAS Serve with Chicken Biriani, Murgh Dilkush or Chicken Do Piaza.

WATCHPOINT It is important to preheat the broiler and cook the eggplant for the specified time. If not well cooked, it will be difficult to scoop out the eggplant flesh.

ONION RELISH

Raw onions with chili peppers and lemon juice often accompany an Indian meal. The flavor of raw onions can be rather strong, so if you prefer a milder flavor, wash the chopped onions in cold water and drain them first.

SERVES 4-6

1 large onion, finely chopped
1 fresh green chili pepper, seeded and
  minced
1 tbsp fresh mint, minced
1 tbsp fresh coriander leaves, minced
½ tsp salt or to taste
1 tbsp lemon juice

1. Mix all the ingredients together except salt.
2. Stir in the salt just before serving.

TIME Preparation takes 10-15 minutes.

SERVING IDEAS Serve with all types of Kababs, Biriani or Tandoori Chicken, and with rice and meat or chicken curry.

APPLE CHUTNEY

*A mouthwatering relish with a sweet and sour, slightly hot flavor. Apples are first
tossed in a few spices and cooked until they are almost pulpy.*

SERVES 8-10

1 tbsp cooking oil

½ tsp black or white mustard seeds

¼ tsp fenugreek seeds

¼ tsp ground turmeric

Pinch of asaphoetida or fennel seeds

2 large apples, peeled and finely chopped

½-¾ tsp chili powder

1½ tsps salt or to taste

3 tbsps soft light brown sugar

1. Heat the oil over medium heat and fry
the mustard seeds until they pop.

2. Add the fenugreek, turmeric and
asaphoetida or fennel seeds and
immediately follow with the apples. Stir and
mix thoroughly.

3. Add the chili powder, salt and sugar, stir
and cook until the apple starts to break
down slightly.

4. Cover and simmer until the apple is
tender (5-6 minutes), stirring frequently.

5. Allow the chutney to cool and store in a
moisture-free air-tight or screw-top jar. It
can then be stored in the refrigerator for 4-6
weeks.

TIME Preparation takes 10 minutes, cooking takes 10 minutes.

SERVING IDEAS Serve with almost all snacks and starters.

Avocado Chutney

Avocado and cottage cheese are combined with a few selected fresh ingredients to make an unusual side dish.

SERVES 6-8

1 ripe avocado

Juice of half a lemon

¼ cup plain cottage cheese

1 clove garlic, peeled and chopped

2 tbsps chopped coriander leaves

1 fresh green chili pepper, chopped and
    seeded for a milder flavor

½ tsp salt or to taste

1. Cut the avocado in half lengthwise and remove the stone. Scoop out the flesh.

2. Put the lemon juice in a blender or food processor and add the avocado along with the rest of the ingredients. Blend until fairly smooth, add a little water if necessary, to make blending easier.

TIME Preparation takes 5-10 minutes.

SERVING IDEAS Serve as a dip with Kababs, Samosas and Pakoras.

GREEN CORIANDER CHUTNEY

*The wonderful flavor of fresh coriander leaves makes this coconut-based chutney
a perfect accompaniment to fried, grilled or roasted dishes.*

SERVES 6-8

¾ cup water

½ cup flaked coconut

1-2 fresh green chili peppers, chopped and
    seeded for a milder flavor

1-2 cloves garlic, peeled and coarsely
    chopped

½-inch cube of root ginger, peeled and
    coarsely chopped

¼ cup fresh coriander leaves, coarsely
    chopped

½ tsp salt or to taste

1 tbsp lemon juice

1. Bring the water to the boil, remove from
heat and soak the coconut in it for 10-15
minutes.

2. Put all the ingredients in a food
processor and blend until smooth. Allow to
cool completely.

TIME Preparation takes 10-15 minutes.

SERVING IDEAS Serve with Onion Bhajiyas, Pakoras of any type, Samosas
or Hussaini Kababs.

341

CUMIN-CORIANDER CHUTNEY

The prominent flavor in this chutney is cumin, even though equal quantities of cumin and coriander are used. Cumin has a stronger flavor than coriander and the mild and sweet coconut base sets it off.

SERVES 4-6

1 tsp cumin seeds

1 tsp coriander seeds

2-3 dried red chili peppers

4 tbsps grated coconut

¼ cup water

½ tsp salt or to taste

1½ tbsps lemon juice

2-3 tbsps roughly chopped onions

1. Grind the cumin, coriander, red chili peppers and the coconut in a blender until the ingredients are smooth.

2. Transfer the ingredients to a bowl and add the water, salt and lemon juice. Mix thoroughly.

3. Stir in the onions.

TIME Preparation takes 10 minutes.

SERVING IDEAS Can be served with almost all fried snacks, Parathas or Rotis, or with rice and any meat, fish or vegetable curry.
Suitable for freezing.

VARIATION Use ½ tsp tamarind concentrate dissolved in a little hot water instead of the lemon juice. If using fresh coconut, substitute some of the liquid in the shell for the ¼ cup water.

MINT & ONION CHUTNEY

This is a delicious relish which will keep well in the refrigerator for 3-4 weeks,
provided no moisture is allowed to get in.

SERVES 6-8

2 tbsps cooking oil

1 large onion, coarsely chopped

¼ cup fresh mint

1 fresh green chili pepper seeded for a
 milder flavor

1 tbsp lemon juice

½ tsp salt or to taste

1. Heat the oil over medium heat and fry the onions until they are soft but not brown. Allow to cool.

2. Put the onions and the rest of the ingredients in a food processor and blend until smooth.

3. Put into a moisture-free airtight container or screw-top jar and refrigerate.

TIME Preparation takes 10 minutes, cooking takes 5 minutes.

SERVING IDEAS Serve with all types of snacks.

DATE SAUCE

A delicious relish with the sweet & sour taste of dates, raisins and tamarind. Tamarind is available from some specialist grocers, dried or in ready-to-use form. The latter variety is called tamarind concentrate and is more convenient to use than the dried variety.

SERVES 6-8

½ cup stoned dates

2 tbsps seedless raisins

1 tsp ground cumin

1 tsp chili powder

1 heaped tsp tamarind concentrate or
   3 tbsps lemon juice

½ cup cold water

¾ tsp salt or to taste

1 tsp soft brown sugar

1. Put all the ingredients in a food processor and add half the water. Switch on and when the ingredients are half ground add the remaining water and blend until fairly smooth.

2. Pour the sauce into a strainer and push it through with a metal spoon until a dry and coarse mixture is left in the sieve – discard this mixture and transfer the sauce to a serving bowl. Garnish with sliced dates, if desired.

TIME Preparation takes 10 minutes.

SERVING IDEAS Serve with Seekh Kababs, Boti Kababs, all types of Pakoras and fried snacks.
Suitable for freezing.

drinks and desserts

NIMBU PANI

Nimbu Pani, or lemon flavored water is a very refreshing drink for summer or with a spicy meal. The sugar and salt replaces energy and natural salt content lost in very hot weather.

SERVES 4

2½ cups water
2 tbsps sugar
1 tsp salt
The juice of 1 lemon
Crushed ice
4 slices of lemon

1. Put the sugar and salt in the water and stir until dissolved.

2. Stir in the lemon juice.

3. Put the crushed ice into individual glasses and strain the nimbu pani into the glasses.

4. Top with the sliced lemon.

TIME Preparation takes 5-10 minutes.

JEERA PANI

Jeera Pani (cumin water) has been a popular aperitif in India from time immemorial. Cumin is noted for its digestive properties.

SERVES 4

2 tbsps cumin seeds
2½ cups water
2-3 dried red chili peppers
¼ cup mint leaves, chopped or
    1 tsp dried mint
1 tsp salt
1 tsp sugar
1 tbsp lemon juice

1. Heat a cast iron or other heavy-based skillet and dry-roast the cumin seeds until they are a shade darker, and crush them lightly.

2. Put the water in a saucepan and bring it to the boil.

3. Add the cumin, chili peppers, mint, salt and sugar.

4. Cover the pan and simmer for 15 minutes.

5. Stir in the lemon juice and remove from heat. Allow the drink to cool, then strain into individual glasses.

TIME Preparation takes a few minutes plus cooling the seeds, cooking takes 15 minutes.

SERVING IDEAS Serve as an aperitif or during meals. Can be served at room temperature or chilled.

RASAM

Rasam is a very popular drink in southern India, where it is usually made by boiling lentils in lots of spice-flavored water. Add a dash of hot oil seasoning before serving.

SERVES 4-6

3¾ cups water

¼ cup masoor dhal (red split lentils), washed and drained

1 tsp coriander seeds

1 tsp cumin seeds

2 dried red chili peppers

6-8 curry leaves (or a pinch of curry powder)

1 tsp salt or to taste

1 level tsp tamarind concentrate or 1 tbsp lemon juice

1 tsp paprika

1 tbsp cooking oil

½ tsp mustard seeds

1. Put the water, dhal, coriander, cumin, chili peppers and curry leaves or powder into a saucepan and bring to the boil. Reduce heat to medium and cook, uncovered, for 6-8 minutes.

2. Cover the pan and simmer for 30 minutes. Remove from heat and allow it to cool slightly.

3. Strain the liquid and sieve the dhal into it. Return the pan to heat and add the tamarind or lemon juice, salt and paprika. Stir until the tamarind is dissolved.

4. Heat the oil and add the mustard seeds. As soon as the seeds crackle, pour the rasam into it or stir the hot oil and the seeds into the rasam. Remove from heat.

TIME Preparation takes 5-10 minutes, cooking takes 35-40 minutes.

SERVING IDEAS Serve as an aperitif or during meals.

Spicy Pineapple Punch

A welcoming drink for guests; serve this warm before lunch or dinner, especially at Christmas time, or enjoy it chilled with barbecues during the long, warm summer evenings.

SERVES 6-8

Scant 2 cups water
4½ cups pineapple juice
5 cinnamon sticks, each 2-inches long; broken up
12 whole cloves
12 cardamoms, crushed
¼ cup fresh mint leaves, chopped
¾ cup brandy

1. Put the water, half the pineapple juice, cinnamon, cloves, cardamom and mint into a saucepan. Bring to the boil, cover the pan and simmer gently for 20 minutes.

2. Remove from the heat and allow to cool. Keep the pan covered.

3. Strain the drink and add the remaining pineapple juice and the brandy. Mix well.

TIME Preparation takes 5 minutes, cooking takes 20-25 minutes.

SPICED TEA

Spiced tea has quite a few variations and is popular in colder regions such as Kashmir, as the ingredients make a warming drink.

SERVES 2

Scant 2 cups water
6 whole cloves
6 green cardamoms, crushed
1 cinnamon stick, 2-inches long; broken up
3 tsps tea leaves or 2 tea bags
Milk and sugar to taste

1. Put the water in a saucepan and bring it to the boil.

2. Add the spices, cover the pan and simmer for 10 minutes.

3. Rinse a teapot with hot water and put in the tea leaves or the tea bags.

4. Bring the spiced liquid to the boil again and strain it into the teapot. Brew for 5 minutes and serve black or with milk and sugar to taste.

TIME Preparation takes 10-15 minutes.

SERVING IDEAS Serve during or after meals.

MANGO SHERBET

Mango Sherbet is a delicious and nourishing drink. The quantities used here make a thick sherbet which can be thinned down by adding more milk or water as desired.

MAKES 2 pints

1lb can of mango pulp
  or 2-15oz cans of sliced mangoes,
  drained
2½ cups milk
4 tbsps sugar
1 tsp ground cardamom
1 tbsp rosewater (optional)
1¼ cups cold water

1. Put the mango pulp or slices, half the milk, sugar, cardamom and rosewater into a blender or food processor and switch on for a few seconds until smooth.

2. Transfer the contents into a large bowl and add the remaining milk and the water.

3. Chill for 2-3 hours.

TIME Preparation takes a few minutes.

SERVING IDEAS Serve during meals or at a barbecue.

VARIATION Omit the milk and use all water. Top the drink with a scoop of vanilla ice cream. Serve as a dessert.

SWEET SAFFRON RICE

This rice is served as a dessert and is cooked in exactly the same way as a pilau rice; the only difference is that sugar is used instead of salt.

SERVES 8-10

1 cup basmati rice

2¼ cups water

1 cinnamon stick, 2-inches long, broken into two pieces

4 whole cloves

¼ tsp saffron strands

4 tbsps ghee or unsalted butter

1 tsp ground cardamom

¼ tsp ground nutmeg

½ cup sugar

½ cup raw cashews, split into halves

3 tbsps seedless raisins

1. Wash the rice and soak it in cold water for 30 minutes; drain thoroughly.

2. Put the water, cinnamon, cloves and saffron in a bowl, cover and microwave on 100% power (High) for 3½ minutes or until boiling. Cover and stand aside for 15 minutes.

3. Preheat a microwave browning dish on 100% power (High) for 4-5 minutes. Melt the ghee or butter in the dish for 30 seconds. Add the rice and 'fry' on 100% power (High) for 5-6 minutes or until it begins to look fairly dry. Stir frequently during this time.

4. Add the cardamom and nutmeg, stir and mix well. Remove from heat.

5. Put the rice into a 5-pint casserole or basin and add the sugar and the spiced liquid; stir and mix until sugar is dissolved.

6. Stir in the cashews and the raisins. Cover with pierced plastic wrap.

7. Cook on 100% power (High) for 10 minutes, then on medium for 2 minutes. Stand for 6-8 minutes.

8. Fork through the rice, remove cinnamon and cloves and serve.

TIME Preparation takes 30 minutes to soak the rice, cooking takes 20 minutes.

COOK'S TIP If you do not have a browning dish, melt the ghee or butter over medium heat in a skillet and fry the rice for 3-4 minutes or until it begins to look fairly dry.

KULFI (INDIAN ICE CREAM)

Kulfi is by far the most popular ice cream in India. It is firmer than conventional ice cream and is often set in small molds. You can, however, use either small yogurt pots or a plastic ice cream container.

SERVES 6-8

⅔ cup fresh milk

2 tbsps ground rice

1 tbsp ground almonds

14½oz can evaporated milk

1 level tsp ground cardamom

¼ cup sugar

Scant 2 cups heavy cream

1 tbsp rose water or 5-6 drops of any other flavoring such as vanilla, almond etc.

¼ cup shelled, unsalted pistachio nuts, lightly crushed

1. Heat the milk to lukewarm.

2. Put the ground rice and ground almonds into a bowl and gradually add the warm milk, a little at a time, to make a thin paste of pouring consistency. Stir continuously and break up any lumps, if any lumps remain, strain the paste.

3. Heat evaporated milk to boiling point and add the ground cardamom.

4. Take the pan off the heat and gradually add the almond/rice mixture, stirring continuously.

5. Add the sugar and cream and place the pan over medium heat, cook the mixture for 12-15 minutes, stirring continuously. Remove the pan from heat and allow the mixture to cool slightly.

6. Add the flavoring and half of the pistachio nuts, stir and mix well. Allow the mixture to cool completely, stirring frequently to prevent a skin from forming on the surface.

7. When the mixture has cooled completely, put it into a plastic container or individual molds.

8. Place in the freezer for 4-5 hours or until very firm.

9. Place the kulfi in the refrigerator for 1½-1 ¾ hours before serving. This will soften it slightly and will make it easier to unmold or cut into desired size. The time required to soften the kulfi will vary according to the size of the container used. Sprinkle with remaining pistachios before serving.

TIME Preparation takes 10 minutes, cooking takes 15-20 minutes.

VARIATION Cream of Rice cereal makes a good substitute for ground rice.

COCONUT STUFFED PANCAKES

Coconut is used for both sweet and savory dishes in southern India. There is no real substitute for freshly grated coconut, but as it is quite time consuming, flaked coconut is a good compromise.

MAKES 6 pancakes

For the filling

¾ cup flaked coconut, finely ground
¼ cup soft dark brown sugar
¼ cup walnut pieces, lightly crushed
1 small can evaporated milk
1 tsp ground cardamom

1. Mix all ingredients, except ground cardamom, in a small saucepan and place over medium heat. As soon as it begins to bubble, reduce heat to low and let it simmer without a lid for 8-10 minutes stirring occasionally.

2. Stir in the ground cardamom, remove the pan from heat and allow the mixture to cool.

For the Pancakes

2 eggs
1½ cups wholewheat flour
1 tsp ground cinnamon
1 tbsp caster sugar
Scant 1 cup milk
Ghee or unsalted butter for frying

1. Put all ingredients, except ghee or butter, in a large bowl and beat with a wire beater until smooth. This batter can also be prepared in a blender or food processor.

2. Place a non-stick or cast iron frying pan over low heat, when hot, spread a little (about ¼ tsp) ghee or butter on it.

3. Pour about 2 tbsps of the batter in the pan and spread it quickly by tilting the pan. Pouring off the batter must be done quickly to prevent it from setting before you have a chance to spread it. It is easier to measure each 2 tbsps into a cup or a ladle before pouring into the pan.

4. In a minute or so, the pancake will set, let it cook for a further minute, then carefully turn it over with a thin spatula or toss it! Cook the other side for about 1 minute (brown spots should appear on both sides).

5. Spread 1 tbsp of the filling on one side of the pancake and roll it into a cylinder shape. Make the rest of the pancakes the same way.

TIME Preparation takes 15-20 minutes, cooking takes 50 minutes.

SERVING IDEAS Serve on their own as a snack or topped with a little whipped cream as a dessert.

WATCHPOINT Use a wide, thin spatula to turn the pancakes; stainless steel or plastic spatulas are ideal.

Durbari Malpura

A great delicacy from the courts of the Mughal Emperors, these small pancakes are smothered with dried fruits and nuts and cream, and delicately flavored with nutmeg and orange rind.

SERVES 6

¾ cup all purpose flour

¼ cup ground rice

¼ cup sugar

1 tsp ground or finely grated nutmeg

Pinch of baking soda

Finely grated rind of 1 orange

¼ cup each of raw cashews and walnuts, lightly crushed

½ cup full cream milk

Oil for deep frying

1 tsp butter

2 tbsps raisins

¼ cup sliced almonds

1¼ cups cream

1 tbsp rose water (optional)

1. Put the flour, ground rice, sugar, nutmeg, soda, orange rind and the crushed nuts into bowl.

2. Add enough milk to make a thick batter.

3. Heat at least 2 inches of oil over medium heat in a deep frying pan.

4. Put in 1 heaped teaspoon of the batter at a time until the whole pan is filled with a single layer.

5. When the malpuras (spoonfuls of batter) start floating to the surface, turn them over. Fry gently until golden brown on both sides (about 5 minutes). Drain on paper towels.

6. Melt the butter over low heat and fry the raisins for 1 minute. Remove them with a slotted spoon and drain on paper towels.

7. In the same fat, fry the almonds until they are lightly browned. Drain on paper towels.

8. Put the cream in a saucepan, large enough to hold all the malpuras and bring to a slow simmer.

9. Put in the malpuras and stir gently.

10. Turn the entire contents of the pan onto a serving dish and sprinkle the rosewater, if using, evenly on top.

11. Garnish with the fried raisins and the almonds. Serve hot or cold.

TIME Preparation takes 10 minutes, cooking takes 20 minutes.

VARIATION Use lemon rind instead of orange. Use Cream of Rice cereal if you can't find ground rice

VERMICELLI KHEER

In this popular dessert, the vermicelli is first lightly fried in ghee, then simmered gently in milk with sugar and spices to make a rich and creamy dish.

SERVES 6-8

2 tbsps ghee or unsalted butter
1oz plain vermicelli
2 tbsps raisins
¼ cup almonds, blanched and slivered
2½ cups whole milk
¼ cup sugar
1 tbsp ground almonds
½ tsp ground cardamom
½ tsp ground cinnamon
1 tbsp rose water or 5-6 drops of other
   flavorings such as vanilla or almond

1. Melt the ghee or butter over low heat and add the vermicelli, raisins and slivered almonds. Stir and fry until the vermicelli is golden brown (2-3 minutes).

2. Add the milk, sugar and ground almonds, bring to the boil and simmer gently for 20 minutes, stirring frequently.

3. Stir in the ground cardamom and cinnamon and remove the pan from heat.

4. Allow the kheer to cool slightly and stir in the rose water or other flavoring.

TIME Preparation takes 10 minutes, cooking takes 20-25 minutes.

SERVING IDEAS Serve hot or cold.

FIRNI (CREAMED GROUND RICE WITH DRIED FRUIT AND NUTS)

*Although firni is basically a rice pudding, it is a far cry from the western variety.
Firni is rich, delicious and temptingly aromatic.*

SERVES 6-8

1¼ cups milk

¼ cup ground rice or Cream of Rice

1 tbsp ground almonds

14oz can of evaporated milk

¼ cup sugar

1 tbsp rosewater (optional)

1 tsp ground cardamom

¼ cup sliced almonds

¼ cup pistachio nuts, lightly crushed

½ cup dried apricots, finely chopped

1. Put the milk into a heavy-based saucepan over a medium heat.

2. Mix the ground rice and ground almonds together and sprinkle evenly over the milk.

Bring the milk to the boil, stirring frequently.

3. Add the evaporated milk and sugar, stir and cook over a low heat for 6-8 minutes.

4. Remove from heat and allow the mixture to cool – stirring occasionally to prevent skin from forming on top.

5. Stir in the rosewater, if using, and the ground cardamom.

6. Reserve a few almonds, pistachios and apricots and stir the remainder into the pudding.

7. Transfer the firni into a serving dish and top with the reserved fruit and nuts. Serve hot or cold.

TIME Preparation takes 5-10 minutes, cooking takes about 15 minutes.

VARIATION Add a few raw cashews (coarsely chopped) while cooking the ground rice and ground almonds.

SWEET VERMICELLI

This quick and easy dessert is a specialty of the Muslims. It is always made during the Muslim religious festival "Idd Ul Fitr"

SERVES 6

4oz plain vermicelli

¼ cup sugar

¼ cup raw cashew nuts, split or coarsely chopped

¼ cup blanched almonds, split whole or coarsely chopped or sliced almonds

2 tbsps raisins

4 cardamoms, split open on the top

½ tsp ground cardamom

½ tsp ground nutmeg

1¼ cups water

4 tbsps ghee or unsalted butter

1. Break the vermicelli into small portions.

2. Melt 1 tbsp ghee or butter over low heat and fry the raisins until they swell up. Remove the pan from heat and transfer the raisins to another plate with a slotted spoon.

3. Place the pan back on the heat, add all the nuts and stir and fry until the nuts turn slightly brown. Transfer them with a slotted spoon to another dish.

4. Return the pan to heat and add the remaining ghee or butter and adjust heat to medium. Add the whole cardamoms and fry for 30 seconds.

5. Add the vermicelli and fry until it turns a rich golden color (about 5 minutes), stirring constantly.

6. Remove the pan from heat, add the raisins, half the fried nuts, ground cardamom and ground nutmeg and stir rapidly.

7. Return the pan to heat and add the water and sugar. Bring to the boil, cover the pan and simmer for 5 minutes.

8. Take the lid off, adjust heat to medium and cook the vermicelli for 2-3 minutes or until the liquid dries up, stirring constantly.

9. Remove from heat and serve hot or cold.

10. If serving cold, using a fork, separate the vermicelli strands as they will stick together when cold.

11. Garnish with the remaining fried nuts.

TIME Preparation takes 25-30 minutes, cooking takes 20 minutes.

SERVING IDEAS Serve as a dessert or with tea and coffee.

Spiced Mango Fool

In India, mango is considered to be the king of all fruits. The taste of this tropical fruit, which grows extensively in India, is slightly like a peach, but more exotic!

SERVES 6-8

2 tbsps milk

¼ tsp saffron strands

¾ cup evaporated milk

¼ cup sugar

1 level tbsp fine semolina or cornmeal

2 heaped tbsps ground almonds

1 tsp ground cardamom

1lb mango pulp or 2-15oz cans of mangoes, drained and puréed

1 cup thick set plain yogurt

1. Put the milk into a small saucepan and bring to the boil. Stir in the saffron strands, remove from the heat, cover the pan and set aside.

2. Put the evaporated milk and sugar into a saucepan and place it over a low heat.

3. When it begins to bubble, sprinkle the semolina or cornmeal over, stir until well blended.

4. Now add the ground almonds, stir and cook until the mixture thickens (5-6 minutes).

5. Stir in the ground cardamom and remove from heat. Allow this to cool completely, then gradually beat in the mango pulp, making sure there are no lumps.

6. In a large mixing bowl beat the yogurt with a fork, gradually beat in the evaporated milk and mango mixture.

7. Stir in the saffron milk along with all the strands for their color and flavor. Mix well.

8. Put the mango fool into a serving dish and chill for 2-3 hours.

TIME Preparation takes 10 minutes, cooking takes 10-15 minutes.

VARIATION Top the dessert with a few strawberries for an attractive look.

MELON BALLS IN MANGO PULP

After a rich and spicy Indian meal, a light and refreshing dessert really cools the palate!

SERVES 6

1lb can of mango pulp or 2-15oz cans of sliced mangoes

1 medium-sized honeydew or canary melon

Finely grated rind of 1 lemon

2 tbsps caster sugar

2 tbsps cornstarch

½ tsp ground nutmeg

⅔ cup whipping cream

1. Drain the canned mangoes and purée them in a food processor, or push through a strainer.

2. Using a melon baller make as many balls as possible out of the melon. Scoop out the remaining flesh and put into a food processor along with all the juice and blend to a purée.

3. Transfer the purée into a saucepan and add the lemon rind and sugar.

4. Blend the cornstarch with a little water and add to the melon purée. Cook over low heat until the mixture thickens. Stir in the nutmeg and remove from heat.

5. Allow the mixture to cool slightly, then mix thoroughly with the mango pulp. Chill.

6. Whip the cream until thick, then stir into the mango mixture.

7. Put the melon and mango mixture into a serving dish and arrange the melon balls in 3-4 rows around the entire diameter.

8. Chill for 2-3 hours before serving. Sprinkle with more nutmeg.

TIME Preparation takes 15-20 minutes plus cooling time, cooking takes 5-10 minutes.
Suitable for freezing.

MANGO DELIGHT

If your budget allows, fresh, ripe mangoes are superb for this dessert. After slicing them, gently scrape off every bit of flesh next to the stones. Though the flesh will not be in neat pieces, it will add a lot to the flavor when mixed with the custard base used for this dish.

SERVES 4-6

½ cup sugar

2 tbsps cornstarch

1 cup milk

2 egg yolks

1 tsp ground cardamom or ground mixed spice

2 fresh ripe mangoes or 2-15oz cans of sliced mangoes

½ cup whipping cream

2 tbsps shelled unsalted pistachio nuts, lightly crushed

1. Mix sugar, cornstarch in a double boiler. Gradually beat in the milk. Place over simmering water and cover. Cook about 8 minutes without stirring.

2. Uncover and cook a further 10 minutes, stirring until thickening.

3. Add egg yolks and cook, stirring constantly until thickened. Add spice and chill.

4. Gradually add the mango pulp to the custard, stirring all the time.

5. Whisk the cream until fairly thick, but still soft.

6. Drain one can of the mango slices and purée them in a blender or food processor. Drain the other can and coarsely chop the mango slices. Peel, slice and chop fresh mangoes.

7. Stir the cream into the mango mixture and gently mix in the chopped mangoes.

8. Transfer the mango mixture into a serving bowl and top with the crushed pistachio nuts. Serve hot or cold.

TIME Preparation takes 10 minutes, cooking takes 10 minutes.

SHRIKAND

Shrikand is a delicious and creamy dessert which is made of strained yogurt. The yogurt is drained until all the water content is gone, the result being a thick and creamy yogurt which is rich but delicious.

SERVES 6

3-15oz cartons of thick set plain yogurt
¼ tsp saffron strands
1 tbsp hot water
⅓ cup sugar
1 heaped tbsp ground almonds
½ tsp ground cardamom
¼ tsp grated or ground nutmeg

1. Pour the yogurt onto a strainer lined with clean, very fine cheese cloth. Place strainer over a bowl until all the water content has been drained off; 4-6 hours or undisturbed overnight in the refrigerator.

2. Add the saffron strands to the hot water, cover and keep aside.

3. Carefully empty the yogurt into a mixing bowl. Beat with a fork, or a whisk, until smooth.

4. Add the sugar, beat and mix thoroughly. Add the ground almonds, cardamom and the nutmeg and mix well.

5. Stir in the saffron strands and the water in which it was soaked.

6. Chill before serving.

TIME Preparation takes a few minutes plus time needed to drain the yogurt.

VARIATION Top the Shrikand with mandarin orange segments, sliced mangoes or chopped pistachio nuts.

SPICED FRUIT SALAD

A novel deviation from traditional Indian desserts, but an excellent one to round off a spicy hot meal. Handle the tinned mango slices very carefully as they tend to be soft. Use fresh mangoes, if available

SERVES 6-8

15oz can pineapple chunks
15oz can papaya chunks
15oz can mango slices, cut into chunks
15oz can guava halves, cut into chunks
3 cinnamon sticks, each 2-inches long
3 cardamoms
6 whole cloves
8 black peppercorns

1. Drain all the fruits and reserve the syrup. Mix all the syrup together, reserve 2½ cups and drain off remainder.

2. Put the syrup into a saucepan and add the spices, bring to the boil, cover the pan and let it simmer for 20 minutes.

3. Uncover and reduce the syrup to half its original volume by boiling for 5-6 minutes. Remove from heat and allow the syrup to cool.

4. Keep the pan covered until the syrup cools, (in an open pan some of the flavor will be lost).

5. Reserve a few pieces of papaya and guava and all the mangoes. Arrange the remaining fruits in a serving bowl.

6. Arrange the mangoes on top, then put in the reserved papaya and guava.

7. Strain the spiced syrup and pour over the fruits. Cover and chill.

TIME Preparation takes 10-15 minutes, cooking takes 20 minutes.

VARIATION Use fresh ripe pear instead of tinned mango.
Add 1 tbsp of brandy to the syrup.

SEMOLINA AND ALMOND HALVA

A quick and easy to prepare candy that's rich and delicious.

SERVES 6-8

½ cup ghee or unsalted butter
¾ cup fine semolina or cornmeal
1 cup ground almonds
½ cup sugar
½ tsp ground nutmeg
1¼ cups whole milk
¼ cup raw cashews, chopped

1. Grease a 7-inch square pan and set aside.

2. Melt the ghee or butter over low heat in a heavy-based pan.

3. Add the semolina or cornmeal and cook until golden brown (6-7 minutes) stirring continuously.

4. Add the almonds, sugar and the nutmeg, stir and mix thoroughly.

5. Add the milk and mix, stirring until the mixture thickens and stops sticking to the bottom and sides of the pan.

6. Put the mixture into the greased pan and spread it evenly using the back of a lightly greased metal spoon.

7. Sprinkle the chopped cashews evenly on top and press them in gently with the palm of your hand.

8. Allow the mixture to cool and cut into 1-inch squares.

TIME Preparation takes 5 minutes, cooking takes 15 minutes.

SERVING IDEAS Serve as a dessert with ice cream or with tea or coffee.

WHEAT FUDGE

This fudge is made of wholewheat flour which is very fine – atta or chapatti flour is ideal for this recipe. The flour is gently roasted with a generous amount of ghee or butter until the wonderful aroma of the roasted wheat is released.

SERVES 10-12

½ cup ghee or unsalted butter

2 cups fine textured wholewheat flour

1½ tsps ground cardamom

¼ cup chopped mixed nuts

2 cups light brown sugar

1. Melt the ghee or butter over medium heat and add the flour, stir and mix thoroughly. Cook for 5 minutes, stirring continuously. Adjust heat to low and cook for a further 10-12 minutes stirring continuously.

2. Add the cardamom and chopped nuts, stir and cook for 2-3 minutes.

3. Remove from heat and add the sugar, stir and mix. If there are any lumps, break them up with the back of the spoon.

4. Lightly grease a large plate and spread the flour mixture on it. Using the back of a metal spoon, spread the mixture evenly and form a rectangle, about ½-inch thick, 6-inches wide and 8-inches long. Allow the mixture to cool, then chill for 20 minutes.

5. Remove from refrigerator and cut into 1½-2-inch squares. Allow to harden before serving. Store in an open container or plate in the refrigerator. They will keep for 3-4 weeks.

TIME Preparation takes 5 minutes, cooking takes 15-18 minutes.

SERVING IDEAS Serve with tea or with after dinner coffee.

389

Besan Ladoo

Besan Ladoos are made of roasted chick pea flour and, like Wheat Fudge, they need constant attention in the first 15 minutes or so. These ladoos have a delicious nutty taste and they really do melt in the mouth!

MAKES 28-30

1 cup ghee or unsalted butter
4 cups besan, sifted
1 cup sugar
1½ tsps ground cardamom
½ cup chopped mixed nuts

1. Melt the ghee or butter over medium heat and add the besan. Reduce heat to low and fry the besan for 12-15 minutes stirring continuously.

2. Add the rest of the ingredients, mix thoroughly and remove from heat.

3. Allow the mixture to cool completely and form into small walnut-sized balls.

4. Store in an airtight container, where they will stay fresh for 4-5 weeks.

TIME Preparation takes 5 minutes, cooking takes 12-15 minutes plus cooling and forming the balls.

SERVING IDEAS Serve with after-dinner coffee or tea.

STUFFED LITCHIS

Litchis grow abundantly in India and the fruit is normally eaten on its own,
when ripe. In this recipe canned fruit is used for convenience.

SERVES 4-6

2-15oz cans litchis, sweetened

1 fresh mango or 15oz canned sliced
　　mangoes

2 tbsps cornstarch

2 tbsps lemon juice

Finely grated rind of 1 lemon

⅔ cup whipping cream

1 heaped tbsp ground almonds

A few drops of yellow food coloring
　　(optional)

Roasted chopped almonds to decorate
　　(optional)

1. Drain the litchis and the mangoes and reserve ¾ cup litchi and ½ cup mango syrup. Mix the syrups together and set aside. If using fresh mango, reserve all the juice from the litchis and add water to make 1¼ cups liquid.

2. Put the cornstarch into a saucepan and add a little syrup to make a smooth paste. Gradually add the rest of the syrup and mix thoroughly.

3. Add the lemon rind and juice and cook over low heat until the mixture thickens. Allow to cool.

4. Beat the cream until thick, and stir into the cornstarch mixture along with the food coloring. Add the ground almonds and mix well.

5. Remove any broken litchis, chop them finely and mix with the cornstarch mixture. Reserve whole litchis.

6. Chop the mango slices coarsely.

7. Stuff each whole litchi with chopped mangoes so that the mango stands about ¼ -inch high on each litchi.

8. Mix any remaining mango pieces or pulp with the cornstarch mixture.

9. Spoon the cornstarch mixture into a 10-inch serving dish and arrange the litchis on top (the mixture will fill a smaller dish too thickly and cause the litchis to sink).

10. Chill before serving. Decorate with almonds.

TIME Preparation takes 20-25 minutes.

SERVING IDEAS So light and refreshing, it will round off any Indian meal
extremely well.

VARIATION Use fresh strawberries instead of mangoes.

glossary

The following glossary of terms is intended to help all Indian cooking enthusiasts to understand the behavior of each individual spice and the effect it has on the flavor of a dish when used not only on its own, but also in combination with other spices.

Ajowan or Carum Seeds (*Ajwain*) Ajowan is closely related to caraway and cumin and is used in many savory dishes. Its flavor is similar to that of thyme. It is used in Indian cooking both for its flavor and its medicinal value. Ajowan seeds are often boiled in a little water and the resulting liquid is drunk to treat stomach ailments.

Allspice (*Kabab Cheene*) Jamaica practically has a monopoly over the supply of allspice to the rest of the world but, although allspice is native to the West Indies, it is now grown in many other tropical countries.

Allspice is not a combination of different spices, but is produced from the dried berries of the Jamaican pepper plant which has a flavor and aroma similar to that of cloves, cinnamon and nutmeg. It is not a traditional ingredient in Indian cooking, but has come to be used in many pilau, biriani and Mughlai meat and poultry dishes.

Aniseed or Fennel Seed (*Sonf or Saunf*) Aniseed or fennel can safely be substituted one for the other, as they have a similar flavor. Aniseeds are similar to cumin seeds but are rather a dull grayish color. They have a sweet, liquorice-like flavor and are used widely in Bengal and Kashmir.

The fennel plant is native to the Mediterranean, though it has been cultivated in India since Ancient times. Both aniseed and fennel seeds are either gently fried or ground with other spices. They are also often chewed at the end of a meal as an aid to digestion and as a breath sweetener.

Asafoetida (*Hing*) This is obtained from the resinous gum of a tropical plant that is closely related to the fennel family. It can be bought from specialist grocers in solid pieces or in powder form.

Asafoetida is used very sparingly because of its very strong flavor. It has quite a powerful smell, but when fried in minute quantities in hot oil with other spices it imparts a certain distinctive flavor that is an integral part of the strict vegetarian diet of the Brahmins. It is never used in recipes for meat and poultry dishes.

Bay Leaf (*Tej Patta*) The bay leaf is not traditional to Indian cooking. The name is a mistranslation, for Western bay leaves are quite different from *tej patta*, which are the tender leaves obtained from the Cassia tree and which have a flavor similar to cinnamon. In the West, bay leaves, obtained from the sweet bay laurel, are more easily available and have become a popular substitute.

Indian bay leaves can be crumbled easily to blend with other spices. Western bay leaves are brighter in appearance and are usually used whole. They also have a stronger flavor than Indian bay leaves.

Black Pepper (*Kali Mirchi*) Black pepper comes from the pepper vines grown in the tropical forests of monsoon Asia. The berries are picked when they are green, and then dried in the sun to give the familiar black pepper. Pepper loses its flavor rapidly and so it is always advisable to buy whole peppercorns and grind them in a pepper mill as and when required. Pre-ground pepper does little to enhance the flavor of a dish.

Caraway Seeds (*Shahjeera*) Caraway seed is closely related to cumin, but has a milder flavor. Unlike cumin, caraway does not dominate the flavour of the dish in which it is used. The flavor of caraway blends easily with meat. Sometimes the seeds are used to flavor the oil before cooking vegetables, pulses, pilaus and birianis.

Cardamom (*Elaichi*) The cardamom plant is a perennial of the ginger family and grows abundantly in southern India. The ripe cardamom seed pods are dried in the sun before being sold commercially.

There are two varieties of cardamom pods: large dark brown, almost black, ones, known as *Badi Elaichi,* and small green ones referred to as *Choti Elaichi.* The dark brown variety is used in certain curries, pilaus and birianis and the inner seeds are often used for making garam masala. The small green variety is used in most curries, pilaus and some sweet dishes. When a recipe calls for whole cardamom, the pods should always be opened up slightly to extract the full flavor of the cardamom, for it is the seeds that have the maximum flavor. The same method can also be used in judging the quality of cardamoms. Good quality cardamom seeds will always appear a rich brownish-black, slightly sticky and have a strong aromatic smell.

Cardamom is sold whole or ground in spice sections of most supermarkets. Ground cardamom is often used in Indian desserts. It is best to grind small quantities at home using a coffee or spice mill. Ready-ground cardamom is not only expensive, but because cardamom loses its natural oil quickly, it also loses its flavor.

Chapatti or Atta Flour This is a fine-textured, wholewheat flour that is used in making most unleavened Indian bread. The whole kernel is a good source of dietary fiber as it contains a high proportion of bran and wheatgerm.

If real chapatti flour is not available, then a fine-textured wholewheat flour or a mixture of equal quantities of wholewheat and all-purpose flour can be used to make Indian breads.

Chickpea Flour or Lentil Flour (*Besan*) This is a very fine-textured flour, creamy yellow in color and made by dry-grinding chickpeas or lentils. It is a very versatile medium which can be used as a base for many dessert dishes, to prepare a batter with which to coat onions and other vegetables before frying to make bhajiyas (as distinct from bhaji), and as a garnish in the final stages of cooking vegetables. Besan should be stored in a cool, dry place.

Chili Peppers, Dried Red (*Lal Mirchi*) These vary a great deal in shape and size. Usually, the tiny ones are very hot, so use them sparingly. They are also paler in appearance. The rich red ones, which are long and flat, are less hot and have more flavor.

When chili peppers are ripe they are usually a rich red color. These are then dried in the sun to give us the dried red chili peppers, which are very different in flavor from fresh green or red chilis.

Chili Peppers, Fresh Green (*Hari Mirchi*) Fresh green chili peppers have a delicious capsicum-like flavor. They also vary a great deal in strength and unfortunately it is difficult to judge the strength. This has to be discovered by trial and error. They are a good source of vitamin C, but have to be eaten in small quantities. Chili peppers are often added to a dish towards the end of cooking to obtain a delicious flavor without the dish being too hot. More often they are ground with other ingredients to make chutneys or are used for pickling.

Fresh green chili peppers vary a great deal in shape and size. It is the long slim variety that is commonly used in Indian cooking. They can be frozen after thorough washing and can be used straight from the freezer.

All chili peppers, red or green, should be seeded if a milder flavor is preferred, as the seeds are the hottest part.

Cinnamon (*Da Uhini*) The cinnamon sticks used in Indian cooking are different from those used in the West. Indian cinnamon sticks have the texture and feel of tree bark, and are actually obtained from the bark of the Cassia tree, which grows in most tropical countries. True cinnamon sticks, which are in the form of a scroll, are available in most supermarkets and have a much more delicate flavor than Cassia bark. True cinnamon is native to Sri Lanka. Both Cassia tree cinnamon and true cinnamon, however, are from the same botanical family.
Cinnamon is an essential ingredient in garam masala. It is also often used whole in certain curries, pilaus and birianis, and is brewed with cloves and aniseed as a medicinal drink to fight the symptoms of colds, coughs and flu. It should be stored in an air-tight container.

Cloves (*Lavang*) Cloves are the buds of the dried flower of the clove tree, which is native to southern Asia. They have a strong and distinctive flavor and are an essential ingredient in garam masala. They are also used whole in certain curries, pilaus and birianis. Whether used whole or ground, cloves should be used in carefully measured quantities as the flavor is rather overpowering.

Cloves should always be bought whole, as ground cloves do not contain the essential oil that flavors a dish.

Cloves are highly antiseptic and are often chewed to relieve toothache.

Coconut, Flaked (*Kopra*) Flaked coconut offers a convenient alternative to the rather time-consuming process of preparing fresh coconut for use in a recipe.

Coconut sometimes has to be ground with other spices to obtain the finer texture essential for making a good sauce. When used for chutneys, it can be ground along with other ingredients as chutneys do not need to be finely ground.

Coconut, Fresh (*Nariyal*) The coconut palm grows along tropical coasts all over the world. The vast coastline of India produces an abundant harvest of coconut, and Indian cooking is well known for its use of coconut in savory as well as sweet dishes.

In India, fresh coconut is generally cracked open and the juice inside the coconut is drunk as a cooling beverage. Various manual gadgets are available to grate the coconut flesh, which is then ground with other spices. Sometimes the juice, or coconut milk, is extracted and used when making a rich sauce. Creamed coconut, if available, is a very convenient substitute for fresh coconut milk.

If you wish to use fresh coconut, a very convenient way to prepare it is as follows: Preheat the oven to 400°F. Crack the coconut shell by striking it smartly with a hammer or other heavy object until the juice starts trickling out. Do not shatter it. Carefully drain the juice and place the cracked whole coconut in the center of the oven for about twenty-five minutes, or until the crack on the shell is visible. Remove the coconut from the oven and gently tap it all the way around with a hammer or meat mallet. The hard outer shell will come away very easily, leaving only the pure white flesh, which has a dark brown outer skin. Cut the coconut into conveniently-sized pieces and peel the skin. Grate the flesh in the food processor. This can be frozen in small quantities ready to use. Coconut prepared in this way will, of course, need to be processed in the same way as flaked coconut.

Clarified Butter (*Ghee*) Ghee is used extensively in Indian cooking, especially in pilaus, birianis and Mughlai dishes. It is the primary ingredient that enhances the richness of Mughlai dishes. Ghee has a distinctive flavor and can be heated to a much higher temperature than ordinary butter without burning because the clarifying process removes the milk solids and salt.

It is not difficult to make ghee at home, the most important point to watch is the temperature. You will need about 1lb unsalted butter, cut up into small pieces. You can use a smaller quantity, and once you have mastered the art, the quantity can be increased to suit your needs. Put the butter in a heavy-based saucepan over a low heat and allow it to melt without sizzling. Adjust the heat to a slightly higher setting to allow the butter to simmer gently for ten to fifteen minutes, during which time all the milk solids will separate and the moisture will be released from the butter. A layer of foam will appear on the surface during this time. When the foam subsides, this is an indication that there is no more moisture left. Let the butter simmer until the milk solids settle at the bottom of the pan and turn brown. Watch carefully so that the milk solids do not burn; keep the heat low. Once the milk solids have turned brown, remove the pan from heat and allow the clarified butter to cool until it is comfortable to handle. Strain the ghee through fine cheesecloth and store in a moisture-free jar. Ghee will stay fresh for about three months.

Coriander (*Nhania or Kotmil*) Coriander is the single most important spice in Indian cooking. Its mild and slightly sweet flavor blends well with almost all Indian dishes and it controls their basic flavor.

Traditionally, coriander is gently roasted before grinding as this brings out its full flavor as well as making it easier to grind finely. Ground pre-packed coriander, if roasted gently and cooled before storing in airtight containers, will significantly enhance the flavor of dishes.

Coriander Leaves (*Hara Dhania*) Fresh coriander leaves are an essential flavoring and garnishing ingredient in Indian dishes. They are also used for many delicious chutneys.

The leaves can be frozen if they are to be used for flavoring a dish or grinding with other spices for chutneys. Fresh leaves should be used for garnishes as frozen ones do not look attractive. The freshness of coriander can be preserved for at least two weeks if, as soon as the bunch is bought, the roots and any yellow/black leaves are cut off and the remaining good leaves are dried on paper towels until all moisture is removed. These should then be wrapped in aluminum foil, sealing all edges, and stored in the refrigerator. During storage it is advisable to remove any yellow/black stalks or leaves as these will spoil the rest of the bunch.

The tender stalks of coriander have the same flavor as that of the leaves. They can therefore be finely chopped and used along with the leaves.

Coriander is easy to grow in any type of soil and it can readily be grown on a window sill throughout the winter and in the garden in the summer.

Cumin (*Jeera*) Cumin is a pungent and aromatic spice, which is also very powerful. There are two varieties: black cumin (*kala jeera*) and white cumin (*safed jeera*). Although both are widely used, one cannot be substituted for the other as they each have their own quite distinctive flavor.

Sometimes black cumin is confused with caraway seeds, which are quite different.

Cumin is used whole to flavor the oil before cooking vegetables, pulses and some rice dishes. Ground cumin, because of its powerful flavor, should be used in carefully measured quantities. A better flavor is obtained by gently roasting the seeds before grinding. Ground pre-packed cumin, if roasted and cooled before storing, will produce more satisfactory results than if used straight from the packet.

Curry Leaves (*Curry Patta*) These are sold dried or fresh. The leaves are small and shiny and are used in many different ways. They can be crumbled before being added to a dish or used whole. Alternatively, they can be fried in oil and then added to the dish.

Curry leaves are used extensively in southern Indian cooking and are one of the main ingredients in commercially prepared curry powder, especially Madras curry powder.

The dried leaves can be stored in a screw-top jar, and fresh ones can be frozen and used straight from the freezer.

Fenugreek (*Methi*) Fenugreek seeds have a slightly bitter flavor and must be used in the specified quantities. They are either fried in hot oil or gently roasted and ground with other spices – each method produces its own distinctive flavor. Whichever method is used, the seeds should not be overcooked, or a very bitter flavor will be the result. Fenugreek is widely used in vegetable, lentil and some fish dishes.

The seeds are brownish-yellow in color and rectangular in shape. The fresh green leaves, which are very much like watercress, are used as a vegetable. They cannot be substituted for the seeds. The leaves are also dried for use as a herb with vegetables and for stuffing breads. In northern India, fenugreek cookies are a great delicacy.

Garam Masala Garam Masala is a combination of hot spices. The word *garam* signifies heat and *masala* means a mixture of various spices.

Garam masala is known to create body heat which helps the body to retain warmth in a cold climate. It is much used in northern India, where the temperature in winter is much lower than in the rest of the country.

Garam masala is sometimes used together with other spices, or it can be sprinkled on as a condiment at the end of the cooking time. Cardamom, cinnamon and cloves are the main ingredients that make up the taste of the final mixture when ground. These spices are also used whole in pilaus and birianis and in certain curries and dry-spiced vegetable dishes.

The recipe for garam masala can vary a great deal; other spices such as whole black peppercorns, coriander seeds, and cumin seeds may be added to to the three basic ingredients.

The garam masala used in this book consists of cinnamon, cardamom, cloves and nutmeg. The quantity of each spice used is: 2 tbsps cinnamon sticks, broken into small pieces, 1½ tbsps cardamoms with the skin, 1 tbsp whole cloves and ½ a whole nutmeg, broken into pieces for grinding.

Heat a cast-iron or other heavy-based pan. When the pan is hot, add the above ingredients and reduce heat to low. Stir and roast the ingredients until they release their aroma. Remove from the heat and allow to cool completely; stir during the first half of the cooling time to prevent them from browning as the pan will remain hot for a while. When completely cool, grind the spices to a fine powder in a coffee or spice mill and store in an air-tight jar. Garam masala prepared in this way is much more aromatic and has a fuller flavor than ready-packed garam masala.The latter does not have the required aroma and flavor because the main ingredients – cinnamon, cardamom and cloves – lose their essential oils very rapidly.

Garlic (*Lasoon*) Fresh garlic is a vital ingredient in Indian cooking. Powdered garlic or garlic salt cannot be substituted as the flavor is so very different.

Fresh garlic will keep well if it is stored in an earthenware pot and the pot kept in a cool, dry and reasonably dark place. Garlic is usually either ground to a paste or used finely chopped. It can be prepared and frozen in ice cube trays.

Garlic also has extremely good medicinal properties. The antiseptic substances in garlic help to tone up the digestive system. Garlic also reduces the cholesterol level in the blood and thereby reduces the risk of high blood pressure.

Ginger (*Adrak*) Root ginger is an almost indispensable ingredient in Indian cooking. Powdered ginger can be used for convenience, but will not produce the same flavour as it does not contain the essential properties of fresh root ginger. Fresh ginger adds a hot taste to the dish and also acts as a thickener. It is either scraped and ground to a paste or grated. The method used to prepare and freeze fresh garlic can also be used for root ginger.

Root ginger will keep well for about four to five weeks if the same process of storage is followed as for fresh garlic.

Ground Mixed Spice This needs no introduction as it is widely used for baking, especially apple-based desserts. The mixture contains the same basic ingredients as garam masala, so it is a good substitute. A teaspoon of mixed spice fried in hot oil will enhance the flavor of any curry.

Mustard Seed (*Rai or Sarson*) Mustard seed has been used as a spice for many thousands of years. There are three different types of seeds: black, brown – which is also known as Indian mustard – and white or Alba mustard.

Brown or black mustard seed is commonly used in Indian cooking. It is not easy to differentiate between the two, though the brown variety is slightly lighter in color.

Powdered or crushed mustard is used in pickles, and the whole seeds are used to flavor vegetables and pulses, and are fried in hot oil to give a nutty flavor. The green leaves are used as a vegetable.

Mustard oil, which is extracted from the seeds, is a popular cooking oil in Assam and Bengal, the two northeastern states in India. It is also used for making pickles.

Onion (*Pyaz*) With a few exceptions, no Indian dish is complete without the use of onions. When a recipe calls for the onions to be fried gently until golden brown, the onion should never be allowed to brown, but should be a pale golden color. Browned onions have a different flavor and are used only for garnishing dishes, and not for making the sauce.

While preparing onions in the blender or food processor, no water should be added at first. Once the onions start to break down, blending becomes easier. The addition of water makes the onions rather soggy. If necessary, however, about one tablespoon of water could be added to make the blending easier.

Onions that have been cut should not be exposed to air for any length of time as this causes them to develop a stale flavor. Onions should be chopped or sliced as finely as possible for Indian cooking. The finer the onions, the better the flavor and the texture of the dish will be.

Green onions and shallots are also used in Indian cooking, except in northern India.

Onion Seeds (*Kalonji*) Onion seeds are used whole for flavoring pickles and vegetable dishes. They are also used in savory snacks and Tandoori-baked bread, such as Naan or Tandoori Roti. In Assam and Bengal, onion seeds are used along with other whole spices to flavor dhals and fish curries.

Onion seeds are not actually derived from the onion plant, but because of their close resemblance to actual onion seeds, they are referred to thus. They actually come from the *Nigella* plant, which is grown in India and the Middle East.

Paprika Indian paprika comes mainly from Kashmir where this mild and sweet variety of pepper, known as *deghi mirchi*, is grown extensively. Its brilliant red color does not mean it is a pungent as the other chili peppers used in Indian cooking. Paprika is primarily used to add that wonderfully rich color to a dish.

Poppy Seeds (*Khus Khus*) Various kinds of poppy flowers are grown all around the world, but the poppy seeds used in Indian cooking come from the opium poppy, which flourishes in tropical climates. The seeds are pale cream, almost white, in appearance and they add a nutty flavor to the dish as well as improving its texture by thickening the sauce.

Rose Extract and Rose-water These are used in many Indian dishes, especially those of Mughal origin. Rose extract is used in sweet dishes and rose-water has its use in both sweet and savory dishes.

The flavor is extracted from a special variety of rose cultivated solely for this purpose. Rose-water is made by diluting rose extract.

Rose-water is also sprinkled on guests to welcome them as they arrive for a wedding.

Saffron (*Kessar*) Saffron consists of the dried stigma of the saffron crocus flower. Though saffron is grown in most Mediterranean countries, the type used in Indian cooking comes from the foothills of the Himalayas.

Saffron is used in Mughlai, Kashmiri and north Indian cooking to add both color and flavor to dishes. The long and laborious process of collecting the stigma makes saffron one of the world's most expensive flavorings. Between 75,000 and 250,000 stigmas are required to produce just one pound of saffron.

Saffron should always be bought in strands whenever possible. Just a pinch of saffron is enough to flavor any dish.

The strands should be soaked in a little hot water or milk for ten to fifteen minutes. Both the infusion and the strands should be used in the dish for maximum flavor. Saffron is used for both sweet and savory dishes.

Do not be tempted to substitute turmeric for saffron, as it has its own distinctive flavor.

Sesame Seeds (*Til*) Sesame is one of most important oil seeds in the world. It is native to India, which, together with China, is the largest grower and exporter of sesame oil to the West.

The sesame seed used in Indian cooking is a pale creamy color and has a nutty flavor.

Tamarind (*Imli*) Tamarind plants grow all over India. The tamarind pods resemble pea pods, but are six to eight inches long, half-an-inch thick, and are a dark brown color when ripe.

Tamarind pulp is sticky and sour and is added to a whole range of Indian dishes to add a distinctive tangy taste. The pod is broken up and the seeds are removed before being packed and sold. The pulp is soaked in hot water and the juice extracted for use.

Ready-to-use tamarind concentrate, a highly concentrated tanarind pulp, is sold in specialty stores and is much more convenient to use.

Turmeric (*Haldi*) Turmeric is native to India and it is the turmeric root that is cleaned, boiled, dried and ground to give the distinctive yellow powder. Turmeric adds color as well as flavor to a dish. It is closely related to the ginger plant and aids the digestive system, as does ginger. Turmeric is also used as an antiseptic.

Turmeric has a certain religious and social significance and is used as a sacred ingredient by the Hindus. In northeast India a bride and a bridegroom are "purified" by being bathed in turmeric paste; it is believed that this prepares them for their new life together. In certain Hindu marriages, a thread, dipped in turmeric water, is tied around the bride's neck by the bridegroom.

Yogurt In India, plain set yogurt, most of which is home-made, is always used for cooking and general consumption.

Yogurt finds its way into the Indian diet in numerous different guises. A vegetarian would always finish off a meal by eating yogurt on its own or by having a yogurt-based drink. Yogurt is used to make salads (raitas) of different kinds and also to tenderize meat and poultry. The enzyme contained in the yogurt breaks up the tissues so that the spices can then penetrate deep into the meat. Yogurt also thickens and enhances the flavor of the sauce in many Indian dishes.

As it is made from buffalo milk, which has a higher fat content than cow's milk, Indian yogurt has a rich, creamy taste. The most suitable yogurt for use in Indian cooking is one that is thick set and is made with full cream milk. Other types of plain yogurt have a high water content and will make the sauce watery and do little to enhance the flavor of dishes.

Aloo Chole 280
Aloo Gosht 140
Aloo Ki Bhaji 284
Aloo Mattar (Microwave) 202
Aloo Mattar 298
Apple Chutney 336
Avocado Chutney 338
Barrah Kabab 22
Batura 238
Bengal Fish Curry 62
Besan Ladoo 390
Bhindi (Okra) Masala 302
Bhindi (Okra) Raita 324
Bhindi (Okra) with Coconut 296
Bhoona Gosht 154
Boti Kabab 28
Cabbage and Mint Salad 314
Cabbage Bhaji (Microwave) 210
Cabbage with Cinnamon 286
Cabbage with Lentil Flour 300
Cardamom Rice 252
Carrot and Coconut Salad 312
Carrot and Mooli Salad 318
Carrot and Peanut Raita 328
Carrot Pilau 254
Cauliflower Cutlets 274
Cauliflower Masala 268
Cauliflower Pakoras 40
Cauliflower Surprise 118
Cauliflower Upkari (Microwave) 200
Cauliflower with Cashews
    (Microwave) 214
Chapattis 232
Chicken and Mushroom Curry
    (Microwave) 186
Chicken Chaat 76
Chicken Dhansak 98
Chicken Do-Piaza 86
Chicken Kohlapuri 80
Chicken Korma 84
Chicken Korma (Microwave) 176
Chicken Liver Masala 112
Chicken Livers with Spinach 114
Chicken or Turkey Pakoras 26
Chicken Tikka 20
Chicken Tikka Masala 92
Chicken with Cashews (Microwave) 182
Chicken with Channa Dhal 82
Chicken with Whole Spices 88
Cinnamon Rice (Microwave) 194
Coconut Stuffed Pancakes 366
Coriander Chicken 96
Cucumber and Onion Raita 330
Cucumber Raita 322
Cumin-Coriander Chutney 342
Dahi Murghi 90
Date Sauce 346
Durbari Malpura 368
Egg and Potato Dum 70
Eggplant Bharta 304
Eggplant Curry (Microwave) 172
Eggplant Raita 332
Firni (Creamed Ground Rice with Dried
    Fruit & Nuts) 372

Fish Bhoona 50
Fish Roe Scramble 58
Fish Shahjahani 60
Fried Brown Rice 248
Gobi Aloo 272
Gobi Mattar (Cabbage with Peas) 278
Green Been and Potato Bhaji 290
Green Beans in Garlic Butter 264
Green Coriander Chutney 340
Jeera Pani 352
Kashmiri Dum Aloo 292
Kheema Mattar 144
Kheema Shahzada 150
Kheema-Palak 162
Kheema-Sali-Mattar 126
Khumbi Aur Besan Ki Bhaji 270
Kofta (Meatball) Curry 124
Kofta Bhoona 134
Kulfi (Indian Ice Cream) 364
Lamb with Butter Beans 146
Lamb with Mung Beans 152
Lettuce and Coconut Chutney
    (Microwave) 218
Loochis 236
Mackerel with Coconut Sauce
    (Microwave) 180
Makkhani Murghi 104
Mango Delight 380
Mango Sherbet 360
Marinated Lamb Chops 138
Marinated Trout (Microwave) 178
Masala Machchi 54
Mattar Pilau 258
Meat and Potato Patties 18
Meat Dilpasand 156
Meat Dilruba 130
Meat Durbari 160
Meat Madras 148
Meat Maharaja 128
Meat Samosas 38
Meat Vindaloo 136
Melon Balls in Mango Pulp 378
Mint and Onion Chutney 344
Mint and Onion Raita 326
Mixed Vegetable Bhaji (Microwave) 208
Mixed Vegetable Bhaji 276
Mixed Vegetable Curry 68
Mixed Vegetable Pilau 256
Mixed Vegetables with Cinnamon
    (Microwave) 204
Murgh Dilkush 108
Murgh Musallam 110
Murghi Aur Aloo 102
Murghi Aur Palak 100
Murghi Badami 106
Murghi Jhal Frezi 94
Murghi Nawabi 74
Mushroom Bhaji 36
Mushroom Pilau 260
Mustard Fish (Microwave) 174
Naan 228
Nargisi Kababs 34
Nawabi Kheema Pilau 132
Nimbu Pani 350

Onion Bhajiyas 24
Onion Relish 334
Parathas 242
Pasanda Badam Curry 158
Pilau Rice 250
Plain Boiled Rice (Microwave) 192
Plain Boiled Rice 246
Plain Fried Rice 244
Potato Gushi (Microwave) 206
Potato Pakoras 32
Potato Raita 320
Potatoes with Garlic and Chili
    Peppers 288
Potatoes with Poppy Seeds 266
Puris 234
Rasam 354
Rogan Josh 120
Rotis 240
Saag Bhaji 282
Saagwalla Dhal 310
Sabji Masala Murgh 78
Saffron Rice (Microwave) 190
Savory Meat and Eggs 164
Savory Rice Cake (Microwave) 224
Seekh Kababs 30
Semolina and Almond Halva 386
Shahi Korma 142
Shrikand 382
Shrimp Chili Masala 64
Shrimp Curry (Microwave) 184
Shrimp with Coconut (Microwave) 188
Shrimp in Garlic and Tamarind
    (Microwave) 170
Sikandari Raan 122
Smoked Mackerel Salad 66
Sour-Hot Potatoes (Microwave) 212
Spiced Almonds (Microwave) 168
Spiced Fruit Salad 384
Spiced Green Beans 294
Spiced Mango Fool 376
Spiced Mixed Nuts 42
Spiced Potato Bites 44
Spiced Sardines 56
Spiced Tea 358
Spicy Channa Dhal 308
Spicy Pineapple Punch 356
Stuffed Litchis 392
Sweet Saffron Rice 362
Sweet Vermicelli 374
Tandoori Chicken 72
Tandoori Chicken Masala 116
Tandoori Fish 52
Tandoori Roti 230
Tarka Dhal (Spiced Lentils) 306
Tarka Dhal (Microwave) 198
Tomato & Cucumber Salad 316
Tomato Chutney (Microwave) 220
Tomato Rice (Microwave) 196
Vegetable Samosas 46
Vermicelli Kheer 370
Wheat Fudge 388
Zucchini Chutney (Microwave) 222
Zucchini with Coconut and Green Chili
    Peppers (Microwave) 216